# THE UNKNOWN
# PAUL McCARTNEY

## McCartney and the avant-garde

# THE UNKNOWN
# PAUL McCARTNEY

## McCartney and the avant-garde

Ian Peel

Reynolds & Hearn Ltd
London

**For Kristianna**

First published in 2002 by
Reynolds & Hearn Ltd
61a Priory Road
Kew Gardens
Richmond
Surrey
TW9 3DH

A CIP catalogue record for this book is available from the British Library.

ISBN 1 903111 36 6

Designed by Paul Chamberlain.

Printed and bound in Great Britain by MPG Books Ltd, Bodmin, Cornwall.

# CONTENTS

# FOREWORD

**B**y the end of the 21st century, the cultural schematics we use today will look very quaint – a bit like those antique maps that would fill some vast area of uncharted territory with a drawing of a poorly observed rhinoceros or spouting whale. Terms such as avant-garde, popular, classical, highbrow, low-brow, mainstream, middle-of-the-road and experimental began to sound bleached out and pointless during the 1960s. Too many movements, individuals and events contributed to that seismic shift to be named here, but The Beatles were as important as anybody.

They created a happy confusion of perception whereby a single record could be appreciated on many different levels without harming either its sales, its artistic impact or coherence. All those genres that recoiled from miscegenation seemed legitimated and somehow socialised within a Beatles album. There was a party. Carl Perkins, Smokey Robinson, Bob Dylan, Karlheinz Stockhausen, Ravi Shankar and the Goons were invited. There were tensions and arguments but by the end of the night, everybody agreed that they had a good time.

Though Lennon and McCartney could write unforgettable songs at a rate that was almost supernatural, they played with sound within each song. Arranging, to use an old-fashioned word, seemed to be an innate skill for all four Beatles. That organic relationship between sonics and structure, reinforced by the experiences of George Martin, led them to electronic music, free improvisation, performance art, minimalism, loops, ambient sound, world musics, collage and noise.

Underestimating the importance of those discoveries is impossible. Composers such as James Tenney, Toru Takemitsu and Terry Riley had sampled and collaged popular musicians to remarkable effect but, even now, their efforts in that area are barely known. Whatever The Beatles did was an event of huge proportions. A general conception of what was possible, or acceptable, was amplified to a similar scale and the influence continues to be felt.

Some of the walls broken down in those heady times have been rebuilt. Somehow it's difficult to imagine a band as complex, versatile and utterly essential as The Beatles existing now, and besides, experimentation no longer has the same impact. Inevitably, an extensive mythology has accumulated since the 1960s. Understanding the events of that time, their context and the interrelationship of all the characters involved demands research that goes beyond that mythology, along with its deeply rooted images and icons.

What did it mean, chewing vegetables with Brian Wilson? In his various guises and disguises over the years, Paul McCartney has suggested some answers to that question. The chewing, the nature of the question and many of the answers are documented in the pages that follow.

**David Toop**
**author of *Rap Attack, Ocean of Sound* and *Exotica***
**August 2002**

# PREFACE

*I remember once saying to John that I was going to do an [avant-garde] album called* **Paul McCartney Goes Too Far.** *He was really tickled with that idea. 'That's great, man! You should do it!' But I would calculate and think no, I'd better do 'Hey Jude'.*

**Paul McCartney on Radio 1, 1990**

Y ou won't believe what you're about to hear. Or if you do believe it, you might be surprised at who you are hearing it from. This is the story of Paul McCartney's sound experiments and pseudonyms, from tape loops to trance.

"Ballads and babies. That's what happened to me," is how Paul McCartney summed up his post-Beatles career in a 1970s interview with *Time* magazine. It was later used as the closing quote of a McCartney biography in 1997, but actually makes the perfect opening for this book, which extends the artist's story a million miles from the ballads, the middle of the road and the rock and roll he is synonymous with.

Since the mid-1960s, Paul McCartney has explored various different fields of avant-garde music on albums, singles, remixes, soundtracks and live performance. Almost every one of these has been carried out either under a pseudonym or completely anonymously, rarely if ever under the name Paul McCartney. Why is this? What avant-garde music has he produced? What are the musical inspirations behind this work? And what are his motivations in continually dabbling away from the mainstream songs he is most famous for?

The Beatles' musical experiments have been examined to death. But from there on in it's uncharted territory. Between MacDonald, Miles and *The Beatles Anthology* you have all you need to build a picture of the 1960s, The Beatles and (most of) their avant-garde work at the time. This book continues the story, connecting all the experimental ideas from that period against a backdrop of influences from the decades before, and linking them to McCartney's work from 1970 to the present day.

*The Unknown Paul McCartney* doesn't set out to paint the artist as being seminally important to the avant-garde. It merely aims to put the experimental ten per cent of his music into the frame. Experimental composers such as Stockhausen and Cage are often mentioned as influences on The Beatles in the psychedelic era. But these and many other musicians, sounds and ideas from the left field of music continue to influence McCartney to this day.

In 1969, McCartney and Ringo Starr were the only Beatles who hadn't released avant-garde solo albums. Lennon and Yoko Ono's *Unfinished Music No. 1/Two Virgins* was already infamous. One hour of screaming, electronic effects and tape loops. It was followed by more madness in music – *Unfinished Music No. 2/Life with the Lions* and *The Wedding Album*. In 1969, George Harrison released *Electronic Sound* – a full album's worth of his (and other people's) Moog synthesiser test-recordings. This followed the early world music of Harrison's *Wonderwall Music* film soundtrack.

Although equally active in the underground experimental scene, McCartney's work was less visible during the sixties. By 1970 the other Beatles had all but abandoned their avant-garde experiments, but McCartney was just getting started. All the influences he picked up in the psychedelic era leaked out from both his solo work and obscure Wings recordings until, in the 1990s, he embraced his avant-garde side and a flood of collaborations and recordings emerged, ranging from freeform post-rock to chill-out.

As his solo career has progressed, Paul McCartney has become increasingly cautious about what music he has released under his own name. Across the past three decades his work has become more and more wide-ranging, but the material that reaches the public under his own name has trodden the middle ground. It's only when you assess the work of Paul McCartney, The Fireman, Percy Thrillington – and his myriad collaborations and hidden tracks for art shows, B-sides and film soundtracks – that you get a full picture of this diverse musician.

McCartney's non-mainstream collaborations are full of surprises. His collaborators include techno/trance producer and founder of The Orb, Youth; Anglo-Asian drum & bass fusion maestro, Nitin Sawhney; Welsh art rock experimentalists Super Furry Animals. To say nothing of a wiggy night-time session with Brian Wilson, a transatlantic rhythm track with Allen Ginsberg and a freeform jazz/rock improvisation with the person you'd least expect McCartney to collaborate with on anything – Yoko Ono.

Major works of official McCartney biography invariably get labelled as either revisionist or propaganda. ("He rewrites history all the time," said Beatles biographer Philip Norman of McCartney in 1987.) Such is the problem of covering an artist who is, on one hand, of vital importance to 20th century music and, on the other, a living breathing human who juggles celebrity with creativity. Rather than pump propaganda (either for or against), all I hope to do in these pages is describe the music I've heard and investigate the influences and processes behind it. As a result, McCartney's story might be seen from a completely new standpoint and the rest of his musical oeuvre might be cast in a new light.

For a period after John Lennon's death (and his immortalisation as rock, and avant-garde rock, guru), McCartney became paranoid. He started making statements about his avant-garde work, questioning who dipped their toes into experimental waters first. In the final analysis, The Beatles' most well-known avant-garde composition is Lennon's – 'Revolution 9' – to say nothing of his random radio broadcasts in 'I Am the Walrus' and his backwards vocals in 'Rain'. Curiously, schizophrenically even, while McCartney the Public Figure was making these statements, McCartney the Private Musician was beavering away making new experimental tracks with no intention of releasing them under his own name. "He's a very interesting musician," says author and guitarist Lenny Kaye. "Certainly he has the wherewithal and the range to try anything and I respect him for that. Even though the general categorisation of John being the radical one and Paul being the pop one is kind of widespread, I remember that in actual practice, they took each other's place in the mirror many a time."

There's another potential by-product of both this book and McCartney's avant-garde musical experiments: some fascinating, out-there genres and musical ideas get put in front of a whole new mass audience. McCartney made his key instrument – the left-handed Hofner violin bass – a musical icon in its own right. This book adds quite a few new, unexpected instruments to the list: olive oil, tape recorders, carrots, pots, celery, radios, apples, glasses, toilets, car horns, twigs and chainsaws. To say nothing of technology. Odd inventions like the 'watery box' and the Gizmotron. Or tools like turntables and samplers, Akais and Mini Moogs – not the kind of gear readily associated with an artist whose first major 1990s album was *Unplugged*.

Tracing the history of the experimental music these odd instruments represent is incredibly subjective. Unless you have a yardstick. How do you know what's off the beaten track, or left of centre, if you haven't established where (or who) the centre actually is? So as well as tracing the 'unknown' McCartney, the book also traces some of the strands of alternative music from the sixties to the present day. The fact that Paul McCartney has a wealth of relatively unknown avant-garde inspirations and collaborations offers the chance to explore an abstract story (the last 40 years of avant-garde rock) with a familiar central character.

Paul McCartney's music – both with The Beatles, Wings and solo – is like a permanent radio, soundtracking our daily lives. Another hypothetical FM station is growing up with his classical music. But coming in on the short wave are these avant-garde transmissions. They begin in the psychedelic era with tape collage, both with and outside of The Beatles, and McCartney's interest in electronic music. These early experiments and the cast of characters and events that inspired them are explored in Chapter Two: 'Influences, Memories and Beatles'. That is, after we have caught up with McCartney's life story and formative influences in Chapter One, which revolve around 'Brass Bands, Vinyl and Pigeon Holes'. One of The Beatles' great lost avant-garde works, 'Carnival of Light', is explored in Chapter Three. "More nonsense has been written about this recording than anything else The Beatles produced," wrote Ian MacDonald in 1994, so this chapter adds some sense and first-hand accounts to the equation.

You could be forgiven for thinking that the avant-garde world – inhabited by unsmiling performers such as AMM and space-age scientists like Delia Derbyshire – was an intensely serious environment. But some people can question the very nature of music or rhythm with a smile or joke as opposed to a lecture. A musical suite performed on gynaecological instruments pops up in Chapter Three. Then, enter the First Vienna Vegetable Orchestra who talk with the Super Furry Animals about McCartney's vegetable-chewing music in Chapter Four, 'From Vegetables to Llysiau (and Back)'. Llysiau is Welsh for vegetables. All will become clear…

Two chapters were originally planned to 'bridge' the investigations of the major works and provide some kind of timeline. One covered the 1970s, another covered the 1980s. But the more I dug around, and listened, the more I heard traces of the avant-garde inspirations and influences from the early chapters. I spotted the seeds of McCartney's relatively recent, prolific experimental output being sown too. So Chapter Five, on the 1970s, became 'Music Made with Moogs and Glasses', a history of Wings viewed from the left field. Chapter Eight, on McCartney in the 1980s, became 'Music Made with Radios and Gizmotrons' and unearths some off-the-wall gems from what is generally regarded as his most lacklustre period.

Between The Beatles and Wings, McCartney flew off in another odd direction, embracing easy listening and exotica to produce Thrillington, an instrumental lounge version of his rocky solo outing, *Ram*. Some of the production techniques and sounds on there were avant-garde but the music was its complete opposite. So why does it qualify for this book? Well, it's 'unknown' to the mainstream market and was certainly experimental. It has influenced some avant-garde musicians since its limited release. And Muzak-style music, which is what Thrillington borders on, is also one of the strongest roots of ambient music, a modern development of the work of 1940s and 1950s avant-garde composers. It also fits in with almost all McCartney's full-blown experimental output in that it was released not under his own name but under an elaborate smoke screen and pseudonym. These and McCartney's other attempts to hide from the public eye and watch his music succeed on its own merits are surveyed in Chapter Seven, 'From Sheep Masks to Pseudonyms (and Baa)'.

Avant-garde as a genre began in the 1940s with some of the composers explored in Chapter Two. At that time, making music with turntables and electronic devices was cutting edge. Further out than that even. Nowadays it's probably just as common as making music with a guitar. These two worlds crossed over in the 1980s in a unique space which grew between song and performance, as Chapter Nine, 'The Chapter Nine Remix', explains. From the 1990s onwards McCartney has embraced his avant-garde leanings while at the same time some of these styles have become mainstream, transforming into techno, ambient and chill-out. Techno might be a daily staple for McCartney's children's generation, but for a rock and roller they're still cutting edge. Some of the other styles he has explored remain truly avant-garde, like minimalism, post-rock, random orchestrations and pure industrial noise.

Chapter Ten examines McCartney's first foray into techno and dance territory as The Fireman, a duo comprising McCartney and dance producer Youth. 'It's a Long Way Off the Frog Chorus' indeed. Chapter 13, 'Crossing the Bridge to Palo Verde', covers the second Fireman album, an ambient epic. The third album in this series wasn't credited to The Fireman, as other players were involved. Peter Blake and the Super Furry Animals joined McCartney and Youth in remixing art into music and drawing long-overlooked parallels between sound collage and pop art. The result is Chapter 15, 'Real Gone Dub Made in Manifest in the Vortex of the Eternal Now'.

McCartney's song-writing collaborators after John Lennon, the likes of Denny Laine (for Wings), Eric Stewart (for *Press to Play* in the 80s) and Elvis Costello (for *Flowers in the Dirt* in the 90s) helped him come up with some catchy melodies and radioplay-friendly arrangements. But it's his avant-garde/non-mainstream collaborators who have stretched McCartney's musical mind and produced results close to those he achieved with his first, iconic collaborator. Youth is one and there follow the stories of two other little-known collaborations with artists you wouldn't expect McCartney to be playing with – Yoko Ono and Allen Ginsberg. Hence Chapter 11, 'In the Studio with Yoko Ono', and Chapter 12, 'On Stage with Allen Ginsberg'.

Not all McCartney's sound experiments have been confined to obscure vinyl or CD. Chapter 14, 'Sound and Sound Spaces', looks at the various bizarre live sessions he has indulged in, far from the mainstream limelight. From continuous 30-minute webcast jams to white noise installed into specially designed steel towers. These are all areas of musical exploration that are relatively alien to his peers. After considering his experimental work at the end of the 1990s and beginning of the

21st century, Chapter 16, 'Music Made for Families and Neuroses', considers the artist's motivations both for experimental work and performance in general.

At the end of Chapter 16, despite hearing the views of musicians and the media on the merits of McCartney's experimental music, I was left with one nagging question. Is it any good? Or, more to the point, is it any good in the context of experimental music, as opposed to in the context of McCartney Music? To answer this question I staged a 'blind tasting', taking CDs and tapes of the recordings unearthed in this book to the studios and lounges of musicians and DJs, all of them renowned in their particular fields, from post-punk experimentalists Wire to Ibiza DJ Chris Coco. We played the tracks and talked about them. And I made sure I didn't let on that they were listening to Paul McCartney until I'd gathered some frank and very revealing opinions.

The book closes with four appendices. The first, 'Listening', is a basic album-based discography of all McCartney's work covered herein, both mainstream and experimental. The second, 'Further Listening', is a lengthy discography of every musician, influence and related performer covered along the way. Musicians like AMM and Cage have often been mentioned in Beatles-related books, but this is the first time a discography has been put together that will actually enable the reader to hear their music. Appendix Three lists 'Selected Articles and Websites' that have provided snippets and pointers in the research process and Appendix Four, 'Bibliography', provides a list of further reading on the artists and eras covered.

"At his worst Paul is twee," wrote Chris Fox once in *Rubberneck*, the UK's longest-running experimental music magazine, "yet how many are aware that for every 'Ode to a Koala Bear' there is a 'Peter Blake 2000' (a 17-minute tour de force of looped and distorted dialogue, some taken from Beatles' studio chat) and for every 'We All Stand Together' an 'Oobu Joobu'?"

If you only hear one Beatles album it has to be *Sgt. Pepper's Lonely Hearts Club Band*. If you only hear one Wings album it has to be *Band on the Run*. If you ask me, the other indispensable McCartney album is *Rushes* by The Fireman. Yet Paul McCartney's best and most groundbreaking work of the past 25 years is missing from every biography on the market. Similarly, his other experimental recordings – such as *Feedback*, *Thrillington*, *Strawberries Oceans Ships Forest* and *Hiroshima Sky Is Always Blue* – are completely ignored in every McCartney book I've ever picked up and are rarely mentioned in the press. The upcoming 200 pages or so should just about plug the gap.

*Ian Peel*
*Winchester*
**August 2002**

# ACKNOWLEDGMENTS

Thanks first and foremost to Richard Reynolds and Marcus Hearn for their excitement and enthusiasm in bringing this book to life.

Thank you to all the musicians and artists who gave me their time, insights and memories: Yoko Ono, Edwin Prevost, Jerry Marotta, Daevid Allen, David Vaughan, Gruff Rhys and the Super Furry Animals, Laurence Juber, Stuart Howell, Steve Anderson, Steve Silberman, David Mansfield, Nitin Sawhney, Arnold Wesker, Youth, Keir Jens-Smith at Black Dog Towers, Adam Sykes at Iris Light, Natalie Rudd, Tim Cole at SSEYO, Guy Fixsen and Laika, Colin Newman and Post-Everything, Brian Wilson, kG and 8 Frozen Modules, Andrew Poppy, Lenny Kaye, J J Jeczalik, the First Vienna Vegetable Orchestra (Stefan Kühn, Barbara Kaiser, Mathias Meinhardter, Ernst Reitermaier), Richard Hewson, Herbie Flowers, Mike Keneally, Mike Flowers, Chris Coco, Trevor Horn, Lol Creme.

Thank you also to all the people who helped me connect with the interviewees, many of whom provided insights of their own: Shazia Nizam, Geoff Baker, Mrs David Vaughan and David's studio colleagues, Robin Eastburn, Julian Carrera, Lindsay Wesker, Darren at Dragonfly, Zak at Big Life, Petrina at Work Hard, Rob Stevens, Mark at deliaderbyshire.com, Jean Sievers, Steve Cohen at Music and Art Management, Bernadette Reitter at the Institute for Transacoustic Research, Karen Foster at the Swingle Singers office. Thanks also to Mark Ellen and the Rocking Vicar, David Hepworth.

And to the listeners, collectors, fans and thinkers whom I have corresponded with. Some have odd, on-line nicknames but all have opened my eyes and ears in some way (or another): Accio; Amrayll, Nowhere Man, cb70, Paul/The Mgnt, Claudio Dirani, Kaikoo Lalkaka, Laila Solum Hansen, Karen Lopez, Nancy, Debbie, Susan, Sue, Cathy (and the Macca-L crowd), Jan Cees ter Brugge, Jorie

Gracen, Jonathan Dancey, Chris Hannam, Bill Smith, David Jacobs, Boris Vanjicki, Carol Cleveland, Amy Titmus, Sari Gurney; Pinstripe.

Like this book, Prendergast's *The Ambient Century* (Bloomsbury) traces the story of experimental music from Stockhausen to Sawnhey but is a road atlas compared to this excavation of one particular path. For dates and facts, two main catalogues were useful and come recommended, namely Madinger and Easter's *Eight Arms to Hold You* (44.1 Productions) and Badman's *The Beatles After the Break-Up* (Omnibus Press). The former compiles music and the second compiles dates and events regarding the solo Beatles.

Thank you to Mum and Dad for introducing me to music in the first place, to Ken for (musical) inspiration, and to Elisiv for (supreme) motivation.

# ONE

# BRASS BANDS, VINYL AND PIGEONHOLES

**P**igeonholes can often be comfortable. Sometimes even cosy. But every now and then they get outgrown. Paul McCartney, musically at least, has always had an odd relationship with the one he got landed with. You can trace his predicament back to a yellowed old copy of the *New Musical Express*, circa 1970:

"James Paul McCartney is home and baby and Linda and ballads and rock 'n' roll ravers and Fair Isle sweaters and dad and brother and the Friday train to Lime Street," wrote the *NME*'s Alan Smith. John Lennon, on the other hand, was "Yoko and Peace and Plastic fantastic; X and Sex; and bang the gong for right and wrong." These sound like epitaphs, yet Smith wrote these boisterous lines at the beginning of the story this book traces...

From childhood, Paul McCartney experienced an array of musical styles. His father was responsible for his musical education and took him to brass band concerts in the local park, as well as making sure the piano at home was rarely silent. Later, McCartney Jr would play telephone pranks with tape recorders, using rude recordings he'd made with John Lennon when the two were in their early teens. At 11 he won a book token in an essay competition to celebrate the coronation of Queen Elizabeth II. He chose a book on modern art, which provided his first insight into the world of Dalí and Picasso. All of these formative moments went on to influence McCartney's avant-garde or experimental music as much, if not more so, than his traditional rock and roll songs.

The avant-garde was never knowingly on The Beatles' agenda. "Avant-garde is French for bullshit," Lennon famously said. "Avant-garde a clue," George Harrison added. But in 1966 McCartney – along with Lennon, Harrison and all of the artists he knew – found his mind exploding. The psychedelic era marked the 'end of the beginning' of The Beatles. By that stage they'd torn through crowds at the Cavern Club, torn across the Reeperbahn in Hamburg and torn up the charts with the first phase of their album catalogue – *Please Please Me* and *With the Beatles* in 1963, *A Hard Day's Night* the year after, and *Beatles For Sale* and *Help!* in 1965.

By the time this book catches up with McCartney's life story he is living at his girlfriend Jane Asher's parents' house, renting their attic room in London's Wimpole Street. All of the relationships are in place that would shape his musical career – John Lennon, George Harrison, Ringo Starr, George Martin – and a host of others are on the fringe, waiting to splinter it into new, uncharted directions.

Before the psychedelic period took hold, McCartney was getting used to experimenting outside of the Beatles unit. With John Lennon he'd produced The Silkie ('You've Got to Hide Your Love Away'), moving on to produce Cliff Bennett & The Rebel Rousers' 'Got to Get You into My Life' on his own. Chapter Seven takes up the thread of these Beatles side-projects with the songs McCartney wrote for Peter & Gordon. But it's important to note that his first major non-Beatles album, released long before the band broke up, was not in the pop mainstream at all. It provided instead the opening chords to McCartney's classical career, later to flourish in the 1990s.

In 1966, McCartney decided to try his hand at a film soundtrack. It was the idea of writing for a new medium that came first, rather than inspiration from a particular film. "I rang our Nems office and said I would like to write a film theme," he told the press at the time, "not a score, just a theme. John was away filming so I had time to do it. Nems fixed it for me to do the theme of *The Family Way*."

Starring Hayley Mills, *The Family Way* was based on a play by Bill Naughton. It gave McCartney a taste of writing outside of The Beatles and for an orchestra. He worked closely with George Martin, who literally had to force him to write the main love theme. "I went to America for a time and on returning realised we needed a love theme for the centre of the picture, something wistful," he reported. "I told Paul and he said he'd compose something. I waited but nothing materialised, and finally I had to go round to Paul's house and literally stand there till he'd composed something." Despite the pressure, the finished result won an Ivor Novello award for Best Instrumental Theme. "John was visiting and advised a bit," said Martin, who himself listened and wrote down what he heard as manuscript. So this first major solo work for McCartney was, as with any solo music, actually channelled and influenced directly by others. As the albums covered in Chapters Five and Eight show, solo music probably only becomes truly so when it's 'isolationist'.

From Hayley Mills' swinging London, fast forward to Bridgewater Hall in Manchester on a Sunday night in 1997. Andrew Poppy is presenting a paper on 'The Presence of Performance in the Age of Electronic Transmission'. He is an avant-garde composer whose work is performed at events like Experiments &

Eccentricities, in which piano and violin interpret works with names like 'Romance in C for Optional Lovers' together with pieces by Cornelius Cardew, the renowned lateral thinker of composition.

Poppy's presentation is part of Cosmopolis, a symposium "exploring the cultural and social transition from post industrial to digital city." The Beatles may seem a million miles away from this musical event but there Poppy puts his finger on the precise moment when The Beatles changed from being a rock and roll combo into a meeting of experimental minds. "The Beatles exploited the early multitrack tape recorder in a particular way," he said. "They were aware of avant-garde composers John Cage and Karlheinz Stockhausen, and they collaged random bits of radio broadcast with George Martin string arrangements and their own rock and roll." Stockhausen and Cage worked in the live environment but The Beatles had their own – the vinyl environment – and the results they were beginning to come up with were the first true record *productions*: "a musical experience that could not happen outside the frame of the loudspeakers," as Poppy described it. "The space it presents is a shameless construction."

The Beatles weren't the first musicians to tackle the avant-garde concepts explored in this book. As the psychedelic era dawned, Lennon, McCartney and Harrison drew on composers dating back decades, centuries even, as well as those around them in the present day. But they were among the first to take these concepts, and new experiments in sound, and press them on vinyl for a mass audience. The composers Poppy mentions – Stockhausen and Cage – were established avant-garde, fringe artists by the mid-1960s. But by their very nature, when The Beatles pressed their own interpretations onto vinyl, they went straight onto several million turntables.

When the band gave up touring they built a massive new concert venue, with Abbey Road on the stage and every teenager's bedroom speakers in the auditorium. "If I sit and play the piano in your presence – is that performance?" asks Andrew Poppy. "If I push the fader up at some point while mixing a recording of the piano playing – is that performance? If I package the recording and send it out into the world – is that performance? A CD is a product of mechanical reproduction. Recordings atomise and fragment musical performance so as to transform its sound materials into a storable form. The sound of a pianist playing is to all intents and purposes *retrieved* and projected in the space that exists between two speakers."

As one of the 20th century's most important avant-garde composers, Karheinz Stockhausen has over 60 years of performance and composition behind him. His selected back catalogue was re-released in 2002, spanning 62 CDs. But as a consequence of the unique sound stage The Beatles had built, as described by Poppy, this is eclipsed by a single Beatles track. The White Album's 'Revolution

THE UNKNOWN PAUL McCARTNEY

9', John Lennon's epic and disturbing sound collage, is perhaps the world's most well-known and most listened-to piece of avant-garde music.

*Paul McCartney Goes Too Far* was an album title bandied around in that Wimpole Street attic in the mid-60s. McCartney wanted to take the array of left field musical ideas he was beginning to encounter and put out an album that would really surprise people. But he was only on the cusp of an ocean of sounds and influences outside of The Beatles and rock and roll. He probably wasn't aware of just how far 'Too Far' could actually be.

# TWO

# INFLUENCES, MEMORIES AND BEATLES

**W**hen the final sensational piano chord crashed in at the end of The Beatles' 'A Day in the Life', the closing song on *Sgt. Pepper's Lonely Hearts Club Band*, pop music came of age in an instant and the psychedelic era had an audible point focus. But that final chord wasn't quite the end of the album. Forty-five seconds of pure ambient sound followed, as the microphones recorded the piano notes slowly mixing into silence. A joyful avant-garde sound collage then burst forth on copies of the LP played on turntables that didn't have 'modern' automatic arms. These unexpected reverberations, an avant-garde PS at the end of one of pop music's most captivating 'letters', lit the blue touch paper for experimentalist pop music.

Chuck Berry, Elvis Presley, Buddy Holly, Eddie Cochran... The influences behind The Beatles' formation and their early songs are well known. Less so the avant-garde and experimental artists that steered them into such new, uncharted waters.

The German composer Karlheinz Stockhausen and the American composer John Cage certainly cast an enormous shadow and their influence on McCartney, and modern music in general, is huge. But they were only a part of the picture. Stockhausen and Cage were the kind of avant-garde composers McCartney learned about in conversation but didn't get to actually hear or see particularly much. Those he did played just as great a part in broadening his field of (aural) vision.

As such, George Martin's influence is immeasurable. Not only for the famous classical influence but also for Martin's off-the-wall electronic experiments (under the pseudonym of Ray Cathode), which are much less well known. Max Mathews, Cornelius Cardew and Luciano Berio were other cutting-edge experimental composers McCartney saw and heard from a distance, their influence balanced by those he actually met and talked to, like Daevid Allen and Delia Derbyshire.

All these influences and more had an impact on McCartney in the mid-1960s and have slowly but surely poured out across the following 40 years in the form of his own experimental music. The early results – McCartney and The Beatles' avant-garde experiments – have been subject to intense scrutiny since the moment they were pressed onto vinyl. 'Tomorrow Never Knows' (featuring McCartney's tape-loop symphony), 'Revolution 9' (Lennon's reply) and the freeform orchestral brilliance in 'A Day in the Life' are the main songs in question.

When put together, these songs act as another major influence on McCartney's later experimental work. There is little point in detailing the exact elements provided by each Beatle in these tracks. As McCartney himself said, "We were four corners of the same square." It was the combined effect of the four players and these recordings that sent shock waves though pop music and made an explosive start to McCartney's musical experiments.

While volumes have been written about 'Tomorrow Never Knows', 'Revolution 9' and 'A Day in the Life', there has been less investigation of The Beatles' other important – and equally freaky – pieces, namely 'Pantomime (Everywhere It's Christmas)', 'Carnival of Light' and 'Sgt. Pepper's Inner Groove'. The latter is the tiny burst of tape collage that extended *Sgt. Pepper's Lonely Hearts Club Band* into an album of infinite length.

'Carnival of Light' was The Beatles' great sound-collage experiment which – although still unreleased – gets a chapter to itself in this book. While all The Beatles' avant-garde work was created for record rather than live performance, 'Carnival of Light' was the exception because it was created for a 'happening'. Tape collage, of course, has become the norm nowadays, 'happenings' having sowed the seeds of the club culture which today provides the framework in which such collages are played.

As soon as The Beatles signed with his Parlophone division of EMI Records on 9 May 1962, George Martin became a fundamental part of the band's sound and a key influence in their musical development. It was Martin who suggested a bluesy harmonica part for the band's first single, 'Love Me Do'. Later on, he would open their ears to classical music, his influence memorably inspiring the strings on 'Yesterday' and the orchestral interludes in 'For No One'. At an early age, George Martin had been blown away by the work of Debussy, especially 'L'Aprés midi d'un faune'. Exposure to both Debussy and Erik Satie – late-19th century composers with a visionary spirit and total disregard for convention – would play a major part in shaping the young McCartney's interests outside rock and roll.

Unlike most other record producers at the time, George Martin was only too ready to work with The Beatles' wackier ideas. He had built up quite some skill in tape looping and editing from producing breakneck comedy records for the likes of Peter Sellers and The Goons. These were almost cinematic radio plays made from dialogue, special effects and breakneck editing of Sellers' sketches like 'Shadows in the Grass'. Martin had a thirst for electronic music too. Inspired by the BBC Radiophonic Workshop, which was located not far from Abbey Road, he cut a bizarre electronic dance single and released it in 1962 under the guise of Ray Cathode.

"Creating atmosphere and sound pictures, that was my bag," remembered Martin. "I did a lot of it before The Beatles even came along." 'Time Beat' and its B-side 'Waltz in Orbit' by Ray Cathode mixed live musicians over a purely syn-thesised electronic rhythm track Martin had created with the Radiophonic Workshop. "It was a resounding flop," he later remembered, "but an interesting flop … Something to learn from anyway!"

One of the leading lights of the BBC Radiophonic Workshop was Delia Derbyshire. Martin described their lab and her colleagues as "people who spent their entire time cooking up freaky sounds with whatever they could lay their hands on. They had, to them, standard equipment of oscillators and variable-speed tape machines, but they also indulged in quite a bit of concrete music [using] milk bottles, bits of old piping…"

Delia Derbyshire was 25 when Ray Cathode's 'Time Beat' was released as a single. At the time she was assisting the experimental composer Luciano Berio (who would later cross paths with Paul McCartney) at his Dartington summer school lectures. Having earned a degree in mathematics in Cambridge she was turned down – or rather, refused to allow to apply – for a job at Decca Records. In the late 1950s and early '60s they simply did not employ women in their recording studios.

Instead she went to work for the BBC as a trainee studio manager and quick-ly moved sideways into the fledgling Radiophonic Workshop, a hi-tech studio set up to push the boundaries of sound and soundtracks. She became their lynch-pin, enthusiastically exploring sound creation (and perception) using the Workshop's vast banks of technology. Modes, moods, tuning and transfer of electronic music all came under Derbyshire's intense research. A lot of it was based around her mathematical training, even if she'd cheerfully break or bend any scientific rule to find a new, emotive sonic experience.

The Radiophonic Workshop and Delia Derbyshire had a job to do too, how-ever. It had been set up to service the BBC's Radio Drama department, effec-tively as a sound effects lab and editing suite. But the team there could not quell their avant-garde spirit and pushed the available technology into new music, the most famous being the theme music for *Doctor Who*. This famous theme 'song' led to a slew of TV commissions for Derbyshire and her team, who between them made orchestras virtually redundant for a time. 'Special sound by BBC Radiophonic Workshop' was how the TV credits ran, with individual staff gaining no recognition at all. Derbyshire's impact is only now being reassessed, with the *Guardian* calling her "the unsung heroine of British electronic music" when she died in 2001, having spent much of the 1980s and '90s away from music, thoroughly disillusioned.

Following on from her work with Berio, Derbyshire worked with other composers, including Sir Peter Maxwell Davies, Roberto Gerhard (on 'Anger of Achilles', which won the 1965 Prix Italia) and Ianni Christou. But the BBC was unable to fit her avant-garde work into their mainstream programming, calling it "too lascivious for 11-year-olds [and] too sophisticated for the BBC2 audience." So she invested her time in Unit Delta Plus, Kaleidophon and Electrophon, three private studios where she pioneered electronic music as we know it today. Another outlet for Derbyshire's work was the emerging psychedelic scene. She provided music for Yoko Ono's pre-Lennon Wrapping Event and got involved in happenings and raves, like those at the Roundhouse in Camden, explored in more detail in the next chapter.

Paul McCartney was inspired by what he'd heard of the BBC's experimental sound installation, and by the work George Martin had done with them. In a moment that could have altered the course of pop history, he seriously considered abandoning the string quartet recorded for 'Yesterday' in favour of a purely electronic backing. In 1998, McCartney recounted how he pulled the Workshop's phone number out of the directory and went there to introduce himself and find out more. He hit it off with Derbyshire immediately and was totally into the experimental work she was producing, most likely because it was reminiscent of his in two key ways – pushing the boundaries while remaining highly melodic and emotional.

But the meeting McCartney remembered (as recounted in his authorised biography *Many Years from Now*) was slightly blurred by the passage of time. It wasn't the Radiophonic Workshop he visited, but the private lab of Derbyshire's friend and colleague Peter Zinovieff, which both used when their experiments became too much for the BBC. Just before she died in 2001, Derbyshire described her meeting with McCartney in an interview with John Cavanagh for *Boazine*.

■ He never came to the workshop. I always did work outside and he came to [Peter] Zinovieff's studio and I played him some of my stuff – that's all … It was the phrase length he was interested in. I've always been non-conformist: I don't like the 8-bar or the 12-bar standard thing. They're all beautiful in their own way, but why not explore different phrase lengths? [McCartney] never came to the workshop … Brian Jones did – golly! There we were with our hand-tuned oscillators and he went into it with his frilly cuffs and things as though he could play it as a musical instrument! He died very young and I cried buckets.

Before going to meet Delia Derbyshire – wherever it was – McCartney had had his mind blown by an album from another unsung pioneer of electronic music. George Martin had played him a recording by Max V Mathews, which had been a major inspiration for his own Ray Cathode alter ego.

Decca Records may have turned Delia Derbyshire away but in 1962 they did release a far-out album, entitled *Music from Mathematics*. It was one of the most influential and important albums in the history of electronic music and featured 18 different 'songs' generated by an IBM 7090 computer and a digital to sound transducer. Mathews was one of seven programmers whose work on the 7090 appeared on the final album, his contributions being electronic interpretations of 'Bicycle Built for Two', 'Numerology', 'The Second Law', 'May Carol' and 'Joy to the World'. Mathews, known as the "father of electronic music" and "the grandfather of techno", had not only programmed a computer to play music but also to simulate vocals. "The computer can also be programmed to speak and sing, as is illustrated by the last verse of this familiar ditty," he wrote of 'Bicycle Built for Two'. "The patterns of human speech are analysed in the same manner as the instrumental sounds. The computer is then programmed to speak the desired words. On this [track] the computer not only was programmed to sing but also to simulate a Honky Tonky type of piano accompaniment that was popular during the era when this song was a hit."

Max V Mathews was 32 when *Music from Mathematics* was released. He had first shown the potential of digital music five years earlier with his 1957 Music I computer program and was a leading figure in acoustic research at AT&T Bell Laboratories, where he worked from 1955 until 1987. In the late 1970s, he also acted as Scientific Adviser to the Institut de Recherche et Coordination Acoustique/Musique (IRCAM) in Paris, whose groundbreaking ideas set the scene for the most non-technical of avant-garde music-making in Chapter Six. His other notable inventions include the Music and Groove software series and the Radio Baton, a computer-linked baton for 'conducting' electronic symphonies.

*Music from Mathematics* is a 'Eureka! moment' album. With the IBM 7090 Mathews had created a new kind of musical instrument and a whole new genre of music was about to emerge as a result. "This new 'instrument' combination is not merely a gadget or a complicated bit of machinery capable of producing new sounds," he declared in the album's liner notes. "It opens the door to the exploration and discovery of many new and unique sounds. However, its musical usefulness and validity go far beyond this. With the development of this equipment carried out at the Bell Telephone Laboratories, the composer will have the benefits of a notational system so precise that future generations will know exactly how the composer intended his music to sound. He will have at his command an 'instrument' which is itself directly involved in the creative process." In an essay that stands as a fitting preface to the history of electronic music in general, Mathews concluded:

> ▮ The human element plays a large role in computer music, as in any art medium. The sounds and sound-producing methods are new; the composer's role is essentially that which it has always been. History tells us that whenever a new concept emerges, it is labelled revolutionary by either its proponents or the public at large. The new techniques and tools of computer music are not meant to replace the more traditional means of composition and performance. Rather, they are designed to enhance and enlarge the range of possibilities available to the searching imagination of musicians. Science has provided the composer with new means to serve the same ends – artistic excellence and communication.

On hearing *Music from Mathematics* in the summer of 1963, composer Ivor Darreg was amazed by the "bass voice with good dynamic range and only the slightest 'electrical accent'" that Mathews had achieved with his computers. "It is important to realise that this was accomplished on machines never intended for musical purposes," Darreg wrote at the time, "but merely for prosaic, non-artistic tasks like adding up the weekly payroll or doing the mathematical drudgery for a roomful of engineers." He was convinced that "the 'psychological moment' for electronic music has arrived."

Paul McCartney, too, was taken aback when George Martin played him this landmark recording, and he continued to listen to it outside the studio – his friend and counter-culture mover Barry Miles had a copy and the two would often play it at Miles' flat. McCartney remains enthused by electronic music to the present day. The light bulbs that *Music from Mathematics* turned on can be heard predominantly on his *McCartney II* album from 1980, the first Fireman album, *Strawberries Oceans Ships Forest*, from 1993, and even his Mellow Extension mix of 'Vo!ce' from 2001.

Of course, in the 1960s, just as John Lennon was the most famous Beatle into tape loops, George Harrison was the band's most visible proponent of this new wave of music. Although he followed a much more traditional path for the rest of his solo career, Harrison's *Electronic Sound* album from 1969 put the possibilities of the Moog synthesiser in front of a huge new audience.

Max V Mathews had inspired the work of Delia Derbyshire and George 'Ray Cathode' Martin in England. In the US one of his main disciples was Morton

Subotnick, whose debut album, *Silver Apples of the Moon*, made it onto the turntables of Paul McCartney and almost every other fan of experimental/freaky music in 1967. Subotnick, then aged 34, had released 30 minutes of electronic sounds from his homemade array of effects gates and early synthesisers. Side two of this album is one of the first hints of techno and modern electronic music, pre-empting the sounds of Kraftwerk by nearly a decade. Subotnick later coined the term Elevator Music with his 1970s installation in a New York elevator system, which triggered pieces of music when passengers selected particular floors.

Karlheinz Stockhausen made Brian Epstein nervous. In 1967 The Beatles' manager needed the composer's approval for Peter Blake to use his image in the *Sgt. Pepper* album's famous front-cover collage. But Stockhausen was touring and was difficult to pin down. He almost didn't make it onto the cover, but an urgent telegram from Epstein saved the day.

■ FURTHER TO LETTER AND ENCLOSED RELEASE FORM CONCERNING BEAT-LES LP YOUR DECISION IS MOST URGENTLY REQUESTED ONE WAY OR ANOTHER BY RETURN STOP SORRY TO PUSH YOU BUT AT THIS STAGE SPEED IS OF THE UTMOST IMPORTANCE REGARDS AND BEST WISHES BRIAN EPSTEIN

Brian Epstein went to such lengths because Stockhausen was so important to The Beatles – to McCartney and Lennon especially. McCartney had been hearing about Stockhausen's work since his teens and began to explore it and actually listen to it in more detail when the psychedelic period arrived. He later described the composer's seamless mix of primitive electronic sound and human vocals, 'Song of the Youths', as his favourite "plick plop" piece.

'Song of the Youths' ('Gesang der Jünglinge') started life as an electronic mass for Cologne cathedral. Stockhausen thought on a panoramic scale and wanted this grand venue to put electronic music in front of as many people as possible. But Cologne cathedral had other ideas and instead a truncated version of 'Song of the Youths' (originally titled 'The Song of the Youths in the Fiery Furnace') was performed via five speaker panels in a broadcasting studio of West German Radio in May 1956. The venue may have changed but the impact wasn't lessened. Stockhausen's 13-minute mix of sin wave, speech and white noise became the talk of the avant-garde and put the new electronic genre firmly on the map.

Born in 1928, Stockhausen had already composed several groundbreaking works as a student in Cologne and Paris before creating 'Gesang der

Jünglinge'. There was a passion and intensity to this and his other 1950s works that transfixed a generation of European composers, influencing both Boulez and Berio.

Following a spell in the USA, where he met John Cage, Stockhausen worked with Cornelius Cardew to produce minimalist orchestral pieces that were both more fluid and more relaxed than his previous work. From the mid-1960s until the end of the decade the composer progressed to concentrate almost solely on music made with tape cut-ups and electronics. He poured and mixed sound as if it was some physical, malleable paint in pieces such as 'Mikrophonie I' (1964), 'Prozession' (1967), 'Kurzwellen' (1968) and 'Aus den sieben Tagen' (1968). All four were being toured around Europe when Epstein started trying to track Stockhausen down.

Outside the live situation and back in his studio, Stockhausen created the seminal early tape compositions 'Telemusik' (1966) and 'Hymnen' (1967). The latter, which pulled together recordings and samples from around the globe, was heard and loved by John Lennon and was a major influence on 'Revolution 9'.

In the 1970s, Stockhausen mixed simpler, classical compositions with full-blown performance art. 'Trans' (1971) was written for an orchestra bathed in violet light, only to be observed through a veil. 'Sirius' (1977) was a scored ceremony for four peculiarly costumed musicians and synthesised and processed audio tape. All were clearly major influences on McCartney's later live performances explored in Chapter 14.

Alongside Karheinz Stockhausen, John Cage is the composer most often cited as The Beatles' and McCartney's prime influence in avant-garde music. Born in 1912 in Los Angeles, Cage casts an enormous shadow over the past 50 years of both avant-garde and electronic/dance music. Nineteenth century piano melodies and the dawn of modern radio invigorated his childhood and provided the foundation for his life's work. His late teens saw him studying for the priesthood before travelling around Europe. Visiting Berlin and Paris, he developed a passion for writing poetry and composing music. At 21 he began studying under Henry Cowell at California's New School for Social Research. There he absorbed all sorts of experimental ideas and an unconventional approach to music making. These were both logistical, such as methods of retuning the piano and use of the electronic Therminvox device, and influential – he was exposed to Eastern music and the visionary ideas of his teacher Arnold Schoenberg.

Schoenberg and Cage impressed each other equally with their disregard for traditional musical understanding and constant questioning and reinvention of what music actually is and could be. In a groundbreaking 1937 lecture, *The Future of Music (Credo)*, Cage identified two of the major directions that modern music would take. Firstly, he predicted how electronic sound and devices would become the crux of composition. Electronics, he said, would mean that "no rhythm would be beyond the composer's earth." He tried to put this theory into practice as part of a quartet, the Magnetic Tape Music Project. Cage also predicted the rise of music created by playing re-engineered machines rather than instruments.

Between 1939 and 1952 Cage started putting both these concepts into practice with the five-part 'Imaginary Landscapes' series. Prefiguring DJ culture by almost 50 years, 'Imaginary Landscapes No. 1' was the sound of vari-speed turntables playing RCA test discs. 'Imaginary Landscapes No. 4' was the sound of overlapping radios being tuned and re-tuned. In the final piece in the series, Cage pre-empted 1980s and 1990s sampling and collage music by creating a new aural landscape by mixing 42 jazz records at once. He would later revisit this merging of previously recorded music into a new, recycled performance with the revolutionary 'Williams Mix', a composition based on the random playback of 600 albums.

Cage's radios-as-music concept in 'Imaginary Landscapes No. 4' was just one piece that sent ripples across the surface of avant-garde music, continuing to do so to this day. McCartney later tried out radio-play for himself on 'The Broadcast' in 1979 and 'Trans Lunar Rising' in 1993. John Lennon was equally inspired and pulled a radio into the mix for 'I Am the Walrus'. Randomly tuning through the stations, he found a BBC broadcast of the Shakespeare play *King Lear*, which is now immortalised in the finished *Magical Mystery Tour* recording.

The 'Imaginary Landscapes' sowed the seeds of modern-day dance and experimental music, but attention is more often drawn to another piece of Cage's revolutionary thinking from 1952. This was the year he first performed '4'33', an avant-garde composition which took music to its most challenging conclusion, when he sat at the piano for four and a half minutes of nothingness. '4'33' was not a performance of complete silence, as is the generally received notion. Instead it made the statement that music could be the random, ambient sound around an audience during a predetermined time-span.

Integrating music with random, everyday elements became a theme of Cage's work across the 1940s and early 50s. He invented the 'prepared piano', writing for pianos whose strings had been entwined with various small, everyday objects to create a new percussive sound. His 'Living Room Music' pieces devolved percussion further into the hands of the listener and the objects that surround them. In the late 1940s Cage composed some of his most important works, inspired by two new influences. An interest in Zen Buddhism and a love of composer Erik Satie pushed him in minimalist, ambient directions. At the same time, an interest in the I Ching and a friendship with surrealist artist Marcel Duchamp created in him a desire to base composition on randomness and chance. 1951's 'Music of Changes' embraced all these concepts, its ethereal piano passages being joined in a structure based on random coin-tossing.

The roots of DJ culture and interactive music can be traced back to John Cage. As can the roots of multimedia art with the primitive, computer-generated elements in 1968's 'HPSCHD', which duetted traditional instruments (harps) with machines and media (tapes and cartridges). In the late 1950s Cage was back in Europe working with Luciano Berio and recording electronic feedback and hiss to create the sprawling 'Fontana Mix'.

Despite clearly working to his own futurist agenda, John Cage was not afraid to collaborate or comment on others' work. He had a love-hate relationship with his closest European peer, Karlheinz Stockhausen. 'Variations' was an attempt to further random composition into true 'indeterminacy', where sounds would be triggered by devices and the movement of dancers, and was a reaction to Stockhausen's 'Klavierstuck' series.

In 1937 Cage gave a lecture in Seattle where he summed up the thinking behind his unique music. "Wherever we are, what we hear is mostly noise. When we ignore it, it disturbs us. When we listen to it, we find it fascinating. The sound of a truck at 50 mph. Static between the stations. Rain. We want to capture and control these sounds, to use them, not as sound effects, but as musical instruments." Outlining his vision for the future of avant-garde music, he went on to set the scene for sampling, remixing and DJ culture when he explained:

■ Every film studio has a library of 'sound effects' recorded on film. With a film phonograph it is now possible to control the amplitude and frequency of any one of these sounds and to give to it rhythms within or beyond the reach of anyone's imagination. Given four film phonographs, we can compose and perform a quartet for explosive motor, wind, heartbeat, and landslide.

Paul McCartney saw these theories put into practice and heard avant-garde music 'live' for the first time when he went with Barry Miles to a lecture by Delia Derbyshire's former mentor, Luciano Berio. Both had enjoyed 'Thema (Omaggio a Joyce)', Berio's pioneering electronic soundscape from 1958 which cut up, looped and 'remixed' a reading of *Ulysses* in homage to its author, James Joyce. Berio had followed this with 'Allez-Hop' (1959), which did the same with a text by Calvino.

Italy's most important avant-garde explorer, Berio was 41 when he came to London to lecture at the Italian Cultural Institute. He had studied as a child with the Milan Conservatoire and then moved into more experimental circles, setting up a laboratory for electronic music in 1955 with fellow experimentalist Bruno Maderna. He would later head the aforementioned institution of academic research into electronic music, ICRAM, in Paris and Milan. Berio spent the 1960s lecturing all over Europe and America, stopping off at Darmstadt, Harvard, the Juilliard School in New York and Columbia University.

During this time, Luciano Berio brought many new influences, such as folk and rock, into his work while extending his passion for the human voice. His muse was his wife, Cathy Berberian, who would perform much of his work – most notably 'Folk Songs' (1964). Berio was also inspired by jazz, the Japanese art of Noh and Indian music.

Although he was yet to create his best work ('Coro' from 1976 took this accolade), there was a buzz when it was announced that Berio would be lecturing at the Italian Cultural Institute in London on 24 February 1966. There McCartney and Miles heard his latest work – in which Berio collaged and remixed the text of Dante into the Bible into T S Eliot into Ezra Pound into Edoardo Sanguineti. They managed to chat briefly with the composer during the interval. It was fresh impetus to McCartney, whose work, publicly at least, had become firmly planted in the middle of the road at that time. February and March 1966 had seen 'Yesterday' receive six Grammy nominations while McCartney wrote another single for his girlfriend's brother's band, Peter & Gordon.

Outside of the Italian Cultural Institute, McCartney could be seen in some of the London counter-culture's most happening nightspots. The UFO Club (he was the only Beatle to visit there, apparently) and the Speakeasy Club were all melting pots for the new psychedelic, acid-induced avant-garde; among the bands that played there were The Pink Floyd (as they were then known) and the Soft Machine. "There was also the Middle Earth, Magic Garden, Sabillas, Bag O' Nails, Ronnie Scott's, the Old and the New," remembered psychedelic artist David Vaughan 35 years later. "There was the Arts Laboratory on Drury Lane that Jim Haines ran. I've got a complete bloody list of them somewhere in my mind…"

The Soft Machine had been formed in October 1966 as a result of a revelation the band's leader, Australian Daevid Allen, had experienced that Easter. "He gained the impression that he was an experiment being supervised by intelligences far beyond his normal level of awareness that he was later to call the octave doctors," reads his official biography. "Seeing himself on stage in front of a large rock festival audience and experiencing an intense connection with them that had the quality of intense LOVE, at the same time being surrounded by an enormous cone of etheric light. Simultaneously drawing astral shadows from deep below us and dissolving them in the downpouring radiance focused at its peak." Seriously.

"For a time I forgot about this revelation," Allen later recounted, "but before long, the act of offering myself to the powers that combine, energise and transform all that lives through music became my only reason to exist. At this point I became aware of my life purpose." Allen and his partner Gilli Smyth then became the Electric Poets, like a psychedelic version of Berio's 'straighter' husband-and-wife avant-garde partnership. The Electric Poets could often be seen at the Speakeasy Club. "The Soft Machine had a Tuesday night residency there,"

Allen told me, "and Hendrix often sat in on bass. Everybody on the scene with the exception of the Stones hung out there – Beatles, Animals, Jeff Beck, Eric Burdon, Zoot Money, Who, etc etc."

Outside of the Soft Machine and the Electric Poets, Allen was a prolific and proficient tape-loop composer. He was the link between the academia of Luciano Berio and John Cage and the psychedelic jamming of The Pink Floyd and the Speakeasy regulars. He cites US avant-garde composer Terry Riley and Floyd's Syd Barrett as his two main influences at that time. Using just a Philips quarter-track reel-to-reel and a kit four track, with no mixer, he created 'Switch Doctor' and other innovative compositions (latterly collected on Voiceprint's compilation CD, *The Death of Rock & Other Entrances*) which pushed the theories of Berio's lecture rooms forward at street level. He met McCartney one hazy night and the two of them planned to collaborate on a new avant-garde piece, but events conspired against them, as Allen remembers:

■ In the aftermath of high hippy spin Paul McCartney spoke of working with me on tape-loop compositions, based on my reputation as a tape-loop and collage composer best circulated by my 30-minute BBC Third Programme piece, commissioned by BBC Radiophonic Workshop and broadcast in 1966. This didn't materialise due to my being banned from entering the UK in 1967 but we had already shared ideas at the Speakeasy Club earlier that year.

Allen was refused entry into the UK because his visa had expired, which meant the end of the tape-loop project with McCartney and the end of Soft Machine too. Instead he settled in Paris and began working on a new form of avant-garde music which mixed electric guitar and 19th century gynaecological instruments processed through an echo chamber. Skipping town briefly after getting mixed up in the Paris riots of May 1968, he formed the band Gong, which continues to push forward with psychedelic music and philosophy to this day.

Like Daevid Allen, McCartney's avant-garde side was greatly inspired by Pink Floyd. Sightings at the Speakeasy Club and elsewhere around London's underground scene clearly left a lasting impression. Although not apparent in his Beatles compositions, Pink Floyd references often come up in McCartney's avant-garde work as The Fireman and on Wings material too, especially *Back to the Egg*.

Cornelius Cardew was another avant-garde musician whom McCartney crossed paths with during this period. Cardew was pushing the boundaries of sound and experimentation in London with the same vigour as John Cage in the USA and Stockhausen in mainland Europe. His work remains sadly overlooked, perhaps because he died young, killed by a hit-and-run driver as he was walking home one night in thick snow in 1981. But in 1967 Morton Feldman decided that "If the new ideas in music are felt today as a movement in England, it's because [Cardew] acts as a moral force, a moral centre. Without him, the young 'far-out' composer would be lost..."

Having worked as an assistant to Stockhausen in the early sixties, Cardew later met and became close friends with John Cage. Both shared a passion for musical notation and the limitless signs and languages that might express music on paper. In fact, when Cage published many of the scores he had collected in *Notations*, a book for the Foundation of Contemporary Performance Arts, it included John Lennon's handwritten score for 'The Word', a birthday present from Lennon and Yoko Ono. Ono is said to have originally approached McCartney for a manuscript to give to Cage, before she met Lennon, but he turned her down.

While Cage was compiling *Notations*, Cardew wrote his own visionary documents on musical expression, *Notations, Interpretations, Etc.* and *Treatise Handbook*. He put his theories into practice too, with the improvisational groups AMM and the Scratch Orchestra. Both bands played music from written words rather than notation, meaning in theory that anyone could play along no matter what their level of competence. One member of the 1969 line-up of the Scratch Orchestra was a 21-year-old Brian Eno, whose first-ever appearance on record would be a 1971 performance of Cardew's political/avant-garde opus 'The Great Learning'.

AMM provided a mix of ambient sound, freeform jazz, avant-garde instruments and electronic sound. At one 'happening', they even mixed the Beach Boys into the equation by preparing a cacophonous loop of 'Barbara Ann', over which the band improvised, trying to drown it out across the course of an entire evening. No surprise that their drummer Edwin Prevost once famously said that "AMM music existed a few minutes before we thought of it..."

In 1966, AMM were holding weekly interactive improvisation sessions at the Royal College of Art. McCartney went along to check them out on the night of 15 September. Barry Miles went too but no other Beatles attended – Lennon was en route to Spain to film *How I Won the War* and Harrison had already decamped to Bombay to study sitar under Ravi Shankar.

There, in a scene often described by Miles although rarely by McCartney, they found many of Cage and Stockhausen's musical theories happening before their eyes. Tapes, radios, prepared piano, pure electronic sound generators and non-musical instruments mixed with drums and guitar and anything else the intellectual audience members cared to bring with them. A drill was used on stage as a musical instrument,a sight which lodged in one side of McCartney's mind for over 30 years until it dropped out of the other when he wielded a chainsaw for a late-1990s avant-garde performance of his own.

On stage that night, AMM comprised Cornelius Cardew (piano, cello), Edwin Prevost (drums, xylophone), Keith Rose (electric guitar), Lou Gare (saxophone, violin) and Lawrence Sheaff (cello, accordion, clarinet). Cardew, Rose and Shaeff also 'played' transistor radios. "For AMM these were important formative moments," remembers Prevost of these sessions. "It was a place of experimentation and a developing confidence in this most mobile of mediums. The sessions were intense, usually conducted in darkness or gloom – depending upon the time of year!" For a live experience that has since passed into avant-garde legend, it's surprising to learn that the whole residency had come about quite by chance, as Edwin Prevost told me:

■ Our continuing presence at The Royal College of Art arose from a misunderstanding. The Colleges' 'jazz club' had invited us for a performance at one of its evenings. Somehow we misunderstood the invitation to be for us to use the space every week. A typically English solution arose. Unspoken of course. The jazz club moved to another night of the week, leaving us to continue our residency. That continued until finally, at the beginning of the New Year (1967), a caretaker decided to ask under whose auspices was our activity placed. As there was no one, we were politely asked to leave. However, during a period of about six months our performances attracted a steady if small stream of curious and interested people. There was no publicity, simply word of mouth. Musicians like Steve Lacy, John Surman, as well as writers and other artists, used to arrive, listen and depart – often without any formal reference or conversations with the musicians. Somehow the occasion did not need any other kind of communication. John Hopkins, 'Hoppy' of *International Times* fame, used to come and cocoon himself in a blanket on the floor. McCartney and co, I think, arrived either with or on the advice of Miles, who we knew slightly from Indica Books sessions and other related events... The sessions had a particular kind of informality...

Casting his mind back to a stage-eye view of that evening, Prevost remembers McCartney dropping in. "I think I can recall McCartney together with two or three other people. Possibly Marianne Faithfull and probably Miles. I seem to remember one or other of them joining in by rattling the radiators. Otherwise I can only recall this group of people – who seemed to keep very close together – sitting on the floor..."

As he sat there on the floor, McCartney was wowed by the concept but not particularly by the music he heard – he would remark, though, that you don't have to like something to be inspired by it. "I think it's painful for a lot of people," said Keith Rowe, who played guitar and transistor radio that night, when he looked back on AMM's performances of the 1960s. "I don't think it's particularly pleasant, AMM, for a lot of folk. I think they listen to it and think, 'God, I'm glad that's over, I don't want to go through that again.'"

The 1970s and AMM just didn't compute. Cardew started bringing a great deal of Marxist-Leninist philosophy into his music, which alienated much of his audience. AMM members came and went and the group lost direction. Cardew and Rowe left to dive headlong into Muzak and easy listening under the guise of PLM (People's Liberation Music). Just as the dawn of the eighties saw a new experimental energy come into Paul McCartney's work, it also saw the tentative reformation of AMM. But this was cut short when Cardew was killed, exactly 12 months after John Lennon.

With an ever-evolving line-up, AMM exist to this day and show no signs of stopping. "This music first attained escape velocity 30 years ago now," wrote Rob Young in *The Wire* magazine in 1995, "and seems less likely than ever to cease. This music that takes root in a bed of silence, sprouts into life from the barest detectable trace elements, evolves intelligence and becomes articulate, expands until it becomes too dense for its own structure to bear, collapses back on itself into new silence and new shape, and tries the cycle again."

John Lennon got to see AMM for himself just over six months after McCartney, on 29 April 1967. While tripping on acid at home with John Dunbar, he saw a TV news item about the 14 Hour Technicolour Dream, a massive rave at the Alexandra Palace. It was being staged as a benefit concert for the *International Times*. McCartney had helped Miles and 'Hoppy' set up this influential underground newspaper the previous year. 41 different acts appeared at the rave, including Pink Floyd, Yoko Ono (her path didn't cross with Lennon's that night), AMM and The Crazy World of Arthur Brown.

*Sgt. Pepper* was finished at this stage and the release date was only a few weeks away. But AMM, the Technicolour Dream and other psychedelic gigs (all four Beatles went to see Procul Harum at the Speakeasy Club a few weeks later) inspired some outrageous, unreleased and relatively undocumented jam sessions. All four Beatles got together between *Sgt. Pepper* and *Magical Mystery Tour* to see if they could emulate these new sights and sounds.

Seven hours of largely instrumental jamming took place featuring electric guitar, vibrato guitar, harmonium, bass, organ, drums and tambourine. Another instrument in the mix was a guitar whose strings were scraped, exactly as Cornelius Cardew had crawled over his piano at the AMM concert McCartney had witnessed, tapping, scratching and playing it in every unconventional way possible. Only a few minutes of this discordant, acid-induced freak-out were recorded and all remain unreleased. However, 'Aerial Tour Instrumental' grew out of these mad sessions to become 'Flying', which appeared on *Magical*

*Mystery Tour.* 'Flying' has little if anything to do with '12 Bar Original' or the other Beatles instrumentals. Its proper place is as the bridge between the high-brow avant-garde improvisation of AMM, the street-level psychedelic bands at the Technicolour Dream and McCartney's later discordant experimental jam, 'Bison', explored in Chapter 13.

The avant-garde scene, perhaps because of the geographical diversity of its originators, has always embraced music from other cultures. Stockhausen's 'Hymnen' for example, pulled together a myriad of national anthems from around the world in a psychedelic audio collage. The Indian sitar guru Ravi Shankar made a graphic impact on the music of The Beatles and the psychedelic era. Less well known is how he stirred one thread of avant-garde music into life, which would make a major impact on Paul McCartney.

In his early twenties Shankar worked in Paris, where he met experimental American composer Philip Glass. The timings and rhythms of Shankar's sitar music simply blew Glass away. This was a flashpoint at the beginning of mini-malist and ambient music which, by the time it had evolved through Terry Riley and Steve Reich, began to show up a great deal in McCartney's avant-garde tracks – such as 'Glasses, 'Church Mice' and 'Feedback'.

Rather more well known is the impact Shankar's Hindustani music made on George Harrison, The Byrds and the flower children who saw him at the Monterey and Woodstock festivals. Shankar made a lasting impression on Paul McCartney too. He inspired McCartney to pick up the sitar for 'Arizona Light' (Chapter 10), 'Riding into Jaipur' (Chapter 16) and the 'Fluid' collaboration with Nitin Sawhney (Chapter 9).

These non-rock and roll influences being absorbed into the McCartney mind were coming from a variety of channels. George Martin and the other Beatles were his key sources, but the Asher family and his friend Barry Miles were also important. In his McCartney biography, Miles highlights the avant-garde sounds and meetings they experienced in the mid-1960s and examines how these influ-enced his musical output up until the *Abbey Road* album of 1969. Miles didn't just investigate avant-garde music with McCartney. The pair also had a thirst for contemporary art (Fraser, Warhol et al) and poetry (Ginsberg, Burroughs et al). This had less of a graphic influence on McCartney's music as a Beatle, but has become more and more of an influence in his solo music and post-Beatles experiments.

Alongside The Beatles and Miles, the Asher family was another important channel of influence. Highly educated and musical, they took McCartney under their wing when he started going out with Jane Asher, introducing him to count-less new styles of music and encouraging him to investigate sounds outside the rock and roll field. His horizons broadened with what George Martin remembered as "modern art, literature, modern music by the likes of John Cage, Stockhausen – the things he heard in the fruitful environment provided by the family Asher." "Although no one could ever say they [the Ashers] had any taste for the avant-garde," wrote Martin in his *Summer of Love* bio of the psychedelic era, "they encouraged Paul in his musical self-education to experiment and to be free, musically, if he felt like it."

McCartney brought Miles into the Apple unit to run Zapple – an avant-garde offshoot label which planned to release everything from spoken word albums to sound effects. Initially conceived as a budget-price spoken word and poetry outlet releasing only albums, Apple had intended this arm to cover works by the likes of Norman Mailer, Eldridge Cleaver, and beat poets Michael McClure and Allen Ginsberg. Interview discs were also planned, with Pablo Picasso and Daniel Colin-Bendit initially pencilled in. The idea was that Zapple releases should be cheaper than normal LPs. With the lower production costs associated with spoken word, they could act as musical magazines, responding quickly to changes in music and culture and priced so they could be bought, listened to once or twice, and then thrown away.

Sadly, like so many projects from Apple at the time, Zapple's ideals were never fully realised and none of these projects ever saw the light of day, despite a cataloguing/price structure having been set up that would take avant-garde music to the masses (15/- for ZAP-coded releases, 21/- for ZAPREC or full price 30/6d for ZAPPLE). The only two albums that ever carried the silver Zapple seal both retailed at full price – John Lennon and Yoko Ono's situationist tape collage *Unfinished Music No. 2/Life with the Lions* (ZAPPLE 01) and George Harrison's aforementioned *Electronic Sound* (ZAPPLE 02).

If McCartney and The Beatles' new-found enthusiasm for far-out music could not find an outlet on their traditional, mainstream albums, they had the perfect opportunity to create a unique platform with Zapple. But The Beatles' newly appointed financial adviser, Allen Klein, had other ideas. He put a stop to the fun and games less than year after the first Zapple release. Typically, Klein stated "There's no use in putting out anything that isn't up to par, even at a reduced price. From now on this company only concentrates on major releases." Rumoured Zapple projects, such as a 24-LP set of Lenny Bruce recordings and *Listening to Richard Brautigan* (the third Zapple release, ZAP01 – scrapped the day before its release only to appear on the Harvest label in the States a year later), were consigned straight to the history books. As Taylor later commented in his autobiography, *Fifty Years Adrift*, "We could have done big things with Apple and Zapple. How did we blow it?"

Throughout the late 1960s, all these avant-garde influences began seeping into The Beatles' music. The most audible influences are the Stockhausen and

Cage-style tape collages and loops which appear in 'Tomorrow Never Knows' and 'Revolution 9'. The electronic influence of Mathews, Derbyshire and co would appear later in McCartney's solo work (as explored in Chapter Eight), but George Harrison beat him to a release of early electronica by some years. Harrison's *Electronic Sound* resembled – as Alan Evans reported for the *New Musical Express* – "noises on a building site, air going into tyres, a machine gun fired by a bird, a rude noise here and there, a dentist's high speed drill..."

'Tomorrow Never Knows' is "probably the most famous use of musique con-crète in history," according to *Rolling Stone*. Lennon's lyrics were inspired by the Tibetan Book of the Dead; he was presumably unaware that French avant-garde composer Pierre Henry was working on an hour-long tape collage that same year, *The Voyage*, inspired by the same literature. McCartney provided equally surreal music to spark off Lennon's lyrics. Inspired by the avant-garde music he had heard, he began experimenting with tape loops in the DIY studio he had set up in the Asher family attic. He adapted his Grundig and Brennell reel-to-reel tape recorders to record infinitely, absorbing and overlaying anything played into them. Thrilled with the "little symphonies" he created, McCartney encour-aged the other Beatles to try the same with their home set-ups. The results formed the bizarre sounds that mix in and out of 'Tomorrow Never Knows', as George Martin remembered.

> ■ They would bring me in these loops, like cats bringing in sparrows. I would listen to them, play them at different speeds, backwards and forwards, at three and three quarters, seven and a half or 15 feet per second, and select liberally from them. From the 30 or so tapes they brought in, I selected 16 [at other times he has stated eight] loops I liked, each about six seconds long, to use on 'Tomorrow Never Knows'.

The finished track introduced LSD and the writings of Timothy Leary to the mass-es. All manner of trips and new possibilities are audible as laughter, orchestral chords, Mellotrons and sitars break into the mix from their respective loops. It was one of, but not *the*, first times such avant-garde techniques had mixed with rock and roll. While in the US, Stockhausen had socialised with Jefferson Airplane and the Grateful Dead. And in 1961, James Tenney (one of Max Mathews' colleagues at Bell Labs) had created 'Collage 1' which, using just phys-ical tape and razor blade to splice it, remixed Elvis Presley's and Carl Perkins' recordings of 'Blue Suede Shoes'. 'Tomorrow Never Knows' has been decon-structed by Beatle-ologists many times and its impact reverberates through rock and experimental music to this day. It was no coincidence that modern-day sound collagists the Chemical Brothers used the track's unique drum rhythm in their crossover hit 'Setting Sun'.

Inspired by the results he was achieving with his Brennell tape machines, McCartney financed the construction of a small recording studio in a flat in Montague Square that he rented from Ringo Starr. Miles' friend Ian Sommerville kitted the place out and moved in as producer-in-residence, working on hours of unreleased sound collages with William Burroughs. To Burroughs, it was more exploratory than creative, as he relied heavily on Sommerville's scientific training and experience of tape editing. Little if any of Burroughs' original experimental material from the McCartney tape lab was ever released, although his ideas and visions from this period would became reality after his death. In 2002, avant-garde electronica band Black Dog prepared modern-day tape loops and mixed them with Parisian poet Black Sifichi's readings of Burroughs for the album *Unsavoury Products*, a project which had been started in collaboration with Burroughs before he died.

Burroughs' experiments aside, McCartney eventually gave his studio premises back to Ringo Starr, the Beatles unit never quite allowing him the time to fully indulge his avant-garde tendencies. No one was quite ready for someone who could produce 'Hey Jude' to produce a clink-clunk experimental soundscape, much to McCartney's surprise and embarrassment. He pressed several acetates of his early tape-loop soundscapes but they remain unreleased, perhaps because the select few who heard them at the time didn't always dig it.

Marianne Faithfull once described how McCartney played one of these demos to Bob Dylan. "I saw him come in once with an acetate of a track he'd been working on which was very far out for its time, with all kinds of distorted electronic things on it," Faithfull remembered. "Paul was obviously terribly proud of it. He put it on the record player and stood back in anticipation, but Dylan just walked out of the room. It was unbelievable. The expression on Paul's face was priceless…"

Following 'Tomorrow Never Knows' (and 'Carnival of Light'), John Lennon led The Beatles' most famous sound-collage experiment. McCartney, Harrison and Starr may not have liked it but by the time of the so-called White Album, The Beatles had a new fifth member in the form of Yoko Ono. 'Revolution 9' was the sound of her and Lennon taking the band off in their own avant-garde direction.

In the same way that this book breaks down McCartney's later avant-garde works, like *Strawberries Oceans Ships Forest* and *Liverpool Sound Collage*, so Beatle-ologists over the years have distilled the noise array that is 'Revolution 9' into its component parts. In doing so they have found violins, orchestral recordings, opera, spoken words from Harrison and Lennon, audience noise and clattering glasses.

McCartney was not actually involved in this most famous piece of avant-garde

Beatles tracks. He was out of the country when Lennon and Ono oversaw its creation. Creating the overall sound of the track was done in the same way George Martin described for 'Tomorrow Never Knows'. With all the tape loops running at once, they were mixed in and out of the finished recording 'live'. This was the genesis of a new form of pop – live mixing of continuous sounds – ie, the modern art of the DJ or remixer. McCartney may have missed out on the fun with 'Revolution 9' but he didn't forget the process, revising it exactly (albeit with updated technology) for a full album's worth of loops mixed up live 25 years later.

One of the loops that floats into audible range in this cacophonous track is actually from *Sgt. Pepper*'s 'A Day in the Life'. If 'Revolution 9' had been the product of Lennon's Stockhausen fixation, then 'A Day in the Life' was a nod to John Cage. But the avant-garde influences here don't detract from the fact that this piece comprises two of Lennon and McCartney's most poetic songs glued together. It's just that the glue they chose to use was the sound of McCartney conducting a terrific, overpowering 40-piece orchestral jam.

McCartney decided against scoring and notation for this orchestra. Taking a leaf out of Cornelius Cardew's book (literally), he gave the players their instructions in words, not musical notes. "We just wrote it down like a cooking recipe," he said. "24 bars, on the ninth bar the orchestra will take off and it will go from its lowest note to its highest note." McCartney was putting the ideal of AMM into action. And he combined them with the outlandish performance art of Stockhausen. To get the orchestra to loosen up, he asked them to attend in full evening dress, with the addition of masks and false noses. This surreal evening became a party with the likes of Mickey Dolenz (who frequently socialised with McCartney at this time), Mick Jagger, Donovan and others all in attendance, roaming the crowd with Super 8 video cameras for The Beatles' shelved *Sgt. Pepper* film. One of the flute players drafted in, Alan Civil, was bemused:

■ Everybody would play their lowest note, say, and go up and play higher and higher. And you'd say "How the hell are they going to use this?" And there was Ringo dashing around with his movie camera. It seemed almost like a party, with booze, fags, and such. It was crazy. You couldn't believe it was a session. A lot of classical musicians didn't really condone this type of session. They thought it was rather beyond, well, beneath their dignity to mess around like that.

If the notation and orchestral instruction were pure Cardew, then the alarm clock-driven rhythm and tempo of this avant-garde injection into *Sgt. Pepper* was pure Cage. Elsewhere on the album, the influence of Burroughs' cut-ups can be heard (the animal sounds in 'Good Morning, Good Morning'), as can McCartney's own "little symphonies" of tape and sticky-tape (the acid fairground trip in 'Being For the Benefit of Mr Kite'). Lennon's daring, McCartney's vision and George Martin's technical dexterity combined to make 'A Day in the Life' a lyrical and musical open door to the possibilities of pop.

The Beatles were at the forefront, and the most visible, but they were not the only band playing with such effects and sounds. Frank Zappa's music comes into play in the next chapter. But other key tracks from 1967 included Love's classic 'Seven and Seven Is', which is split in half by the sound of an A-bomb explosion. Brian Wilson used all manner of found sounds in The Beach Boys' *Pet Sounds*; and The Box Tops had the sound of a jet airplane shooting through their song 'The Letter'.

'A Day in the Life' ended with a heart-stopping, "scary" (as Brian Wilson found it) piano chord, played by Lennon, McCartney, Ringo Starr, Mal Evans and George Martin in unison across three pianos, 12 days after the orchestral session. This final punctuation mark was the end of the album, save for 'Sgt. Pepper's Inner Groove,' a riotous sound collage dismissed as "silly nonsense" by George Martin. "We mumbled a few words into tape, cut the tape up, and recorded the result backwards," he explained. They then placed their creation in the run-off groove of the vinyl, something which only those with a manual turntable would ever hear, as McCartney explained:

■ A lot of record players [in the 1960s] didn't have auto-change. You would play an album and it would go 'tick, tick, tick,' in the run-out groove – it would just stay there endlessly. We were whacked out so much of the time in the sixties – just quite harmlessly, as we thought, it was quite innocent – but you would be at friends' houses, 12 at night, and nobody would be going to get up to change that record player. So we'd be getting into the little 'tick, tick, tick' – 'It's quite good, you know? There's a rhythm there.' We were into Cage and Stockhausen, those kind of people. Obviously, once you allow yourself that kind of freedom… well, Cage is appreciating silence, isn't he? We were appreciating the run-out groove! We said, "What if we put something, so that every time it did that, it said something?" So we put a little loop of conversation on.

George Martin took up the story several years later in a radio interview.

■ I think it was probably Paul that said, if ever people don't have the modern machines, they will hear something that will knock their socks off. So we said, all right, giggle, lets do it. They just went down into the studio and I said "Just sing the first thing that comes into your head when I put the red light on." All four of them sang something quite ridiculous, and I lopped off about two seconds of it, and then stuck it round into a circle and laid that in the groove.

Pre-Beatles, the groundbreaking performances of Stockhausen and the avant-garde had always been limited to either stage or radio. There was no market for albums by these composers in the sixties. Conversely, by 1966 The Beatles had given up live concerts and ploughed all their creative energy into songs they knew would only ever be heard on vinyl. As such they pushed this medium to its limits, hence some experimental music even in the run-off groove.

As to what The Beatles actually said when Martin recorded them for this collage is anyone's guess. General consensus is that "I never could see any other way" rings out above the noise (although when played backwards the phrase "We'll f*** you like you're Superman" becomes clear).

Few listeners eventually heard the collage, as it was not included on US pressings of *Sgt. Pepper's Lonely Hearts Club Band*, Capitol pressing plant employees apparently thinking it was a mistake on the master reel and discarding it. The first time American listeners got to hear the track was years later when it was included on Capitol Records' 1978 *Rarities* compilation, where it had a title for the first time, 'Sgt. Pepper's Inner Groove'. UK record buyers, on the other hand, were treated to two quite different versions on the mono and stereo pressings of *Sgt. Pepper*.

The Beatles weren't breaking any new ground musically with the collage they created for 'Inner Groove', they were merely repeating the Cage/Stockhausen-inspired loops of previous tracks. What was new, however, was the combination of this music with a new medium, the run-off groove of a pop record (it had been used in classical circles on 1940s 78s). It inspired a host of imitators and homages. One of Brian Eno's classic post-Scratch Orchestra albums, *Taking Tiger Mountain (By Strategy)*, ended side one with infinite chirping crickets in its run-off groove. Released soon after *Sgt. Pepper*, Pink Floyd's *Atom Heart Mother* locked in the sound of water dripping. The Dukes of Stratosphere (XTC's Pepper-inspired psychedelic alter ego), the James Gang, M, The Who, Sonic Youth's Lee Ranaldo and Peter Gabriel have also tried it. 'White Shadow', the end track on side one of Gabriel's *Scratch* album, is infinitely long thanks to The Beatles' run-off groove trick.

A further, playfully avant-garde use of the vinyl medium was hit upon when The Beatles decided to cut a 20,000-hertz tone into the vinyl, just before the 'Inner Groove' collage. George Martin had been telling the band about how certain tones are only audible to certain species so they decided that there should be a part of the album that only dogs could enjoy.

Another new medium that The Beatles used as a stage for their avant-garde ideas were the records used to distribute their Christmas messages to fan club members. These flexi discs are all but unheard-of these days, but right up until the 1980s they were a cheap way of distributing music without the costs of pressing (or mailing) hard vinyl, as Paul McCartney reminisced years later on *Oobu Joobu*, his radio show that's investigated in Chapter 16.

> ■ In the early sixties, one of the little gimmicks that had come out was that you could buy a birthday card and it had inside it a little disc that you could actually play. It was a floppy, but not what you mean now by a floppy disc, but it was just a little record you could put on your record player and play it. And it was a cheap little thing that you could play and it would say "Happy birthday to you" and these were in birthday cards and greetings cards. And our publicist at the time, a bloke called Tony Barrow, brought one of these in and he said "Wouldn't it be great if we could send one of these out to the fans? We could give everyone one and it could be an actual, their own personal record from The Beatles." So we got into that idea and the first one was sort of "Hello this is George, hello this is Paul, hello this is John here, hello this is Ringo, hello fans." It was one of those kind of fan club records which was very nice but over the years we started to realise this was quite a little opportunity we had here. So they got more and more complicated as we got more and more into them and we'd made up special little pieces of music that would only appear on these fan club records.

These special records were released over seven consecutive Christmases, from 1963 to 1969. As McCartney described it, the first four were scripted, Goons-style larking and music. But it was no surprise that, after all the new influences that permeated the band in 1966, the Christmas record that year was a little different. Coming in a psychedelic sleeve painted by McCartney, *Pantomime (Everywhere It's Christmas)* had The Beatles 'acting' their way through the kind of skits Lennon had written in his *Spaniard in the Works* and *In His Own Write* books. At the same time George Martin was given the chance to wheel out Ray Cathode's box of tricks and special effects library.

"It was recorded at [Beatles publisher] Dick James' studio," explained the *New Musical Express*, "the first time they have waxed outside of EMI since they came to fame." Their news article, 'Beatles Goon It Up Again', from 17 December 1966 continued, "It's all rather obscure humour and if there are any funny lines then they are obliterated by some of the noises which make up the background." *Christmastime (Is Here Again)* arrived a year later and took things further, mixing a special composition with a psychedelic game show. But by the 1968 and 1969 recordings the acid trip was starting to wear off. The content was as freaky as before, but the band were recording their contributions separately, DJ Kenny Everett was editing them back together and George Martin was nowhere to be seen.

All this experimentation died down by the end of the sixties and the end of The Beatles' collective life, as they knee-jerked away from the avant-garde to a back-to-basics approach for their final albums. "'Get Back' is the new Beatles single," proclaimed an Apple advert in April 1969. "It's the first Beatles single which is as alive as can be, in this electronic age. There's no electronic watch-macallit." But the spirit of experimentation was still there, just philosophically rather than electronically, as Abbey Road (and later McCartney/Wings) engineer Alan Parsons remembered.

> ■ I think I was enormously impressed at that time by the way they didn't use normal, conventional musical instruments to make the record. They used all sorts of strange ideas and processes, with instruments. Remember, they were one of the first pop bands, if not *the* first, to brilliantly use the Moog synthesiser, and earlier they were the first to use the Mellotron. The Moog was used on *Abbey Road* quite a bit. It was actually George Harrison's ... I was surprised when I saw Ringo blowing through a straw into a glass of water to get the underwater effect for *Octopus's Garden*. Then, on *Maxwell's Silver Hammer*, he banged an anvil for the hammering sound on the track.

It would be impossible for any artist or musician to name the exact influences that show up in their work. By their very nature influences are subject to memories, moods and the passage of time. Arnold Browne would be the first to agree. He's a fictional character, made up by me. In combining the stories of Tara Browne and Arnold Wesker, he proves that it's impossible to ever chart "exactly" what happened with The Beatles and the stories of its four musicians. Those who were there at the time have even less hope. They were either absorbing musical and artistic influences so readily that one merged into the next. Or they were absorbing so many mind-altering substances that memory took second place to new experiences.

George Martin always thought that in 'A Day in the Life' John Lennon was singing about Tara Browne, a friend of his, Paul's and David Vaughan (who takes up the story of the experimental McCartney in the next chapter). This was an assumption echoed by Beatles biographers Miles and MacDonald. "Typical of John, the lyrics were taken from things he'd read all over the place," remembered George Martin (as cited in *The Beatles – An Oral History*). "The person who 'blew his mind out' in a car crash was a friend of his named Tara Browne."

However, in his chronicle of the making of *Sgt. Pepper*, Martin changed his mind. "I must confess that I had always thought, like most people, that the lyric 'He blew his mind out in a car' referred to the death of Tara Browne, who was a close friend of John and Paul," he wrote. "No so. Some Beatle analyst somewhere had put two and two together to make five." It wasn't a car crash that blew the character in the song's mind out, it was an acid trip, he had now decided.

"In the mid-60s, Paul patrolled London with his antennae out, omnivorous, wide open for experience," wrote author Barry Miles in a 2002 article on McCartney's avant-garde awakenings in 1966. Miles, who worked and socialised with McCartney in the mid-1960s, plying him with various avant-garde musics and ideas, continued: "Through Jane Asher he met playwrights, actors and film directors: Bernard Miles, Harold Pinter, Arnold Wesker."

True, Wesker does remember meeting Paul McCartney in the sixties. But that's about it, with no recollection of Jane Asher. *The Kitchen* (1957), *The Wesker Trilogy* (1958/60), *Chips with Everything* (1962) and *The Four Seasons* (1965) had by 1966 established Arnold Wesker, then 34, as one of England's most important playwrights. "These are my memories of Paul McCartney…" he wrote to me in a letter. "Harold Pinter used to give huge parties. I was invited to one with my wife, Dusty, and The Beatles were among the guests. I seem to remember getting them, or one of them, a drink. I think I was a little over-eager to please. The next occasion was when I visited John Lennon in a house in the south somewhere…" Wesker went to visit Lennon to help raise funds for the Camden Roundhouse, a pivotal venue in the development of Paul McCartney as avant-garde musician, the story of which we take up in Chapter Three. "At the time my publisher, Tom Maschler of Jonathan Cape, was publishing John Lennon's book (forget the title) and said he'd arrange a meeting. A date was set for morning coffee – or was it afternoon tea?"

■ Whenever I visit someone I take something. This time I thought as we're having a beverage of some sort I'd take a Jewish gift of smoked salmon, cream cheese and bagels. We drove to the house. A bored, utterly uninterested and unwelcoming young woman opened the door to us. I gave her my gift. She seemed surprised that anyone would bring anything, took it, and told us to wait. I remember there was a large room with a sunken part in the centre. Some other young people were lounging around. The atmosphere was unanimated.

Finally we were taken up to a small room where Lennon and McCartney were rehearsing with their guitars. They stopped to talk. It was Lennon I was interested in. I explained the aims of Centre Fortytwo – which were to establish an arts centre where all the arts, including jazz, would function and from where we'd target a popular audience. I told him about The Roundhouse and the funds we needed.

I can remember little of the details of the conversation we exchanged, I know only that McCartney was sceptical and couldn't see the point of it, and that Lennon contradicted him. They communicated an air of agreeing on little.

Lennon said he'd think about it. He did and finally wrote his support in time for the appeal's launch but not in time for his name to be on the appeal's invitation card. We couldn't have been together for more than 30 minutes. I was looking forward to sharing the smoked salmon bagels with them but no one offered us anything to drink. We left dry and cold. They seemed not to be familiar with the basic rules of hospitality.

Although this seemingly uneventful meeting casts a new, intriguing light on the Lennon-McCartney partnership, it was hardly the inspirational meeting Miles alludes to. Unless McCartney remembers it differently. But the continual cataloguing and archiving of the Beatles oeuvre which drives so many is of little or no interest to either McCartney or this book. "It could have been subconscious," McCartney said in 2002 on hearing that his new song 'From a Lover to a Friend' could be a letter to his first wife about his second. "Only years later was it suggested 'Yesterday' could have been written about my dead mother," he added. He'll readily admit that his own memory of events and meetings is fading too. "We forget – who cares?" he once told *Bassplayer* magazine. "We did some great stuff. But exact analysis was never our bag..."

# THREE
# 'CARNIVAL OF LIGHT'
## AT THE FANTASY-
## LOON/BLOWOUT/DRAG BALL

*The Beatles Anthology* project of 1994, which saw six CDs' worth of tracks pulled from the archives, left most people under the impression that we'd heard everything there was to hear from The Beatles. Not so. Aside from the complete final 'Rooftop Concert', some 200 unreleased tracks from the *Get Back* film sessions and the legendary 20-minute version of 'Helter Skelter', fans of The Beatles' experimental works are yet to hear the 'Carnival of Light' Rave sound-track, a cut-and-paste sound collage featuring all four members in an explosive prequel to 'Revolution 9'. For Paul McCartney, 'Carnival of Light' is "the coolest piece of music since sliced bread."

'Carnival of Light' is an unpredictable sound collage explosion – bursting with random percussion and vocal effects in a melody-less powerpack of random-ness. It was recorded for one of the late-1960s London underground happenings where lightshows met with experimental dance music to take performance – and public interaction – to a brand new level. They were the forerunners of con-temporary club culture. This Beatles track was heard once – for one night only – and has since sat on top of the pile of recordings waiting to find a legal cus-todian after the Beatles' divorce. 30 years on, McCartney remains in love with 'Carnival of Light', although George Harrison and George Martin's disdain for it has become just as legendary as the music itself.

1966 and the dawn of club culture as we know it... The Roundhouse Theatre, a rickety, not-quite-converted locomotive winding-house in Chalk Farm, London. Light shows and bubbles. Giant jellies and Syd Barrett's Pink Floyd. LSD and minimal lighting. Yoko Ono pre-Lennon. The *Sunday Times* would describe scenes of "throbbing music ... bizarre coloured shapes flashed on a huge screen behind ... a mountain of jelly which people ate at midnight

... All apparently very psychedelic."

The highly influential *International Times*, the underground paper Barry Miles had started with a little help from Paul McCartney, was launched at the Roundhouse and described what resulted as "Two and a half thousand people dancing about in that strange, giant round barn. Darkness, only flashing lights. People in masks, girls half-naked. Other people standing about wondering what the hell was going on. Pot smoke." The dawn of club culture was heralded by the dawn of club flyers, and the *IT* launch was no exception. Miles and co mailed anyone and everyone they knew, promising:

> ■ "Pop/Op/Costume/Masque/Fantasy-Loon/Blowout/Drag Ball. All night rave to launch *International Times*, with the Soft Machine, Pink Floyd, steel bands, strips, trips, happenings, movies. Bring your own poison and flowers & gas filled balloons & submarines & rocket ships & candy & striped boxes & ladders & paint & flutes & feet & ladders & locomotives & madness & autumn & blow lamps."

The music was equally outlandish. "The Pink Floyd, psychedelic pop group, did weird things to the feel of the evening with their scary feedback sounds," wrote the *International Times*, "slide projections playing on their skin (drops of paint run riot on the slides to produce outer space/prehistoric textures on the skin), spotlights flashing on them in time with a drum beat. The Soft Machine, another group with new ideas, drove a motor bike into the place, in and around the pillars that held up that gallery we had been warned wasn't all that safe." *IT* concluded, breathlessly, "It was a good party"!

The Soft Machine, the archetypal four-piece combination of psychedelia and Englishness, was fronted by Daevid Allen. These events at the Roundhouse saw the start of his lifelong journey through musical experimentation. Still touring intensively to this day, he was tracked down in Australia and told me that:

> ■ The first Roundhouse gig with Pink Floyd playing under an earlier name and Yoko Ono appearing in the middle of our Soft Machine set to create a 'happening' was most memorable for me – for the atmosphere of incredulous realisation that we were not isolated individuals with futuristic notions but rather a large group of likeminded individuals with a shared revolutionary vision. So the feeling was of sudden transition from a lonely yet inspired egocentricity into a powerful group consciousness of ever-expanding possibility. What a moment! Was this how the Dadaists felt in the 1920s? It was a total cultural/sociological paradigm switch and its purest expression was through its music.

Paul McCartney was mesmerised by these concerts. "As the Soft Machine finished," wrote Julian Palacios in his biography of Syd Barrett, *Lost in the Woods*, "the Pink Floyd began their set on the stage set up on the opposite side of the Roundhouse. With the house lights off and their light show on, Barrett and Co began with the low, ominous rumble of 'Astronomy Domine'. Their light show, though appallingly primitive, made quite an impression on the assembled crowd, not least of all Paul McCartney, who made his approval plain."

Surprisingly, Paul McCartney fitted in perfectly among the clubbers at the Roundhouse – by disguising himself in white Arab robes, complete with headdress. Also spotted was Marianne Faithfull in a slightly more conspicuous micromini nun's habit. Other regulars at the Roundhouse included Douglas Binder, Dudley Edwards and David Vaughan, an artistic trio who plastered psychedelic overtures over public spaces. The most often photographed example of such painting at the time was the first incarnation of Apple's shop in Savile Row. Same style but actually by Simon Postuma and Marijke Koger, who also recorded for Apple Records as The Fool. At the time, Binder, Edwards and Vaughan kept their art on a slightly smaller scale: multi-coloured cars and psychedelic pianos.

David Vaughan was a graduate of the Bradford College of Art and The Slade School of Art. On moving down south he began developing what has become a lifelong passion for public-scale artworks, taking walls, pubic spaces, musical instruments and furniture and sandblasting them with colour until they became something entirely new. Cars were a particular speciality. As for his artistic partners: "I never found out much about Binder, or Edwards either!" he told me. "Douglas Binder was a painter at the Royal College of Art, Dudley Edwards was doing graphics at Bradford and I met him when I was at the Slade and he was working nearby. The two of them came to live with me and we got a big place in Chalk Farm."

Binder, Edwards and Vaughan took the most gas-guzzling antitheses of hippie culture – Buicks, AC Cobras and the like – and turned them into the ultimate statements of the alternative lifestyle. Vaughan is probably the only furniture restorer, or furniture 're-imaginer' as Tim Burton might put it, whose customer list includes Henry Moore, Lord Snowdon, the British Admiralty and Paul McCartney.

In 1966 Vaughan's work really exploded. At the height of the psychedelic era he received multiple commissions for public murals – for Knightsbridge, Carnaby Street, London Zoo and Montreal's Expo 67. He continues this unique style today. Having returned to the north of England in the early 1970s, he has lectured, illustrated songs by Bob Dylan ('The Masters of War' series) and produced numerous important murals. Among these is an entire corridor of Tameside General Hospital in his hometown of Ashton. Another copies and merges pre-Raphaelite images across the walls of an Ardwick homeless shelter.

Along with Edwards and Binder, David Vaughan also become involved in the Roundhouse's groundbreaking events, staging 'happenings' for the likes of The Jimi Hendrix Experience. He takes up the story of the venue, and the emerging avant-garde, where Arnold Wesker left off in the previous chapter: "The Roundhouse was originally 'given' to Arnold Wesker, a very famous and notorious Jewish playwright of the sixties," Vaughan told me. "Slightly older than the sixties lot, but fancied himself a bit 'with it'. They got together and were given government money to put this place together as some kind of centre to hold plays in." Wesker gives his side of the story, tying up with his reminiscences quoted in the previous chapter:

■ I was running an arts organisation called Centre Fortytwo in the (very) early sixties. We had just discovered a building in Chalk Farm owned by Gilby's the Wine Merchants that was going on the market to a property owner called Louis Mintz. It was called The Roundhouse. I persuaded Louis to give me the remaining 19-year lease for our centre. We hired French architects to design and cost its conversion. The amount was around £450,000. I wanted to run the place for two years without government grants and so needed to raise an extra £200,000.

We therefore had to raise £650,000. I needed names to support the appeal. John Lennon was one I sought. His agreement came too late for the invitation card. The others who agreed to sign were: Lord Harewood, Dame Peggy Ashcroft (actress), Prof A J Ayer (philosopher), Sir Arthur Bliss (composer), Benjamin Britten (composer), Albert Finney (actor), Graham Greene (novelist), Yehudi Menuhin (violinist), Henry Moore (sculptor), John Piper (painter), J B Priestley (playwright), Terence Rattigan (playwright), Sir Herbert Read (art critic), Vanessa Redgrave (actress), Sir Carol Reed (film director) and Sir John Rothenstein.

However, as far as David Vaughan was concerned, Wesker and his team "couldn't do it! They were too in the clouds!" – which is when he stepped in with Binder and Edwards. Vaughan's memories of his first visit to the Roundhouse are vivid. Not least because, while he was there, he managed to pull off the kind of art stunt that would make modernday Turner Prize Terrorists like Tracy Emin or the K Foundation proud. "The Roundhouse was held for all kinds of events, like the Young Contemporaries exhibition," he remembers, adding:

■ The Young Contemporaries is an award that everyone chases. They send work in from all over the world, all over Britain. So it got millions and millions and millions of different parcels, different shapes and sizes, sculptures, paintings, the lot. And the Roundhouse one day was full of this crap. We saw them going in and out with it. So I went in and I was just stood there weighing up this fantastic

Turneresque, dark scene of this massive engine shed, with all these millions and millions of parcels and sculptures and paintings, half-opened and all sorts, at the time when they were being judged by the boffins of the day. And then what they considered the best would go on show at somewhere like the Royal Academy or some big venue and the student that won it would get, like, fifty million quid!

I was stood there and this chap came along who resembled John Cleese. He was very, very tall like him. Six and a half foot, ramrod straight. Bowler hat, pinstripe suit and a brief case. And he walked up to me and he gave me this ticket and said, "I've come for 167, it's been rejected and I've been sent on behalf of my client." I said, "Oh, very good, give me the ticket." So I went outside and tied it to a road lamp. You know the old-variety road lamp, with the hook on the top with a candlewick inside. A train had run over it about 50 years ago and it was lying there rusty and rotten and desolate. I thought, "The poor bugger." So I tied the ticket around the handle and I walked back and gave it to him! I said, "There you are, my boy, there's your 167!" He said, "Oh yes, very good", never batted an eyelid, walked outside and flagged down a cab! And off he went! We were in f***ing hysterics! I never found out who the hell he was. Never saw him again. Never got his name or his poor client or anything, but can you imagine the performance? So I thought, "This is the place for me. This has got my kind of vibes!"

At the end of 1966, one of David Vaughan's most important musical instrument commissions became Paul McCartney's piano. A complete overhaul of the traditional upright, used for composing in the music room of his flat in London's Cavendish Avenue. For £300, Vaughan covered the piano in a psychedelic rainbow. He also added a new wooden back to the upright, for an extra fee. As soon as the piano was finished McCartney was back at work – he used it to compose 'Penny Lane' and other songs, which The Beatles and George Martin were soon to commit to tape as recording for *Sgt. Pepper's Lonely Hearts Club Band* kicked off. Back in Chalk Farm, Binder, Edwards and Vaughan were about to make the Roundhouse their own, as the latter remembers:

■ I met this here Arnold Wesker and they obviously couldn't hack it. So I ended up taking the place over. The three of us together, but I was like a bit of a battering ram for anything I wanted to do. I'd just go ahead and do it. And the first thing was the Million Volt Light and Sound Rave. Million Volt named after, for obvious reasons, lysergic acid. If you take enough of it, it's like a million volts. And I brought over a fellow called Richard Ardent from San Francisco who ran the light shows for Bill Graham at the Fillmore West in San Francisco, or was it Los Angeles? I can't remember which. But I went there in the 1960s and this fellow was a bit of a genius. So I brought him over.

And first of all, I got the locals from Gloucester Avenue – Jim Cleary, an Irish fellow and his mate Tom, I still remember them two, to put the toilets in. Which of course Wesker and whatnot didn't do. So that was the first fundamental I thought to do, and that was at our expense, Binder and us all paid for that. And then we sheeted the entire round auditorium so it looked like a great big round cinema. And that was at our expense. And then we put behind it all the liquid lighting and overhead projectors we could lay our hands on, and all the back-projectors and Kodak carousels. They were advanced for the time. They were slide projectors. They went around in a circle and were dead new at the time.

Then there was the Pop Caterers. They came out of the ether. And they turned out to be a right bunch of villains who previously worked for the Krays, who decided they were going to turn caterers overnight. They got it completely wrong. They'd serve beefburgers and hamburgers and they'd make a killing. I think they had a bit of a protection racket going on as well. They got everything wrong. I'll never forget that night that they were there – nobody bought a bloody beefburger or hamburger or bugger all and they ended up fighting between us. They thought, this is a good word, the Pop Caterers, but they were really a bunch of villains from the East End who were muscling in. Anyway, they came out of the ether and I didn't pay any attention to them. Anyone that wanted to do anything was all right with me, so long as they didn't charge. And I just let the thing happen, let the story unfold...

Having finished McCartney's psychedelic piano re-spray by Christmas 1966, Vaughan told him about the new Roundhouse event which he, Binder and Edwards were planning for the New Year and asked The Beatles to provide the soundtrack. McCartney convinced Lennon, Harrison, Starr and Martin that the Roundhouse would be a great testing ground for an experimental Beatles sound-collage. A recording session had already been booked at Abbey Road for 5 January 1967 but the planned vocal overdubs for 'Penny Lane' were pushed aside in favour of some New Year madness. Almost 14 minutes of randomised 1960s audio freaking – aka The Beatles' 'Carnival of Light' – was assembled.

Assembled is the word. 'Carnival of Light' wasn't written, it was a cut-and-paste collage of found sounds. Cutting edge at the time but now just like almost every sample-laden dance track in the clubs. The music may have been nothing like anything the band had recorded to date but, like any Beatles track, it's based around some familiar pillars. Ringo is there at the core, thumping out, under-pinning the epic and trading off some classic period organ. This is the basis for various other elements to come in and out of the mix. Sound effects, overdriv-en guitar, percussion, church organ, cinema organ. The vocals are equally extreme. If 'Penny Lane' was 20th century poetry, this was 21st century anti-poetry with the lyric sheet – had any of this madness not been spontaneous – reading something like:

■ **All:** general screaming
**McCartney:** whistling
**Lennon:** gargling
**All:** Barcelona!
**McCartney:** coughing
**Lennon:** Are you all right?
**McCartney:** Can we hear it back now?

The effects are equally freaky. Elements drowned in reverb surround sloweddown drums and organ, with some more traditional musicianship leaking out as one instrument plays off another. And it's worth noting that this experimental track – where shrieking is key – was not only recorded before Yoko Ono and John Lennon's *Two Virgins* (derided for over three decades now on account of Ono's ear-piercing vocals), but before the two even met.

Ten days before 'Carnival of Light' was aired at the Roundhouse (and the day after Tara Browne's death), McCartney gave an interview to Granada TV about the underground scene he was becoming increasingly involved in. In a special entitled *So Far Out It's Straight Down*, McCartney talked about the divide between straights and hippies that he was currently straddling:

■ I really wish the people that look sort of in anger at the 'weirdos', at the happenings, at the psychedelic freak-out, would instead of just looking with anger – just look with nothing; with no feeling; be unbiased about it. They really don't realise that what these people are talking about is something that they really want themselves. It's something that everyone wants. You know, it's personal freedom to be able to talk and be able to say things. And it's dead straight! It's a real sort of basic pleasure for everyone. But it looks weird from the outside.

In order to find out what 'Carnival of Light' actually sounds like, look no further than Frank Zappa's rich back-catalogue. The track has been likened in the past to both 'The Return of the Son of Monster Magnet (Unfinished Ballet in Two Tableaux)' from Zappa's debut album *Freak Out!* and 'The Chrome Plated Megaphone of Destiny' from *We're Only In It for the Money*. The latter appeared in 1967 and was a direct, irreverent, six-and-a-half minute response to The Beatles' experimental work. This mould-breaking composition, which required you to read Franz Kafka's *In the Penal Colony* before listening, was described by

*Rolling Stone* as "perhaps the most mercilessly derisive raspberry ever flung at the rock scene by an actual participant therein."

'The Return of the Son of Monster Magnet' came out in 1966, directly inspired by and in memory of the experimental composer Edgard Varèse, who had died the previous year. It was "what freaks sound like when you turn them loose in a recording studio at one o'clock in the morning on $500-worth of rented percussion equipment," explained Zappa on the sleeve notes. Stockhausen, Burroughs and many of the other influences that were weighing on McCartney and The Beatles are also apparent in Zappa's work from this period, which came to a head with 'Lumpy Gravy', a symphony merging rock with all manner of avant-garde strains – spoken word, electronics, tape loops and so on – realised by the Abnuceals Emuukha Electric Symphony Orchestra & Chorus. In later years, incidentally, McCartney remixers and producers Art of Noise used many of the same elements, rejigged to equally dark effect, on 'Who's Afraid of the Art of Noise?' in 1984.

'Carnival of Light' is no simple psychedelic dreamscape. Recordings of this type allowed The Beatles to break free from traditional song structures and produce music that was rawer and, as a result, more emotional. Those who actually heard it, however, were of the same opinion as Bob Dylan on McCartney's early avant-garde attempts – comprehensively underwhelmed. David Vaughan:

> ■ We booked Jimi Hendrix for fifty pounds. That was his first gig in the British Isles. And of course we were dead chuffed about this. And then we got The Pink Floyd on the bill, and The Soft Machine. So all the music was live, apart from these f\*\*ing awful tapes that Paul McCartney did. You know, where he thought he'd do something without words, that was very mysterious. He just proffered his services and that's what we got. I can't remember but I don't think it was up to much. It didn't last with me. It was more or less how he came to turn himself on, and everybody else on, to this new abstract music without words.

McCartney's 'Carnival of Light' didn't make a lasting impression on Daevid Allen, either. "I dimly remember the sound collage because it was not particularly memorable," he told me. "He had obviously improved a bit by the time *Sgt. Pepper* was made." He may not have dug the music, but David Vaughan at least felt that with 'Carnival of Light' The Beatles were working their way out of the commercial rat race.

> ■ They'd been known for 'Love Me Do' and all that. And the idea was that, of course, he did it before John. They were a pain in the arse, the pair of them, I can tell you. In fact they all were. They were always trying to upstage each other. I

mean, who gives a f*** who was first for that one, do you know what I mean? They invented rock and roll music, you know, and psychedelia and God knows what else. But people their age, or older, or a bit younger, who travelled more, or had seen more or heard more, they knew it was all bullshit. It's like Hear'Say now – once they got hold of them, they turned them into dummies. The media men pressganged them into these suits and funny haircuts. But I felt sorry for Lennon because he was desperately, all his life, trying to get away from it once he'd realised what he'd been sucked into. That's why he married that warbling Okay Yony. But this is just asides. This is what you conjure up in my memory…

'Carnival of Light' came in stark contrast to 'Penny Lane' (recorded the same week). Negative reaction and all, it evoked the Summer of Love's precarious sunset. And rightly so. Such a dark sound collage more eloquently describes the time than a three-minute pop song ever could. As *Time Out* magazine later recalled, "After the '67 Summer of Love, Vietnam splashed blood on our pretty faces and our acid-educated ideals had to face the real world." Rather than being a forerunner for chill-out Ibiza soundtracks, the darker and deeper tone of 'Carnival of Light' makes it more of a basis for Primal Scream's groundbreaking *Screamadelica*, released on Creation post-'second Summer of Love', 1991.

Working on 'Carnival of Light' at Abbey Road split the Beatles down the middle. McCartney was finally putting all he had heard of Stockhausen and the avant-garde into practice. Lennon was following his instincts. Starr was following. Harrison and Martin, on the other hand, were quite simply not digging it. George Martin thought the whole process was nonsense and was itching to get back on course with 'Penny Lane' overdubs and re-orchestrations. Harrison put his views in print, on the sleeve notes to his first solo album, the equally experimental (but rather more focussed) *Electronic Sound* (1969). "It could be called avant-garde," he said. "But a more apt description would be (in the words of my old friend Alvin) 'Avant-garde a clue'!" This oft-quoted witticism presumably came from Harrison's fellow guitar solider Alvin Lee of Ten Years After/Ten Years Later fame.

Although Alvin Lee was not averse to fusing guitars with technology in later years, Harrison has stuck by his view. 'Carnival of Light' was set to be included on *The Beatles Anthology 3*, the third and final compilation of classic and rare material, released in 1996. But Harrison used his right of veto on the track listing and it was put back in the tape locker.

The Carnival of Light Rave was finally staged at The Roundhouse on 28 January 1967, and repeated on 4 February. 'With music by Paul McCartney and Delta Music Plus,' proclaimed the flyers. "Yoko's part was significant as a first tentative pre-echo of the 'new age interpersonal therapy group'," remembered

Daevid Allen. "She had the lights turned out and then each audience member was instructed to touch the person next to them. One of my guitar solos was accompanied by a motorbike (parked next to me for the whole gig) being revved wildly in energetic empathy."

Despite their efforts, none of The Beatles attended the rave, although Delia Derbyshire was there to see the public's reaction to her Delta Music Plus. Bouncing to the other side of the musical spectrum, McCartney and Harrison instead spent the night at an Albert Hall concert by The Four Tops. McCartney was out the next night with Lennon at the Saville Theatre for a double-header of The Jimi Hendrix Experience and The Who. He may not have noticed, but Hendrix had one less guitar on stage at the Saville following his previous gig at David Vaughan's rave, as Vaughan explains: "I can't remember much [about The Beatles' 'Carnival of Light' collage] but it paled into insignificance when you heard this guy, this Hendrix on the stage. What happened there with Hendrix was also very comical, because at the end of the night somebody pissed off with his guitar!"

'Carnival of Light' had been a last flicker of the wild, off-the-wall experimentation which was about to be set to one side as the Beatles embarked on a new phase. The day before the rave they had signed a new, nine-year recording contract with EMI, and by the end of that month had delivered finished masters of 'Penny Lane' and 'Strawberry Fields Forever'. The tracks were pressed up and on the radio in days, marking a high point of creativity (if not sales).

The rave's unique Beatles soundtrack was never to be heard again and quickly passed into Beatles legend. Fans and musicologists have discussed, debated and dreamt about how it might sound ever since. Years later, 2001 to be precise, Mark Ellen managed to pin McCartney down and get him talking about the track during an interview on another subject entirely. He reported his findings to The Rocking Vicar, a kind of private members' club for music journalists and collectors of 'pop apocrypha' run by fellow Old Grey Whistle Test and VH-1 presenter David Hepworth. The Rocking Vicar's pet subjects include classic quotes from "the world's most inane DeeJays", compiling lists of the worst album titles of all time and generally letting slip mirthful observations of celebrity excess. "Deepend Beatles obsessives like myself have lost a fair amount of sleep over the years fantasising about the possible existence of 'Carnival of Light', the highly legendary 'lost' Fabs out-take," Ellen mused. "Although no one has ever heard it – it remains intriguingly unbootlegged … No Beatle, to my knowledge, has ever gone on record to offer any official insight."

Ellen was interviewing McCartney in his London office (noting for the Rocking Vicar, incidentally, that the album collection there includes Vocal Selections of Fats Domino and the musical The Unsinkable Molly Brown). "I was at that point of the encounter where you're almost being physically dragged out of the door as there's another interviewer waiting in the wings, and I decided to pop the all-important question and managed to solicit the following for Rocking Vicar…"

■ **Rocking Vicar:** Just one last question – 'Carnival of Light', does it actually exist?

**Paul McCartney:** It does exist, yeah. We recorded it in about 15 minutes. It's very avant-garde – as George would say, 'avant-garde a clue' – and George did not like it 'cos he doesn't like avant-garde music.

**Vicar:** Who wrote it?

**McCartney:** It's officially me. I instigated it. No, there's no lyrics, it's avant-garde music. You would class it as… well, you wouldn't class it actually, but it would come in the Stockhausen/John Cage bracket … John Cage would be the nearest. It's very free-form. Yeah, man, it's the coolest piece of music since sliced bread!

**Vicar:** This is early '67?

**McCartney:** I was asked about '67 to do it by Barry Miles – you know, who did my book *Many Years From Now* – and he asked me to do it for this event at The Roundhouse called Carnival of Light, so that's how it got its title. I went into the studio and said to the guys, look, we've got half an hour before the session officially starts, would you mind terribly if I did this thing?

**Vicar:** So this is with the other Beatles?

**McCartney:** With the other Beatles. This is a Beatle record. And they all just fell in with the spirit of it and I just said, "Would you go on that?" and "Would you stay on that?" and "Would you be on that?" and "We'll just take 20 minutes to do it in real time." And they all just got into it.

**Vicar:** Why don't you release it?

**McCartney:** I actually have a project I would like… I'm involved… One of the many things I did, I did a thing called *The Grateful Dead Photo Film*, using Linda's snapshots and making them move, dissolving between them and making them into a film, a short art film, which I showed at festivals and things. And I'm actually in the process – although everything else and its uncle is holding it up – but I've got a Beatles photo film on the go and I would love to use it as part of the soundtrack of that.

**Vicar:** There was a rumour it was going to come out on *Anthology*. What happened with that?

**McCartney:** It was up for consideration on *The Anthology* and George vetoed it. He didn't like it. Maybe its time hadn't come…

McCartney may have finally spilled the beans on 'Carnival of Light' but he also seemed to have suffered a major 'Arnold Browne'/Chapter 2-style memory lapse when stating that the sound collage was put together at the behest of Barry Miles. Miles, McCartney and David Vaughan had all agreed four years earlier during the writing of *Many Years From Now* that it was Vaughan's idea.

McCartney's photo film project looks the most likely possibility for an airing of the Beatles' most avant-garde work. At the time of the Roundhouse events, Binder Edwards and Vaughan and the makers of *International Times* were getting heavily into the medium of photo collage. Exactly 30 years later McCartney is using modern techniques to approach the same style and follow up his and Linda McCartney's experimental film of the Grateful Dead, achieved by morphing hundreds of Linda's still photographs to create a moving image. The finished effect is 'otherworldly' to say the least. Whether it will get a public airing or go the way of McCartney's other unissued film projects – such as *The Backyard* from the 1970s and *Tropical Island Hum* from the 1990s – remains to be seen.

Regardless of McCartney's film plans, the perfect 'Carnival of Light' visual had already been created. The Beatles 1969 Christmas Fan Club album had a front cover photo image by Ringo Starr. His long-exposure photo of red and orange neon blurs matched the title and mood of the track perfectly. The same year, The Beatles would remember the Roundhouse during the protracted *Let It Be* project, when they were looking for a venue for their final gig. The Chalk Farm venue was suggested but eventually they settled for the rooftop of their Apple offices in Savile Row.

Despite the views of those who heard it – and those who performed on it – interest in this great, unreleased Beatles experiment continues to grow. By the summer of 2001, EMI were acknowledging the existence of the track but stating categorically that it would not be released as a single.

The proto-raves of Binder, Edwards and Vaughan were not built to last. They were a momentary flash of what was to come for British youth in future decades. Having talked with Lennon and McCartney at that meeting where "they communicated an air of agreeing on little," Arnold Wesker secured the funding he needed and David Vaughan moved on, as he explains:

> ■ They [the raves] didn't last very long. We did about three or four and then we were thrown out. There was some crew behind it that decided they were going to open this Centre Fortytwo and get local firms in Camden to invest loads of money in it. And eventually they did sort of a good job. They redid the venue so it can stage events and exhibitions and so on. We would have never got it to that level at all. We liked it the way it was…

FOUR

# FROM VEGETABLES TO LLYSIAU (AND BACK)

**P**aul McCartney has often used his most traditional musical instruments for his most experimental compositions. An upright double bass, originally played by Elvis Presley's band on 'Heatbreak Hotel', can be heard throughout The Fireman's *Rushes* album. Simple six-string guitars and basses, like the Epiphone Casino and McCartney's trademark Hofner violin bass, were the basis for live experiments with both The Fireman and Allen Ginsberg. But experimental music doesn't really need instruments at all. McCartney's 1966 Montague Square sound lab, with its tape machines and editing equipment, is one example. Vegetables are another. As French composer Pierre Boulez wrote in 1976 on founding the Institut de Recherche et de Coordination Acoustique/Musique (ICRAM) in Paris, "Research/invention, individual/collective. The multiple resources of this double dialectic are capable of engendering infinite possibilities..."

It was most likely recreational drugs, rather than the convoluted strategies of Boulez, that led Paul McCartney to munch carrots into a microphone in Brian Wilson's studio in 1966. At that time, Wilson, co-founder, songwriter, singer and producer of The Beach Boys, was slipping into a paranoia which, he would later say, was nurtured by "the pot, the speed [and] the constant pressure." It drove him to some legendary obsessions. At times, he would only talk with musical collaborators if they were in his swimming pool, at others he could only compose at a piano positioned in a giant sandbox. Vegetables were another obsession. In the mid-sixties, despite continual drug use, Wilson became a health obsessive. At first, he wanted to turn his garden into an organic vegetable patch, whose goods would be sold through a drive-in window built off the kitchen. Later, in the summer of 1969, his paranoia would hold him back from following up The Beach Boys' classic *Pet Sounds* and he became a non-performing member of his own band, instead managing (disastrously) a health food store, the Radiant Radish, in partnership with his cousin and roadie.

Back in 1966, Paul McCartney found out about Brian Wilson's vegetable fixation when he made an impromptu visit to The Beach Boys' studio while visiting Jane Asher in LA. There Wilson was working on 'Vega-Tables', one of first few tracks to be recorded for the follow-up to *Pet Sounds*. It would become a legendary Beach Boys song, whose lyrics were classic Wilson of that era. Childlike and psychedelic, humorous and touching, "I threw away my candy bar and I ate the wrapper," he sang, "And when they told me what I'd done, I burst into laughter."

"In a white suit and red leather shoes, he epitomised cool," Wilson later said of McCartney's visit to the 'Vega-Tables' session. "The studio was overflowing with different kinds of vegetables strewn across countertops, tables, amps and instruments. I'd even played a game of pool with Hal Blaine [Phil Spector and Wilson's session drummer] using celery stalks for cues, cherry tomatoes and radishes as balls, and Dixie cups as the goal. McCartney raised an eyebrow at the sight."

But the two got on famously in a meeting described by one critic at the time as "like Van Gogh meeting Constable meeting Turner meeting Rembrandt in a time machine fuelled by adrenaline and Dexedrine." Juggling the experimental with the traditional, McCartney gave two private performances that night. For the first, he sat at the piano and premiered 'She's Leaving Home', the then-unrecorded *Sgt. Pepper* track, for Wilson and family. For the other, he was recorded chewing carrots which were dubbed into 'Vega-Tables' to add extra authenticity.

The finished recording of 'Vega-Tables' has since passed into Beach Boys folklore, such is the intrigue that surrounds the enigmatic Wilson. It was mooted more than once as a possible single from the follow-up album to *Pet Sounds*, *SMiLE*. It was one of several songs that followed the album's theme of natural elements. 'Vega-Tables' was 'earth', 'Wind Chimes' was 'wind', an unreleased piano instrumental would be 'air' and so on. However, as Wilson slipped further and further into a mania that would last well into the next decade, *SMiLE* became one of rock music's great lost albums. The album that eventually appeared, *Smiley Smile*, featuring a slightly retitled 'Vegatables', which was a shadow of what Wilson had planned. It still featured McCartney's percussive chewing but whether he did this for the original 'Vega-Tables' sessions, or for the final *Smiley Smile* sessions, is a question dear to fanatical researchers. No one present at that blurry, inspirational sixties session can remember.

Such antics looked set to become just another entry in the bizarre diary of Brian Wilson had it not been for a drunken Welsh keyboard player who bumped – literally – into Paul McCartney at the 2000 *NME* Premier Music Awards.

McCartney was there to accept the *NME*'s Best Band Ever award on behalf of The Beatles. Said Welsh keyboard player was 24-year-old Cian Ciaran of Super Furry Animals, there with his band to pick up the gong for Best Live Act.

Formed in 1993, Super Furry Animals comprise Gruff Rhys (lead vocals, guitar), Huw 'Bunf' Bunford (guitar, vocals), Guto Pryce (bass), Dafydd Ieuan (drums) and Cian Ciaran. Between a US tour and recording a new album, I found Rhys having a cup of tea at home in Cardiff. "I think we were at the *NME* Awards a few years back," he told me, "and I think he [Ciaran] was coming back from the toilet and he bumped into Paul McCartney. He'd been drinking heavily and he got chatting to him and brought him back to our table and introduced us all. And in the meantime he'd asked us if we could remix his stuff."

"That was a direct reference," Rhys said of Brian Wilson's 'Vege-Tables' when discussing his band's song 'Receptacle for the Respectable', which features its own carrot-chewing percussion by Paul McCartney. "We found ourselves in the unexpected situation where we could call up Paul McCartney to try out some chewing and because we'd done *Liverpool Sound Collage* [as explored in Chapter 15] we thought we'd ask him the favour back. And I think he was up for a bit of fun."

Super Furry Animals can rightly claim to be at the forefront of experimental British pop, notable for effortlessly moulding a variety of genres into something as unique as it is sustainable. They are perhaps one of the few bass/drums/guitars/electronics/vocals bands that can pull off songs which bounce from punk rock to techno to progressive and, often, all points in between. This musical innovation, combined with a pop idealism, set the band apart from other contemporaries of the mid-1990s Welsh scene, which saw the likes of Catatonia, 60 Foot Dolls and Gorky's Zygotic Mynci break towards the mainstream. Their 1996 debut *Fuzzy Logic*, including the hit single 'Something for the Weekend', followed independent Welsh-language EPs such as *Lianfairpwllgywgyllgoger Chwymdrobwlltysiliogoygoyocynygofod (In Space)*.

In 2001 they released their fourth album, *Rings Around the World*, a multimedia affair which was mixed in 5.1 Surround Sound and simultaneously released on DVD with a set of short films. This followed previous multimedia experiments like the band's purple tank, which blasted techno across the UK music festivals of 1996. "A OES HEDDWCH?" read the inscription on the side, Welsh for "IS THERE PEACE?" *Rings Around the World* was notable too for its collaborations. The Velvet Underground's (and Wales') John Cale appears, playing piano on a song about Bill Clinton and Monica Lewinsky. Elsewhere, on 'Receptacle for the Respectable', a certain Liverpudlian songwriter appears rhythmically chewing carrots.

Following some secret tape-swapping ("We'd only get a fax with a map of the studio, then an hour before it would be cancelled," Rhys told reporters), the carrot rhythm track was in the bag. McCartney's fans were bemused, the Super Furries' were unsurprised and the BBC didn't know quite what to make of it all. "Sir Paul McCartney has collaborated on the new album by the Super Furry Animals by chewing on a piece of celery," the BBC reported. "The former Beatle can be heard chewing in rhythm to the song 'Receptacle for the Respectable' on the Welsh band's new album *Rings Around the World*, which is released on 16 July," they explained. "This is not Sir Paul's first foray into vegetable chewing for his art – he also munched his way through the Beach Boys' song 'Vegetables' in 1967."

Gruff Rhys told me more about putting the llysiau (Welsh for vegetables) track together:

■ It took months to arrange. It was shrouded in secrecy and heavy security. We'd planned to go to his studio in a secret location, we had to be on standby on a certain day and then we'd receive a fax in the morning with the directions to his studio. This all took quite a while but then we'd get a call from his secretary saying "Oh, he can't come, he's got to go to his daughter's fashion show in Paris." We were going "Yeah, yeah, yeah, whatever," you know what I mean? Then we looked at the newspaper the next day and there he was, at his daughter's fashion show in Paris!

We got the idea that he wasn't bullshitting us, so we thought it would all work out in the end. Then eventually it got too complicated for us to come over with our veg so in the end he sent us a DAT [Digital Audio Tape] of himself chomping on various vegetables. A carrot and a celery and he also did a very bad impression of Tom Jones. He did quite a few Welsh accents as well, which we're holding back as future blackmail...

Aside from the vegetables, the track itself is uniquely Super Furry Animals and, as *Guitarist* magazine noted, "sums up the band's remarkable vision". Rhys described it to *NME* magazine as "A song in four parts. It goes from '60s harmony pop to early '70s glam rock in the Bacharach balladry then goes death metal."

"We were in America at the time and had spent two weeks watching Blink 182 on TV every day," Bunf told *Guitarist* about that metal injection towards the end of the track, "and I think 'the rock' just got to us. It was almost like a joke, because I didn't have any heavy metal pedals, so it sounds like a sixth form band trying to do death metal, and it's just as funny really."

As with Brian Wilson's vegetable pool game, the Super Furries took this idea and ran with it. "Yeah, we've got plenty of strange-sounding things going on," Bunf told *Guitarist*. "For that rhythm, as well as Paul McCartney chewing his celery, we used olive oil. What you do is, you get olive oil in a jar and you shake it to get this really unusual type of rhythm sound."

*Rings Around the World* was also experimental in that it was one of the first albums to be mixed especially for a five-speaker set-up (5.1 Surround Sound) as opposed to two (traditional stereo). "The difference between stereo sound and 5.1 sound is you have five speakers that encompass you," Ciaran told the press at the time, "and you can send any sound you want to the five speakers instead of to the traditional two. You can make sound travel around the room, you can make it bounce around your head. It just gives you more depth and space to play with, if you can position sounds around the room, making you feel like you're in the middle of the musicians. We just liked the idea that the medium was there to be used and hadn't been exploited, really."

"That's the most effective way to hear Paul," Rhys told me of the 5.1 mix of 'Receptacle for the Respectable', "because it's a bit more separated, on the actual track it's not very clear what we actually did. His role on the song's pretty peripheral, but we thought we'd get it on for good luck. We'd given him specific directions to use the celery for the top end, you know, and the carrot gives out more of a low-frequency crunch, so we thought we were covering our frequencies pretty well."

Super Furry Animals managed to recreate this new culinary rhythm section on tour. As well as giant screens and post-millennium 'ZOO TV', the *Rings Around the World* gigs featured a roadie – in McCartney mask – standing in on celery in a spectacle witnessed with awe by *The Stage*. "They look so eager, full of energy, and enjoying it every inch as much as the audience," they said of the band's Brixton Academy show on 2 October 2001. "The venue piled out with utterances of this gig being the most bizarrely fantastic, creatively original you are possibly ever likely to witness, experienced with constant surprise and undivided attention ... The tongue-tied 'Receptacle for the Respectable' featured Gruff's announcement of 'featuring a special guest appearance' – a stage hand with a cut-out mask as the celery-munching Paul McCartney..."

"We found a magazine with large masks of the Beatles," Rhys told me, "so we had various Beatles – we've had them all on stage, much to the amusement of the audience." They also used the stage show to take their experimentation with vegetables even further:

■ When we were on tour, on that song we play on the guitar on the synth. I use a harmonica holder and I insert usually pieces of celery or both, depending what's available. With a hectic tour schedule sometimes it's impossible to find celery late at night or on the move so I've also tried out cucumber, which I don't recommend, as it hasn't got a particularly good crunch but, surprisingly, asparagus is very effective. Unexpectedly it's a very loud vegetable.

McCartney's work with vegetables is groundbreaking in some ways but not in others. He is certainly the most well-known muncher of musical carrots; indeed, his efforts afford this genre much-deserved and otherwise unavailable space in a rock biography such as this. It's groundbreaking in the sense of a superstar songwriter doing something 'different', but he was certainly not the first, and won't be the last, to use vegetables to make music.

Traditional music from around the world has often seen dried beans used for percussion, and yarrow leaves are a staple of Romanian folk music. John Cage wrote three pieces for vegetable material. 'Child of Tree' (1975), a percussion solo using amplified plant materials, was followed by 'Branches' (1976) and 'Cartridge Music' (1980), for amplified 'small sounds' and loudspeakers. Before Cage, the Fluxus movement, the 1950s experimental New York art movement which counted Yoko Ono among its members, played with pumpkins, cacti and melons. Then there's Lindsey Pollak, an Australian performance artist who is often seen performing on a handmade carrot flute, to say nothing of the vegetable-inspired work of Frank Zappa on Pumpkin Records.

The works of Cage, Pollak and Zappa are mere stir-fry, however, by comparison to the First Viennese Vegetable Orchestra. Formed in 1998 by Joerg Piringer, this orchestra comprises nine musicians and a chief cook who perform classical and jazz compositions exclusively on vegetables from the stalls of Vienna's Naschmarkt.

As a bemused Peter Finn reported in the *Washington Post* of a 2001 performance: "The First Vienna Vegetable Orchestra blows carved-out carrots, taps turnips, claps with eggplant cymbals, twangs on rhubarb fibres, and rustles parsley and greens to create an experimental sound that eventually winds up, literally, in the audience's stomach." That's right. As any recital from this orchestra progresses, there's a natural wear and tear on their hand-peeled instruments. So as soon as one carrot recorder or cucumber didgeridoo starts to falter it's tossed into a live, rhythmically stirred soup cauldron, which is then served to the audience as a grand finale.

The Vegetable Orchestra believe they perform an "autonomous and totally novel type of sound which cannot be achieved with conventional musical instruments", providing a "playful departure from the conventional way of looking at vegetables as mere means to still an appetite." One of their most elaborate instruments is the 'cucumber-o-phone', which comprises a carrot mouthpiece on one end of a hollowed-out cucumber, which has a bell pepper attached at the other to amplify sound.

It's easy to make light of the Vegetable Orchestra, but there's a serious side to any group that tries to push the envelope. "Anywhere else this would be a gag," noted Finn. "In Vienna, it's an aesthetic. They are artists intent on the idiosyncratic cultivation of a new music form." The First Viennese Vegetable Orchestra itself is part of a wider body aimed at forcibly expanding musical boundaries or, as they put it, "breaking open socially induced functional deafness." This body is known as IFTAF, the Institute for TransAcoustic Research. In manifesto-like documents they aim to be "a platform for the ear-training arts/sciences and auditory phenomenology..." and to explore "the borders between acoustics and their tangential realms: science and art, everyday life and research, sound and noise, tone and light, acoustic and other modes of perception."

"None of us knew that Paul McCartney had worked in the area of vegetable music," says Stefan Kühn from the First Vienna Vegetable Orchestra. "But any track that uses vegetables is important because the world of vegetable music is still rather small. The favourite record of one of our members is from The Dead Kennedys, called 'Fresh Fruit for Rotten Vegetables'. We also like the work of some newer sound-artists who reproduce measurements from plants into sound, though this is very different from what we do."

McCartney's love of carrots is echoed by the Vegetable Orchestra. They use a carrot xylophone "because it can be tuned exactly," says Barbara Kaiser. "We all love carrots, because their consistency allows you to work on them with a knife or drill and they can be made into percussion or wind instruments. You can do anything with carrots, they are basics, very versatile for making flutes, chewing sounds, definitely one of the main instruments in the vegetable orchestra. Root celery is great for making bongos or dried castanets. The orchestra occasionally uses a celery violin and we also work with radish, because you can make big wind instruments out of it and a sort of marimba. And the 'Gurkophon' – a wind instrument made from cucumber with a carrot mouthpiece and a bell pepper (preferably in red) bell/horn."

The Orchestra's Mathias Meinhardter told me that their "dream collaboration" would be on Aardman Production film 'The Great Vegetable Plot,' but they have also name-checked Bowie, McCartney, Christian Wolff, Daevid Allen, Kruder & Dorfmeister and Fatboy Slim as possible collaborators. Perhaps the next stage for McCartney's animate percussion techniques is to take a leaf out of Super Furry Animals' or the Vienna Orchestra's book and take to the stage. "On recordings the vegetable music sounds like electronic music, but a live performance is more of a show," says Ernst Reitermaier. "The audience gets more sensorial impressions, they can smell and see parts of instruments flying around. It usually takes some time at concerts until the audience can focus on the music ... We prefer performing in small spaces, before an audience interested in the philosophical background of expanding the traditional music vocabulary and in exploring the new dimension of sound."

But why vegetables? Perhaps chewing on a carrot is a playful way to wake up anyone (from a child to a cynical music industry hack) to where rhythm – and inspiration – comes from. It's the silly things – like Super Furry Animals' purple tank – that tend to help musicians and listeners turn a corner. As Gruff Rhys once noted, "There's certain ways the music industry works and people for some reason just accept it. And there is no reason. You don't have to do things by the rule book."

Throughout the seventies and eighties, Paul McCartney's night-time vegetable-chewing session with Brian Wilson was locked away with the memories of many other bizarre sixties encounters. But a knock-on effect of his return to carrot percussion with Super Furry Animals was that these memories began to get unlocked. In New York City in June 2000, McCartney gave a rare long-form speech when he inducted Wilson into the Songwriters' Hall of Fame. He paid homage to Wilson's simple gift for melody, as well as his experimental flair.

> ■ In the sixties particularly, Brian Wilson wrote some music [which], when I played it, it made me cry. And I don't quite know why. It wasn't necessarily the words or the music ... there was just something so deep in it that there's only certain pieces of music can do this to me. Just reaching right down in me and I think it's a sign of great genius to be able to do that with a bunch of words and a bunch of notes. And I would take, in later years, I would take my kids aside, and say "Listen to this bit of music here." And they would watch me crying, and they understand.

"Thank you, sir, for everything you've done for me," McCartney said to Wilson, "for making me cry, for having that 'thing' you can do with your music. You just put those notes and those harmonies together, stick a couple of words over the top of it and you've got me. Any day."

It was also no coincidence that McCartney's high-profile US tour of 2002 was called Driving USA, with posters and logos reminiscent of the Beach Boys' 'Surfin' USA'. While on tour, the 'Vegetables' song made national news in the UK when McCartney staged a typical publicity stunt. He called in to an LA radio show to answer their concert ticket competition, the question being "On which track did McCartney chew vegetables as percussion?" He was the only caller to get the question right and, funnily enough, the whole thing was filmed for the *Driving USA* DVD.

If nothing else, 'Vegetables', Super Furry Animals and the First Viennese Vegetable Orchestra prove that avant-garde music and experimental musical thinking don't have to be highbrow. No one cracked a smile when McCartney saw AMM in concert in 1966. "They were serious in intent and intensity," Edwin Prevost recalled, "but the only kind of appropriate response seemed to be silence.

Even we, as musicians, rarely talked about these sessions immediately afterwards. Often we would meet some other time in the week for any discussion."

By contrast, all the music covered in this chapter is as much about laughter as it is about questioning the nature of music-making. As such, the final word on the subject should go to the First Viennese Vegetable Orchestra:

> ■ Vegetable music can be a good way to reawaken the ability to listen. There is a humorous aspect to vegetable music, it includes sensuality and a whole experience. We would like to see these instruments in concert halls and music schools around the world, to take away the stiffness from the traditional music teaching, in order to teach children the possibility to explore new sounds, invent instruments and take a relaxed and fun approach to music. We approach music from a respectful but playful standpoint. We are preparing a vegetable music revolution!

# FIVE

# MUSIC MADE WITH MOOGS AND GLASSES

In the early 1970s, the pioneering spirit of the 1960s crashed and burned. Rock and roll became pop, disco was born, and punk fought back. As The Beatles collapsed into personal and business acrimony that would last longer than the decade itself, McCartney was on a mission. He went back to basics, building up a band from 'college gig' scratch, taking Wings to stadium greatness in the space of just ten years.

Only one thing suffered in this frantic period, most recently catalogued in Wings' *Wingspan* 'anthology' film and compilation: McCartney's avant-garde works. The idea of a whole album of tape loops – *Paul McCartney Goes Too Far* – went out the window. McCartney had to convince his public that there was life after The Beatles. Wings were vying for chart positions against a new breed – ranging from David Bowie to The Osmonds – and McCartney just didn't feel the public was into experimentalism. As he explained on Radio 1 in 1989, it would be a case of "Wait a minute, you've just been writing 'Here, There and Everywhere'. Now you've come up with whoo-weee, plonk!?"

His one key 'unknown' work in the 1970s was less avant-garde but certainly an off-the-wall experiment – the *Thrillington* album examined in the next chapter. Truly out-there ideas and sound trickery were hidden away on album tracks and B-sides. On one he put minimalism in front of a worldwide audience. On another the influence of John Cage was clearly audible. But the great ideas and potential collaborations forged in the sixties were shelved in favour of more traditional pursuits – songs, albums, ballads, bands and families – leading most to conclude that, in leaving The Beatles, McCartney had left the counterculture too.

To some extent, McCartney was only following the trend. The seventies saw a major swing back towards the middle of the road. Delia Derbyshire was one of the first to suffer. In 1972 she left the BBC, taking her unique and pioneering spirit in the field of electronic music with her. "Something serious happened around '72, '73, '74," she remembered years later. "The world went out of tune with itself and the BBC went out of tune with itself..."

Derbyshire was caught in a shift from pioneering to penny-pinching, blaming this directly on the fact that the BBC had hired an accountant as Director General. And there was no room for compromise – "A hip capitalist is a pig capitalist," said activist Jerry Rubin in 1970. While The Beatles and Apple fought with lawyers and accountants, David Vaughan saw a similar change of mood at street level:

> ■ It was what was happening on the street that made me realise quickly that things were changing. I could feel it. The climate was changing, people were getting money-conscious again. The minds had opened like the parting of the Red Sea. And as soon as the people got through they closed back again. So that everything had a monetary bias to it again. The thinking just in ordinary people – "Er, how much is this? How much is that going to cost? Is it worth it?" – and so on and so forth. A free spirit will take you wherever it wants to go, rather than you pressganging it into what you want it to do. That had gone; the freeness of the spirit had been shackled again. And all of a sudden it started the road to where we are now.

By 1969 the sixties dream was as good as over. Hard to imagine that just two years earlier The Beatles played 'All You Need is Love' – the classic peace and love anthem – live on worldwide TV across 18 countries. But the acid-induced dream that had inspired music like this and the whole psychedelic era was heading for a wake-up call, with the 1970s as one massive hangover.

Having come out of his 'gynaecological instruments' period, Daevid Allen had formed Gong, a loose collective of almost comic transcendental visionaries who continue to this day touring, recording and existing on just the right side of self-parody. By 1971 he was back in the UK and back on stage at the Roundhouse. Although the mood he found was quite different from the 'Carnival of Light' nights…

> ■ Well, from front of stage at the roundhouse in '71, which was actually before it moved on, the situation was getting a little out of control. Gong is fundamentally focused more on raising consciousness than raising pocket money for new toys so the feeling was that the overall focus was blowing out at the seams and that the energy was lurching from very light to very dense with alarming emotional side effects for the vulnerable. In other words, we were suffering from a gigantic spiritual/psychic/acid/DMT/STP/whatever hangover which at the

> drop of a b flat could turn dangerously nasty, as per Altamont. So some of us had
> to rethink, clean up our acts and try for newer, safer ways to lift off.

The "b flat" turn Daevid Allen refers to is the giant free concert The Rolling Stones staged at the end of their 1969 tour, playing alongside Santana, The Grateful Dead and Jefferson Airplane at Altamont Motor Speedway in San Francisco. A combination of drug excess and the Stones' choice of show security – the Hell's Angels – made for what Gerry Garcia of The Grateful Dead described as "an afternoon in hell." The Hell's Angels had been paid $500-worth of beer for their services and patrolled the audience with pool cues and knives. 10,000 people were expected but 300,000 turned up. By the time The Rolling Stones were on stage doctors had attended to over 800 LSD trippers and a member of Jefferson Airplane had been beaten unconscious. As the concert turned into a riot, a member of the audience, 18-year-old Meredith Hunter, was stabbed to death right in front of the stage. The spirit of the sixties died with him there and then.

Maysles, Maysles and Zermin's 1970 documentary account of Altamont, *Gimme Shelter*, remains deeply unsettling. On seeing an image from that day – of a Hell's Angel with a pool cue, reprinted in *Mojo* magazine in 2002 – reader Marc Noel Hunter remembered that "The Angels were beating up an unfortunate obese man who had unwisely removed his clothes, probably thinking he was among the peace and love generation. I remember the picture in *Rolling Stone*, which ran the caption 'To the Angels the sight of a fat man was so repulsive he had to get beaten.' I was 16 at the time, but it was one of those images that stays with you. I find it just as disturbing now as I did then." *Gimme Shelter* ends with flower children wandering away from the festival site at dawn the next morning, looking as distraught and bewildered as the Stones when they fled the stage.

For David Vaughan, Altamont was a violent end to an era of peace and love. It came as a great personal blow not only to him but to all those who, for a moment, thought times really were changing.

The psychedelic approach, the psychedelic feeling had gone, replaced by the psychotic attitude, which you get through different drugs. When people start taking things like speed, heroin and so on and so forth it sort of hardens the mind. And before you can say Jack Robinson you've got skin-encapsulated egos again. People saying "I was here first, and this is my right of way" and all that. Banging and colliding like they are now. And that all came together in the Altamont concert and that black fellow that was stabbed to death by those idiots that Jagger thought were cool, you know, the Hell's Angels. And that would epitomise it in everybody's mind, that time. And that really was the end of a dream.

Such an emotional and disappointing end to an era sent ripples through its artistic community which are still visible today. For many it meant an exodus from

London. Peter Blake moved to Avon, beginning the ruralist movement, which we catch up with in Chapter 15. Paul McCartney had gone from London psychedelic socialite to living as a recluse in the Scottish highlands. Daevid Allen and Gong partner Gilli Smyth were living almost permanently in France and David Vaughan relocated back to his home town of Ashton in the north of England.

The seventies had begun with Phil Spector producing the last overblown sounds of The Beatles, for *Let It Be*. At the same time McCartney was recording mostly at home with no effects, no plan, no band even. His finished demos became the eponymous *McCartney* album with a press release slotted into advance copies in which he stated: "I do not foresee a time when the Lennon & McCartney partnership will be active again in songwriting." With that, and before *McCartney* was even released, The Beatles were over, with front-page newspaper stories quoting McCartney's press release.

The critical reception of the *McCartney* album was completely symptomatic of the times. The sixties were very much over when *Melody Maker* referred to some tracks (presumably the grating 'Man We Was Lonely') as "the worst example of his music-hall side" and to the end The Beatles as "possibly the non-event of the year." At the same time, George Harrison deemed McCartney's debut song album "a little disappointing" while Lennon called it "rubbish", thus starting an era where comparisons and 'what ifs?' were a permanent fixture of the four former bandmates' solo careers.

With the *New Musical Express* calling *Let It Be* a "cardboard tombstone," perhaps The Beatles as a unit just weren't made for the 1970s. But then neither was avant-grade music, or the 'rock concrete' of Love, The Box Tops and The psychedelic Beatles. The most pivotal collaboration between 1970s rock and early avant-garde composers – Spooky Tooth and Pierre Henry's Ceremony – was a disaster. And compilations that attempted to give some historical background to the story – like Limelight's *The Total Experience in Sound* (featuring both Henry and Luciano Berio) – bombed.

The music on *McCartney* was patchy and unfinished, its homespun simplicity the complete opposite to *Let It Be* and Phil Spector's strings, brass, sound walls and overdubs, which McCartney despised. "I have a better time with my family," he said in his infamous press release, and it's evident in these songs. Tracks like 'The Lovely Linda', though melodically arousing, fortunately clock in at just under a minute long. But simplicity was the key, a new musical direction totally opposed to Traffic, T Rex and other new bands of the time. This "homemade affair," as George Martin described it, represented a new style which McCartney, Donovan and a few others were tapping into.

'Junk' (which McCartney had first written in 1968 while in India with Donovan, The Beatles and the Maharishi) was a perfect example of McCartney's new isolationist approach. DJ John Peel, who in 1970 had already carved himself a niche as one of the UK's most important curators of leftfield pop music, was a fan of Donovan and McCartney's new direction. "I don't think Lennon is leaving McCartney behind or vice versa," he told Bob Harris in an interview for *UNIT* magazine. "I think they are just going in opposite directions."

Instrumentals accounted for almost half the *McCartney* album and they showed that, outside the confines of The Beatles, he had a lot of exploring he wanted to do. While 'Valentine's Day' would not have sounded out of place on *Let It Be*, McCartney's final solo version of the old Beatles rehearsal jam 'Hot as Sun' would have, with its reggae-influenced Caribbean vibe. The album's finale, the instrumental 'Kreen Akrore', stood for the next ten years as the longest experimental track McCartney issued on his mainstream albums. Effectively a thoughtful, if rudimentary, drum workout, it was inspired by an ITV documentary he had seen on the Kreen Akrore tribe. The documentary, *The Tribe that Hides from Man*, about how the Kreen Akrore kill any outsiders that attempt to interfere with their isolated lifestyle, was a perfect, if extreme, analogy for McCartney's new musical and personal lifestyle.

Cinematic and stereo-separated, 'Kreen Akrore' was directly inspired by the '3D' instrumentals (and vocal harmonies) of Brian Wilson. It featured McCartney's heavy breathing during the 'chase' sequence, and the sound of both Paul and Linda screaming, whooping and making animal noises during the opening 'discovery' sequence. Just as Wilson had once done in one of his more chemically enhanced sessions, McCartney built a fire in the studio, although he stopped short of lighting it, instead just overdubbing the sound of snapping twigs into the opening sequence.

The *McCartney* album is often accused of sounding rushed and unfinished. It was certainly put out in a hurry compared to the multiple-take overdub sessions of The Beatles' albums from the years that preceded it. But proof that this material could stand the test of time came when two of the instrumentals – 'Momma Miss America' and 'Singalong Junk' – appeared on the 1996 *Jerry McGuire* film soundtrack. Both sounded as fresh as any of the contemporary artists the compilation featured.

Another of these instrumentals, 'Glasses', is a curious avant-garde composition. It comprises layers of ambient hum, which McCartney achieved by simply recording himself and Linda rubbing the rims of wine glasses, and then playing them back over the top of each other. It distilled the abstract, avant-garde ideas that McCartney had been exposed to in his latter years as a Beatle right down to their very essence: pure sound.

The year before the *McCartney* album, minimalism as a genre had been ignited by Steve Reich, an artist McCartney had discovered and been impressed by in the late 1960s. In a groundbreaking Reich concert at the Whitney Museum in New York, each member of the audience found an essay on their seat, entitled *Music as a Gradual Process*. It described a new sonic form of "pulse music," one which "happens extremely gradually" and "facilitates closely detailed listening." 'Glasses' is more influenced by Reich than by Cage or Stockhausen. This is because the type of avant-garde music Reich described at the Whitney Museum was one in which the process of its creation was exactly the same as the end result. Thus, the act of McCartney rubbing wine glasses was music, as was the sound they produced.

Following another of Reich's principles, 'Glasses' is a track that could go on indefinitely. "Once the process is set up and loaded it runs by itself," he wrote in *Music as a Gradual Process*. It was testament to McCartney's adventurous musical spirit in 1970 that he was happy to put a track like this in front of the same audience and on the same album as instant singalong classics like 'Maybe I'm Amazed'. In doing so he put an emerging experimental genre, minimalism, in front of a global audience.

Of course, most buyers of the *McCartney* album would probably have dismissed 'Glasses' as an odd joke. Or they might not have even noticed the track at all, such was its ambient qualities. As Steve Reich once said of minimalism, it's like "watching the minute hand of a watch – you can perceive it moving only after you observe it for a while." But whatever *McCartney* buyers thought of it, they'd still been given the chance to hear it and consider it. Although putting 'Glasses' on one of the most anticipated pop albums of 1970 was a daring step, McCartney did hide it away a little. Rather than making it a track in its own right, he just spliced a minute's worth in between two other tracks, 'Hot as Sun' and a short section of 'Suicide', a catchy vocal track that is yet to receive a full release.

The roots of minimalism can be traced back much further than Reich – back to composers like Mozart and Schoenberg. It continues to develop to this day, having been directly influenced by the likes of Terry Riley, La Monte Young, Philip Glass and Brian Eno. Without minimalism, Eno would not have hit upon ambient music which, by the time it had matured for a couple of decades, directly influenced McCartney's late-1990s avant-garde work.

Some years later, McCartney revisited this strain of minimalism. At the end of a rehearsal session he recorded a 'duet' version. Linda played the glasses and Paul played piano, attempting to discern the key of the glasses' whines and hums. Despite being quite a bizarre recording even by McCartney's standards, he decided once again that 'Glasses' should get an airing. This second recording was featured on his 1995 radio series *Oobu Joobu*, described in Chapter 16. Paying homage to one of his main inspirations for the track, he followed this by playing Mozart's 'Glass Menagerie Music for Glass Harmonica'. The music for McCartney's

*Feedback* installation, explored in Chapter 14, is a pure piece of minimalism also.

Seven solo Beatles albums had been released by the time of *McCartney*, all of which were avant-garde or experimental to some degree. But the public's curiosity for the first studio album of songs to come from one of the band took it to over a million sales, in the US alone, in just four weeks.

1970 was a bold-type full stop at the end of the peace and love era. In a single year the world saw the death of Jimi Hendrix, the break up of The Beatles, the underground *Oz* magazine shut down by police, and Timothy Leary imprisoned for ten years for offering drugs to a plainclothes policeman (although he would escape a few months later). On New Year's Eve, McCartney began legal proceedings against his former bandmates to end 'The Beatles & Company'. "I think the group is finished," he said.

McCartney's second post-Beatles album, *Ram*, began life at the start of 1970 when he and Linda relocated to New York to write songs and audition players. In a highly productive spring session (which concluded at home on his farm in Cambletown, Scotland), McCartney recorded some upbeat, confident material that was worlds away from the *McCartney* album. Enough material was finished for *Ram* and other future Wings LPs, including the tracks which would start the 'running battles' in song with John Lennon: '3 Legs', 'Too Many People' and 'Dear Friend'. By February, one track, 'Another Day', was already out as a single and by July *Ram* was a UK number one album.

*Ram* has a consistency and direction that McCartney would not always manage to muster for his solo and Wings releases. Its 12 songs are punchy and confident, but avant-garde concepts are kept almost completely locked away, save for the odd, fleeting hint of his experimental streak. Like gunshots on the track 'Oh Woman Oh Why' (used as the B-side to 'Another Day') or the organic electronic burst (strikingly similar to one heard at the beginning of 'Why', the opening track on Yoko Ono's 1970 *Plastic Ono Band* album) and audible studio talk at the start of 'Ram On'. Elsewhere, Paul Beaver's primitive synthesiser work enhances 'Dear Boy', as does atmospheric tapes of thunder and rain on 'Uncle Albert/Admiral Halsey'.

The influence of Brian Wilson is clear throughout *Ram*, from the production on 'The Back Seat of my Car' and the vocals on 'Dear Boy' to the vibes on 'Uncle Albert'. "Paul is the greatest bass player in the world," said Ringo Starr at the time, although this was in an affidavit to Morris Finer QC as The Beatles and Apple continued to burn themselves out in the High Court.

Following *Ram*, McCartney took a new direction, steering even further towards the mainstream. New recruits Denny Laine and Denny Seiwell joined for a secret session at Abbey Road, before moving to Cambletown to start recording with the McCartneys. On 3 August 1971, the formation of the new band was announced, and on 13 September McCartney's second baby, Stella, was born. The birth is said to have inspired the choice of band name, when he prayed the baby would arrive on the wings of an angel.

The results of the Cambletown sessions, *Wings Wild Life*, was released at the end of 1971 to little fanfare. Often underrated, it contains some pure, classic early Wings like 'Mumbo', the intense title track, and another blast at Lennon, 'Dear Boy'. But sales were disappointing and the first single, the reggae-flavoured cover of 'Love is Strange', was cancelled. As the press delighted in pointing out, Wings were not off to a 'flying' start.

Undeterred by the sales of *Wings Wild Life*, McCartney finished 1971 with a little off-the-wall experimentation. While in New York on promotion, he recorded 'The Great Cock and Seagull Race', also known as 'Breakfast Blues' or 'The Rooster', a strange rock instrumental featuring spoken word sections, seagull sound effects and weird guitar. It's a loud, heads-down, rough track – the precursor to 1998's 'Bison', recorded as The Fireman – which closed quietly with keyboard jamming and comedy percussion.

"I can't really describe what direction I'm going in musically, because it's ever-changing and that's what it's all about," he had told *Life* magazine in April 1971. "I have my personal influences, and they come from everywhere," he said, "from age nothing to today. Sounds I heard on the radio. Sounds I heard my father play on the piano. Sounds I found myself in rock and roll. Sounds that the group made..."

The violence that Daevid Allen and David Vaughan talked about continued in 1972. The situation in Northern Ireland was worsening and, incensed by Bloody Sunday, McCartney recorded and released Wings' first single, 'Give Ireland Back to the Irish'. It was banned by the BBC and several other radio stations. "I think the British government overstepped their mark and showed themselves to be more of a sort of repressive regime than I ever believed them to be," he told one TV station.

There was a flicker of musical experimentation with the B-side of 'Give Ireland Back to the Irish', which was a dub reggae version. Perhaps the most un-Beatlelike of rhythms, McCartney has had an ongoing fascination with reggae. In June 1977, the Wings entourage stopped off in Kingston Jamaica to record with Lee 'Scratch' Perry. Pivotal to the worldwide impact of the genre, Perry's Upsetter label had released over 100 singles between 1969 and 1974. The visit to his infamous shack of a recording studio, Black Ark, saw McCartney record two 1950s standards, 'Sugartime' and 'Mr Sandman'. Linda was on vocals and these tracks were intended for her solo album, which was eventually released posthumously over 20 years later.

McCartney and Perry worked together for a very short space of time, but both were on the cusp of taking their music and individual styles in new directions. Perry was experimenting more and more with synthesisers, drum machines, special effects and multi-layered production. This became his late-1970s trademark, most notably on the Upsetters album *Return of the Super Ape*. McCartney, too, was beginning to think along more electronic lines, having played with Moogs and primitive beat-boxes in his home studio the year before. But at the time, the world wasn't quite ready for either man to veer too left of centre. In fact, the reception given to Perry's 1978 album *Roast Fish Collie Weed and Corn Bread* was one factor that lead to the artist's complete disillusionment with the music scene he had so strongly influenced. In 1980 he burned down Black Ark studios and left Jamaica for the next ten years.

Wings became a real live band in 1972, starting with their legendary tour of UK universities, where they'd just turn up unannounced and play for an entrance fee of 50p. To McCartney it was just "rehearsing," but at the same time it was bringing him back down to earth from Beatlemania. There were no Beatles tracks in Wings' set, and his share of the takings each night was the first time he'd actually handled money for over ten years.

Following the college tour, Wings flew to Los Angeles to start recording their second album, *Red Rose Speedway*. There they recorded a brace of mellow McCartney tracks, like 'One More Kiss', 'Single Pigeon' and 'Little Lamb Dragonfly'. All were of middling quality, the only high-point being 'My Love', with strings from *Thrillington* mainspring Richard Hewson. Wings were certainly finding their own sound but it was a long way from the raw demo sounds of *McCartney* and *Wings Wild Life* and – despite following the release of 'Give Ireland Back to the Irish' – closer to the middle of the road than McCartney had ever been.

Despite this mainstream focus, Wings did steer into experimental territory at one point, with 'Loup (1st Indian on the Moon)'. This *Red Rose Speedway* instrumental was clearly inspired by the progressive and concept rock scenes that were springing up at the time. In fact, McCartney had worked extensively with the king of the concept album, Alan Parsons, who had been sound engineer on *Abbey Road*, *Thrillington* and *Wings Wild Life*. Parsons would also go on to produce Pink Floyd's *Dark Side of the Moon*. It was these kinds of futurist rock experiments that inspired 'Loup'. Carrying on from where 'Glasses' left off, it features short sections of experimental minimalism. Cage-style, random, seemingly homemade instruments can be heard popping up too. The track ends with birds tweeting in an echo chamber. But the whole thing is bonded together with funky laidback jamming. "This is the difference between Cage and me," McCartney once said, explaining how his sound experiments "would just be in the middle of a song as a little solo; his would be the whole thing."

'Loup (1st Indian on the Moon)' was a competent (if short) nod to the experimental, underground end of rock music that was taking firm hold as McCartney and band set out on the rather more commercial *Wings Over Europe* tour. Travelling in their painted-up open-top bus, they played to crowds much more aware of The Osmonds and David Cassidy than The Alan Parsons Project. Pot busts, continued touring, a monumental Bond theme ('Live and Let Die') and McCartney's increasing love of the media meant that Wings became bigger and bigger as the seventies moved on. But this would also mean that the likes of 'Loup' were only momentary brushes with avant-garde techniques.

1973's *Band on the Run* solidified Wings' position as an independent unit, totally distinct from McCartney's 'former band'. "The best post-Beatle effort," said *Time Out*'s review, "and one that may do a lot to overcome the prejudices of those who see him [McCartney] only as a middle-of-the-road writer, drastically reducing the tweeness quota here." Recorded in Nigeria and propelled into the charts on the back of 'Jet' and the title track, the album sold over 3,000,000 copies in America alone. It was this halcyon period which, alongside avant-garde projects, McCartney harked back to in preparing a *Band on the Run* 25th anniversary box set when Linda McCartney died in 1998. The album's penultimate track is an ethereal soundscape, 'Picasso's Last Words (Drink to Me)'. Recorded with the band as a straightforward song, McCartney later remixed it into Cubist style, in that he chopped it up and rearranged it into four distinct sections.

'Picasso's Last Words' is a little burst of leftfield fun set in McCartney's most mainstream and acclaimed album of the seventies. It offered up some sounds never before heard on a McCartney record, not least the section comprised simply of drum machine, lush strings and vocals. Elsewhere this trio is complimented by Ginger Baker on percussion, or rather, shaking a metal bucket of gravel. The track also used long sections of 'found' dialogue, namely tapes of a French-language tourist guide. One of McCartney's early references to his love of painting, he had also started a song during the *Ram* sessions called 'When the Wind is Blowing', which was inspired by Picasso's 'The Old Guitarist'.

Buoyed by the success of *Band on the Run*, McCartney produced a solo album by his pseudonymous brother, Mike McGear, collaborated with Peggy Lee and even recorded the soundtrack to a Mother's Pride bread commercial. But by the end of 1974 he was working on Wings' next album, *Venus and Mars*, writing some songs with how they'd sound on the following UK and Australian tours in mind. With much of the album being put together in New Orleans during Mardi Gras, *Venus and Mars* is perhaps one Wings LP that is waiting to be rediscovered in future years. When it is, the play-off between electronic sounds and orchestral strings on 'Love in Song' will sound way ahead of its time, and the computer sound effects behind 'Venus and Mars (Reprise)' will sound pure retro.

Post-Mother's Pride, McCartney's interest in music for TV continued and his political songwriting waned. Leaving the political poignancy of 'Give Ireland Back to the Irish' behind him, in the year that Margaret Thatcher was elected Tory party leader and the Khmer Rouge came to power in Cambodia, McCartney was covering the theme from *Crossroads* for the finale of *Venus and Mars*. His soundtrack for the ATV adventure series, *The Zoo Gang*, is worthy of note, however, for its pure 'spy-cheese' sound.

Testament to McCartney's tireless and prolific output is the patchiness of his seventies albums, 1976's *Wings at the Speed of Sound* being a prime example. 'Warm and Beautiful' and 'She's My Baby' are McCartney classics, the latter being his first dalliance with keyboard-based funk and a foretaste of the greatness to come in 'Arrow Through Me' on *Back to the Egg* four years later. The rest of the album is best forgotten, although it does venture momentarily into non-mainstream production twiddling. On one track, the most upfront tape loop since the pioneering days of the sixties sounds like the start of a McCartney avant-garde composition, only to turn out to be the intro to the infuriating 'Silly Love Songs'. Elsewhere, the sounds of a fry-up in the McCartney kitchen start off Linda's lead vocal track, 'Cook of the House'.

There was turmoil in music in 1976. England had punk and America had Patti Smith. Those that needed a safer option had Wings. They also had some nostalgia too – in that year's *Wings Over America* tour, the band was established enough in its own right to start playing the odd Beatles track, with 'Lady Madonna', 'Blackbird' and 'Yesterday' all coming out of the McCartney archives. He also used the tour to publicly nod to his interest in classical music, playing Vivaldi's *The Four Seasons* across the auditoria each night as the pre-show music.

Another style McCartney started to play with in 1976 was electronic music – something he had all but abandoned since the days of Delia Derbyshire. Before heading back out on Wings' second European tour, McCartney sat down in his home studio in Cambletown and started messing about with Moog synthesisers. Combining them with the beats of his early drum machine purchases, he assembled various private experiments. Into the tape locker went 'Rhodes/Moog/Drum Track', 'Linda Melody with Moog', 'Moog Melody' and (the best title of all) 'Fishy Matters Underwater'.

Wings' most comfortably middle-of-the-road album, *London Town*, followed in 1978. His Moog experiments and sixties heritage had given McCartney a confidence and slick style in electronic pop, as evidenced on the funky instrumental 'Cuff Link' and the intro and breaks in 'With a Little Luck'. When Wings did experiment musically it veered off into overblown 1970s 'epic' rock. The use of Mellotron and Morse code picked out on electric piano did nothing to save the album's stodgy finale, 'More Moose and the Grey Goose'.

The *London Town* sessions saw McCartney nailing down the mainstream pop formula with tracks like 'Girlfriend', 'With a Little Luck' and 'Mull of Kintyre'. Never averse to stating the obvious, "It's definitely not punk," was how he described the latter to *Melody Maker*. The public wisely overlooked the double A-side flip to 'Mull of Kintyre', 'Girls School' ("about a pornographic St Trinian's"), and the single consolidated McCartney's public profile as MOR song-smith. With over 2,000,000 sales, 'Mull of Kintyre' became the biggest UK single ever until the release of Band Aid's 'Do They Know It's Christmas'.

For the media and the public at large, 'Mull of Kintyre' pushed McCartney so far into his 'safe balladeer' pigeonhole that they could lock the door and throw away the key. But, thankfully, this judgment had the opposite effect on McCartney's music and his experimental tendencies. With Wings now an established household name for kids and housewives alike, there was room to experiment again. He headed back to Scotland with a new line-up to start on what would become Wings' last album. Aside from the *Thrillington* side-project, it would include some of his most playful, leftfield ideas since the end of The Beatles.

# SIX

# "AN ABUNDANCE OF MELODY"
## AS EASY LISTENING FIGHTS BACK

**B**y the start of the 1970s The Beatles were finally over and Paul McCartney was a free agent. Personally he may have been on the verge of a nervous breakdown but creatively he was firing on all cylinders, in all directions, pouring out a string of songs direct into the tape deck for the *McCartney* album, and following it up with more homegrown solo compositions for *Ram*. But his work during this flashpoint period between The Beatles and Wings was not just concerned with rock and roll.

McCartney used his newfound freedom to play with classical, exotica, muzak and easy listening. He experimented with new effects and sounds too, from early phasing and flanging units to stereo recordings of dripping taps and toilets, aided and abetted by colleagues from previous Apple and Beatles projects, Richard Hewson, Tony Clark and super producer-in-training Alan Parsons. Once finished, McCartney intentionally shrouded this experimental work in mystery, locking it away for seven years before finally releasing it under a pseudonym – that of a fictional character whose profile he had built up via name-dropping and media games. For Pipe Down, the "anti-Muzak pressure group", their Anti-Christ was about to be born in the shape of Percy 'Thrills' Thrillington.

But McCartney's muzak experiment wasn't released during the Beatles-Wings abyss in which it was conceived. As if to further distance it from reality, it was held up until 1977, the height of the punk era. Was Percy Thrillington out to impress or just looking for a fight?

Maybe confrontation is what it was all about. When The Beatles were at their prime, they were as dangerous as hell. But the middle of the road fought back. *Sgt. Pepper's Lonely Hearts Club Band* didn't just chart with other psychedelic records. It was released at the same time as Andy Williams' *Music To Watch Girls*

*By.* Or take *Late Night Sounds in Stereo*, a classic easy listening album from 1968 issued on Marble Arch Records and available now at a car-boot sale near you. Here, bandleaders like Cyril Stapleton and John Schroeder scored the hits of the day into instrumental swing that was either the height of latenight lounge or intensely irritating elevator music, depending on your disposition (or age). Nestling between covers of 'The Pink Panther' by Sounds Orchestral and 'While the City Sleeps' by The Tony Hatch Singers & Swingers are Beatles songs, already standards by 1968. Not covered, but safely reworked from the edge of youth culture into the middle of the road. "Hear Sounds Orchestral tackle 'Michelle'," wrote David Norman in the liner notes for *Late Night Sounds in Stereo*, "and you realise all over again the musical value of this quieter type production from the Messrs Lennon and McCartney."

But that was then. By 2000, easy listening had left the middle of the road for the height of cool. James Calrje's *Blow Up a Go Go* was the soundtrack to a GAP TV advert a little after Freakpower's easy anthem *Turn On Tune In Cop Out* had topped the UK charts. Easy listening had developed into lounge, via muzak, exotica and, rather more descriptively, space-age bachelor-pad music. Even the archetypal exotica artist, vibes player Arthur Lyman, was revived on 2002's *Ocean's 11* soundtrack. The boundaries had blurred and kitcsh was cool. In the sleeve notes to their landmark compilation *Easy Tune* in 1995, the Dutch label Drive In noted that "it's sometimes difficult to discern where Latin, soul and bachelor-pad music begin and easy listening and club-pop end."

The growth of more cutting edge, experimental forms of music, like chill-out and ambient, are very much anchored in lounge. Ambient would not have existed had it not been for Muzak (the original elevator music company), according to Brian Eno as quoted in Chapter 13. As for chill-out, "just as chilling out has become a euphemism for staying in," noted the *Guardian* in February 2002, "so-called lounge music has become the acceptable face of easy listening, ranging from cha-cha-cha versions of Kraftwerk right through to the edited back catalogues of original easy swingers such as Mel Torme and Andy Williams…"

1971's *Ram* album would mark the end of McCartney's short, post-Beatles solo career, essentially a confidence-boosting and angst-clearing session in preparation for the long and winding college tour which took Wings from the penny stalls to stadiums across the rest of the decade. But before he set off he wanted to try an experiment. Before *Ram* was even in the shops, McCartney began assembling collaborators to help him put together a completely orchestrated instrumental version of the album. Not a full classical orchestra, but the classic 1970s-style 'pops' orchestra found on *Late Night Sound in Stereo* and the like. Cyril Stapleton would have been proud.

Of course, this was not McCartney's first attempt at a full-length orchestral work. *Thrillington* is very much the forgotten bridge between *The Family Way* – the 1967 George Martin soundtrack collaboration – and McCartney's 1990s orchestral works such as *The Liverpool Oratorio* and *Working Classical*. As with these later albums, McCartney had to choose an arranger to make *Ram* into something an orchestra could perform. This task fell to Richard Hewson, who remembers *Thrillington* as a career highlight. "I would say *Thrillington* was most rewarding," he says, "because Paul gave me a completely free hand to do whatever I wanted. Although I do have a soft spot for Mary Hopkin's 'Those Were the Days' because it was my first job straight from music college!"

In the mid-1960s Richard Hewson was a classical music student in London. There he formed a jazz trio which featured Peter Asher (of Peter & Gordon) on bass. And it was while the three of them rehearsed that Hewson met McCartney – who was going out with Jane Asher, Peter's sister. By 1968 Peter Asher was Head of A&R for Apple Records and was drafting in Richard Hewson for orchestral arrangements on tracks such as 'Those Were the Days'. By the end of 1970 Hewson had completed more orchestral work for Apple Records, scoring James Taylor, more Mary Hopkin and some legendary über-dub/over-dub sessions on The Beatles' *Let It Be*. Hewson added strings to 'The Long and Winding Road' and 'I Me Mine'. Not just a few strings either – this was for the musical megalomaniac Phil Spector, so he was instructed to draft in multiple harps and as many violinists as would physically fit into the studio at Abbey Road.

Hewson was only too happy to take the call from Paul McCartney about a 'secret' experimental session which would be released under a pseudonym. He was on a path of scoring himself firmly into the middle of the road with more string sessions in the 1970s for Supertramp, Carly Simon ('Nobody Does It Better') and McCartney (notably the 1973 number one single 'My Love'). He would later turn this around by returning to experimentation, and hiding under a pseudonym himself, using his initials to form The RAH Band, which scored the massive eighties hit 'Clouds Across the Moon'. Inspired by Kraftwerk and the DIY spirit of late-eighties dance music, Hewson continues in this vein today, charting in 1994 with 'Looks Like I'm In Love Again' under the more techno-oriented guise of Key West.

It was two weeks before the *Ram* album hit the shops (28 May 1971) when Hewson met with McCartney and heard about his idea. "He just handed me the *Ram* album," he remembers, "and said 'Let's make this into an instrumental, replacing all vocals, guitars and keyboards with orchestral instruments,' so it was quite experimental for me."

Hewson hadn't even heard the album in question but gave an instant "Yes!" – although the more obvious initial response might well have been "Why?" While some cynics have suggested that the album was thought up to fulfil obligations to Capitol Records, Hewson is sure that McCartney's intentions were experimental rather than contractual. "Back in the seventies we didn't have samplers to use for testing out how sounds might be transformed from vocal to, say, flugel horn," he told me, "so it was all down to imagining the result in your head and hoping it worked in the studio. I think some of it worked quite well…"

Hewson's arrangements were to be realised by an array of session musicians – violinists (19 in total), cellists and alto-saxophonists, plus assorted trombones and trumpets, clarinets, piccolos, flutes and recorders, a harpsichord and a tuba. A boy's choir was also drafted in for the *Thrillington* version of 'Ram On'. But in true seventies lounge style, these instruments were offset against a core of more traditional pop performers. According to Hewson, "The musicians I chose were the small group of top players that I regularly used. Herbie Flowers on bass, Clem Cattini of The Tornadoes on drums, Vic Flick – a legendary guitarist, Roger Coulan on keyboards, the Dolmetsch family on recorders, The Mike Sammes Singers and various top jazz players on saxes and brass, because I was and still am heavily into jazz. The strings and woodwind were all drawn from the top session players of the day."

McCartney drafted Tony Clark into the control room. They had some history together after Clark, then an 18-year-old new recruit at Abbey Road, acted as tape op on *The Beatles For Sale* album. He would later oversee the mastering – the transference from master tape to vinyl – of the 'Paperback Writer' single and work with McCartney producing Badfinger's 'Come and Get It'. Joining Clark and Hewson in the control room was Alan Parsons, The Beatles and Pink Floyd engineer who would later use some of the ideas he experienced on this project in his own renowned series of conceptual orchestral-rock albums under the guide of The Alan Parsons Project. All three were overseen throughout the recording session by McCartney himself, who remained firmly in the producer's role and resisted the temptation to perform on the album in any way.

The recording of *Thrillington* was structured and swift – three days (although each was at least 14 hours' long) in Abbey Road and it was all over. Herbie Flowers and co laid down their tracks on the first day (15 June 1971) and the rest of the sessions were used for building up the various orchestral parts. The Mike Sammes Singers came in to deliver their vocals on day two and, for day three, McCartney, Parsons, Hewson and Clark decamped to Studio One, where The Beatles had recorded the avant-orchestra for 'A Day in the Life', for a full orchestral session. Contrary to reports at the time (and since), it was The Mike Sammes Singers who performed on *Thrillington*, not the quavering experimental jazz vocalists The Swingle Singers. "Mike Sammes was my vocal contractor at that time," says Richard Hewson, "and, if memory serves me correctly, he would have booked a section of freelance vocalists, some of whom were in The Swingle Singers, as were some members of the strings and brass from the big

London orchestras." The Mike Sammes Singers had crossed paths with The Beatles before when they performed on 'I Am the Walrus' in 1967 and on 'Good Night', the closing track of the so-called White Album, a year later.

Right from the start of the *Thrillington* album, you can hear the work of Herbie Flowers. The 'bass player's bass player', who performed the legendary bassline on Lou Reed's 'Walk On the Wild Side', literally dances all over the exotica version of 'Too Many People', *Thrillington*'s opening track. During the early seventies, Flowers was one of London's most in-demand session players, for bass and also tuba, which he had been practising since joining the Royal Air Force. Like other session musicians of the day, he skipped from one job to the next, literally taking a booking, reading from the manuscript and moving on to another appointment, barely looking up to see who was in the control room or who the session was for. As such, there's a mountain of albums out there featuring the work of Flowers and his contemporaries, all of which, he told me, are having to be tracked down if only to secure future (and back-dated) royalties:

■ At that time it was like an explosion of pop music being made. And as such there was a great requirement for a bunch of session musicians who could read what producers wanted. Especially as those producers couldn't afford to spend ages in studio. But I wasn't just a session player, thank goodness. Half the work I was doing was West End shows and nightclubs. I formed a band called Blue Mink too, which made life a bit more interesting than just rolling up and playing what was put in front of us. Although when it all started we had to make up what we were playing because there was nothing to copy ... 99 per cent of what we produced was dreadful – as was 99 per cent of our behaviour!

Maybe some of that behaviour was captured on *Thrillington*. "In the back office with a bottle of scotch," is one of the lines of studio chatter that can be heard between tracks on the finished album. "During that time as a session player, I spent 15-20 years running from one studio to the next," Flowers remembers from his home near Brighton. "No one knew what it was or what was going to be next! People employed me to work for them and I treated that like a confidential arrangement, because it's my living."

Also on the scene in the mid-1970s was Laurence Juber, who would go on to join Wings at the end of the decade. He had similar experiences to Flowers' – playing regularly but rarely knowing who for. "I used to do orchestra dates at Abbey Road," he told me. "I played on *Tales of Mystery and Imagination* for Alan Parsons. I played acoustic guitar on a couple of the tracks. There was some stuff that was all acoustic instruments with mandolin and strings and harpsichord. I always have a good laugh about that when I see Alan because I didn't know who it was for. I read it in a magazine 20 years later."

Herbie Flowers has had no ordinary session career. His credits include David Bowie (1969's *Space Oddity* and 1974's *Diamond Dogs*), Harry Nilsson (1971's *Nilsson Schmilsson*), Lou Reed (1972's *Transformer*, which featured Herbie on tuba too) and Elton John (1978's *A Single Man*). To say nothing of appearances on the solo eighties work of The Beatles – George Harrison's *Somewhere in England* and *Gone Troppo*, Ringo Starr's *Stop and Smell the Roses* and *Starr Struck* and Paul McCartney's *Give My Regards to Broad Street*. But this is not something Flowers dwells on much. "I'm a bit of an obscurist," he says. "I don't like to be thinking about a lot of that because, like most things, when you listen to it now the playing doesn't sound as good as it should."

He does, however, have a great respect for the collaborations and creations of the man once known as Thrillington. "McCartney is brilliant. He always was a class act, everything about the man. We were good buddies and I felt very honoured that one of the world's greatest bass players would sometimes ask for some bass playing from me. Whether it be The Scaffold (McCartney's brother Mike's pop comedy trio) or *Give My Regards to Broad Street*. I'd be on bass because he was producing or playing piano. Or maybe, like all of us, he felt like it needed another input. If someone writes something and shuts themselves away with a workstation it goes up and down together, like living inside a balloon."

So for Herbie Flowers, the *Thrillington* project began just like the dozens he was booked for in May 1971… consequently, he says, "I'll have to cast my mind back – because it was only one day's work! I can remember people like Jim Lawless being on it and Clem Cattini was on drums. Richard Hewson was a brilliant arranger and he was up in the control box with Paul, who produced it and financed it. It was one of Paul's little excursions. I don't think his name appears anywhere on it – apart from on the writers' credits."

The finished result – *Thrillington* by Percy 'Thills' Thrillington – and the quality of the playing that Hewson and McCartney inspired sticks in Flowers' mind. "When you listen back to it, it's absolutely remarkable the quality of playing that's on there," says Flowers. "I can remember walking out the studio and thinking 'Blimey'. Just the fact that I can remember the session – not because Paul was in the box but because of Richard Hewson and the others. I remember thinking, 'There's a good writer, and a good rhythm section too.' I remember it as a really good day, not least because we were at Abbey Road, the quintessential recording studio. It was and still is."

The critics – those who heard it at least – agreed with him. "*Thrillington*," according to *GetMusic*, "avoids the temptation to deliver flaccid elevator music, in favour of very precise playing and finely detailed arrangements. The orchestrations incorporate elements of big-band swing and very elegantly realised pop music, with occasional backing by scatted and vamped choruses, courtesy of the Swingle Singers [sic], who call up memories of the Hi-Los at various points…"

The opening song, 'Too Many People', sets the pace for the entire album. Rock and roll is transformed into funky jazz with more than a hint of studio experimentation. It ends with the whole track going through a new sound tool which had been delivered to Abbey Road studios during the recording of *Thrillington*. The 'watery box', as it become known, was developed by Bernie Speights, who would go on to create various quadraphonic studio tools for Pink Floyd. This box was an early stereo phaser, the effect being to take all the sounds put through it and slosh them around as if in some psychedelic echo chamber.

'Ram On', the next track, is pure easy listening, stepped up even further with 'Dear Boy', which in *Thrillington* form has The Mike Sammes Singers scatting throughout. 'Uncle Albert', on the other hand, has McCartney's vocals replaced by the expert recorder playing of the Carl Dolmetsch family, which trades off a spy-thriller horn section before moving into a Vaudeville 'Admiral Halsey' with a manic bass solo from Herbie Flowers in the outro. *Thrillington*'s version of 'Smile Away' is much more accessible 30 years later than the glammed-up rock version found on *Ram*. It's covered in percussion, including some mad grunting noises courtesy of Chris Karen (the drummer from Dudley Moore's jazz trio) trying to figure out how to play a guica, a South American percussion instrument. Flute, bass and jazzy, wordless singing characterise 'Heart of the Country' and the Austin Powers-style brass returns for 'Monkberry Moon Delight'. Two of the highlights for *GetMusic* were 'Eat at Home'- "a big-band reggae instrumental that would have delighted big-band ska king Byron Lee" – and '3 Legs', which "swings like a latter-day Count Basie cut."

Like many of the albums covered in this book, *Thrillington* is omitted completely from most critical overviews of McCartney's work. But the few that cover it love it. "*Thrillington* is perhaps the most obscure album to be issued by a former Beatle," says *Excite*, which goes on to praise Hewson's "delightfully eclectic interpretation of *Ram* … While the album was not a commercial success, it does feature some lovely music, including jazzy versions of McCartney compositions like 'Dear Boy' and 'Smile Away' and a big pop production number of 'Uncle Albert/Admiral Halsey' that will be of interest to both McCartney fans and aficionados of kitschy, lounge-oriented instrumental music."

*Thrillington* closes with its most off-the-wall idea of all, as the sounds of the Abbey Road lavatories mix seamlessly with 'The Back Seat of my Car'. "The dripping water at the end of the record actually came about when Paul and I went to take a pee at the end of the sessions," says Hewson, "and we could hear the playback coming from the control room through to the loo, mixed with the sound of the dripping of water in the cistern. So we got a mike in and recorded it!"

'3 Legs' is one of the album's highlights for former Frank Zappa guitar-slinger, Mike Keneally. '5 Legs' on his own *Wooden Smoke* album (described in *Guitarist* as "the best headphone-to-oblivion album since Floyd's *Wish You Were Here*") is a direct tribute. "To me *Thrillington* is reminiscent of incidental music from a late-sixties British spy TV show, something with a lot of cars in it and very bad editing," he says. "Maybe Roger Moore on a lark, acting badly for the fun of it."

Mike Keneally learned to play guitar in 1971 at age ten, on hearing Frank Zappa's 'Help, I'm a Rock'. Sixteen years later he was hired by his inspiration and played guitar and keyboards on many of Zappa's final albums, including *Broadway the Hard Way*, *Make a Jazz Noise Here*, *The Best Band You Never Heard In Your Life* and *You Can't Do That On Stage Anymore*. In the 1990s he became a fixture in Z, Dweezil Zappa's band, and collaborated with equally experimental guitarist Robert Fripp. "He gave me answers to questions I had felt for myself, but never had the courage or capacity to find an answer [to]," Fripp said of him. Keneally still sees *Ram* as an exciting if unknown highpoint in McCartney's solo output.

■ Paul was still being visited by the melody gods in those days. The arrangements are creative and sophisticated without being freeze-dried or over-thought. Everybody on the album plays really well and the lyrics capture the content-edness of his home life in a way which I find charming and warming. I was around nine years old and still terribly mourning the end of The Beatles [when it came out]. They'd been just about the most important thing in my life for several years so any news of solo releases was always of the greatest interest to me. I'd been somewhat confused by the *McCartney* album, so when I began hearing *Ram* tracks on the radio I was heartened that the sound seemed fuller and, to my unsophisticated, nine-year-old ears, more Beatle-like than the rough-hewn demo style of *McCartney*. At nine, one doesn't worry about the same things about an album like *Ram* that a music critic might concern themselves with, so all I perceived when I finally bought the album was an abundance of melody and good sounds and great spirits. Which is what I still hear.

Keneally finally heard the *Thrillington* version of *Ram* in the 1990s when it appeared on CD. "I read about *Thrillington* in a Beatles book, sometime in the late seventies or early eighties most likely. I didn't actually hear it until a couple of years after the CD issue came out. At that point it was background music for the piece I was writing for the Beer For Dolphins (his touring band since 1994) website, and I think that's what the album is best suited for – fun, engaging background music with a really interesting concept at its core. *Thrillington* is a very groovy collection of arrangements of all of that album's songs… it's simply utterly lovely and fun. And makes me smile as I sit and type to you and sing along: 'Ram on… give your heart to somebody... soooooooon! Right away! Right away!' Not bad advice."

After Richard Hewson's manic three-day session in May 1971, *Thrillington* was complete, but it sat in the McCartney archives for the duration of Wings. Literally days after the last notes of *Thrillington* were mixed, McCartney was in the studio with the first line-up of his new band recording their debut album, *Wings Wild Life*. Six years later, and at the close of Wings' last world tour, contracts were sent out to Hewson and others to actually get the project released.

The reason for this delay has been the source of much speculation, but in retrospect it seems perfectly natural. In that short, highly creative gap between The Beatles and Wings, McCartney experimented not just with sounds but with whole styles. Not all of these experiments fitted with the hard-rocking post-Beatles solo image he was trying to build up. When Wings was over there was a certain amount of house-clearing and stock-taking going on. "Paul has always been very keen on this project, and we might be able to arrange for it to be released in due course," read a letter from McCartney Productions Ltd to Richard Hewson, which arrived on his doorstep on 18 October 1976. Although some of the players on the record had all but forgotten about the recording seven years earlier... Herbie Flowers: "To get this record through the post, seven years later, signed 'Dear Herb, thanks very much, Paul Mac'... I was quite flattered."

McCartney himself points to a more obvious reason for the delay. "[*Thrillington*] came about because I wanted someone to do a big band version of the *Ram* album – but seeing as there were no takers I thought I'd better be that someone!" he recalled. "Well, what I didn't realise was that no one would want to release an album like that! Not even then," he told Mark Lewisohn in spring 1992. "And no way would you get it released now"! As such, the 'greatest record you never heard' is a tag which (yet again) springs to mind. Despite being heralded as "a very potent work in its own right" by the *All Music Guide*, they also note its rarity value as "one of the few genuinely rare, legitimate commercial LP releases in Paul McCartney's output, mostly a result of its never having been officially credited to McCartney or publicised as one of his releases."

So why did McCartney turn one of his best early works into what many might call 'muzak'? Maybe, at the time of its recording, McCartney wanted to fight his way out of the musical pigeonhole in which he was rapidly being incarcerated. Mike Keneally agrees: "I think it's telling that Paul chose *Ram* as the album for such treatment," he told me. "It indicates that he, too, felt there was an unusual concentration of good melodic content to be dealt with there. And I wouldn't be at all surprised if he relished the opportunity to shine a different light on material which was so unfairly treated the first time around. It may also have been an ironic comment on the prevailing opinion that he was pretty much turning out muzak anyway..."

# SEVEN
# FROM SHEEP MASKS TO PSEUDONYMS
## (AND BAA)

So who exactly was (or is) Percy Thrillington? Of the many smoke screens and fictional characters created by Paul McCartney to release his more left-field, experimental work, this one was the most elaborate. McCartney decided that such an off-the-wall album needed equally off-the-wall publicity:

> ■ We invented it all, Linda and I, and we went around southern Ireland and found a guy in a field, a young farmer, and asked if he minded doing some photographic modelling for us. We wanted to find someone that no one could possibly trace, paid him the going rate and photographed him in a field, wearing a sweater and then wearing an evening suit. But he never quite looked Percy Thrillington enough…

With the bemused farmer's moment of glory consigned to the cutting room floor, the McCartneys decided to build the profile of Percy Thrillington by using words instead of pictures. "Percy Thrillington has been persuaded to prolong his stay in Paris as he finds the springtime atmosphere most conducive to creativity," read a tiny announcement in the classified ads section of the London *Evening Standard* one night in 1976. Few people noticed, but a second ad started to turn a few heads, and a third a few more. "Percy Thrillington, despite excesses on both social and business time, hopes to lend his support to today's daffodil ball," read one classified, to be followed another evening with "Percy Thrillington will be attending tonight's production of *Don Giovanni* and awaits with eager anticipation a stimulating performance from Miss Hayashi."

"In the period August 1976 to August 1978 I regularly commuted from Hammersmith to The City by tube," recalls Tony Shackleton, then a city worker and the exact target for what today would be called ambient advertising. "I'd read the London evening papers cover to cover. At that time there were two – the *Evening News* and the *Evening Standard* – but the *Evening News* was soon to close down, leaving the *Evening Standard* as the only London evening paper." Indeed, the paper itself picked up on the hotbed of activity within its classifieds, with an article on Friday 18 March 1977 entitled 'The Perambulations of Percy Thrillington'.

"Percy Thrillington is alive and well and living in the country. But he has been gadding about somewhat, hence the frequent messages in the *Evening Standard*," wrote *Standard* journalist Stephen Clackson. The scam had worked, at least to the point where avid readers were demanding to know who Thrillington was. "Every day, it seems, curious readers and others telephone demanding to know more about this man," he reported. When the album was released, the sleeve's fictional biography of Percy Thrillington carried the story further.

▪ What is known about this enigmatic figure is that he was born in Coventry Cathedral in England in 1939. As a young man he wandered the globe. His travels took him to Baton Rouge, Louisiana in the United States where he studied music for five years. He later moved to Los Angeles where he gained expertise in conducting and arranging as well as the marketing end of the music business. Eventually his path lead to London where his long ambition to form an orchestra and record was finally realised after he met Paul McCartney who helped Thrillington secure a recording contract.

And so it went on. The biography was credited to Clint Harrigan, another of McCartney's pseudonyms. He used this *nom de plume* again on the next album he recorded, *Wings Wild Life*, in a short essay on the formation of Wings. "When Paul and Linda McCartney were in New York recording *Ram…*" he said of their search for the first Wings drummer, "they found a sweaty old basement in the West 40's and invited some drummers to play on a battered old drum kit. One of those who turned up and went straight for the tom toms was Denny Seiwell, a tall type with eight generations of drummers in his family, who played well and left the drum kit throbbing…" But modesty prevented McCartney from putting his own name at the bottom of this write-up, which closed simply with "Can you dig it?" and a sketch of the band at play. "I thought, I can't just sign it Paul McCartney," he recalled in 1992, "having written about how great the group is, so I made up the name Clint Harrigan. It was the easiest way of doing it, to put someone else's name there, do a little cartoon and put it out."

With Thrillington reported to have sent a single red rose to every female member of London's press on Valentine's Day 1977, the character's reputation as a bit of a womaniser began to grow. In a press release, McCartney Productions told how Percy's assistant, Miss Telfer Smallett, had been interviewed on the radio stating that her boss wasn't married but was most certainly "an appreciator of women." EMI's publicity department were roped in too, and issued a denial to the journalists – this was nothing to do with them, they said. "Percy Thrillington certainly isn't Paul McCartney as some people seem to think," they said. "Percy Thrillington does exist as an individual and it is surprising how many people are following his activities through the personal columns ... Hopefully he will make a personal appearance soon, but he does spend a lot of time rushing around the country and seems to wish to remain anonymous."

Thrillington's addiction to the opposite sex was directly inspired by the hilarious liner-note hyperbole that surrounded the creators of some of the classics of exotica and easy listening. On the back cover of Arthur Lyman's masterful *I Wish You Love*, released on Hi-Fi Records many years earlier, his sleeve biographer oozed...

■ In his many personal appearances, the romantic and personable Lyman has had particular appeal for feminine listeners of all ages. This charm is a sort of personal magnetism accented by a movie idol appearance, but without any particular intent, and unaccompanied by the twisting and carrying on of the many popular purposeful charmers. Obviously Arthur Lyman gets through to girls young and old; in fact to everyone, with much natural personal appeal and sensual sounds.

As the media interest grew, McCartney used this new platform to directly address the weary commuters that were picking up on the ads. Some classifieds even hinted at McCartney's own orchestral ambitions. "Percy Thrillington is extremely flattered that rumours suggest that he is to be invited to advise on Modern Music at the Paris Conservatoire, while he is visiting that city," he wrote.

Some readers got in on the joke and started to place equally bizarre adverts by response. What to most were fun and games beside the crossword panel became interactive art to others. "Dear Percy," wrote the equally ridiculously-named Guy Bugland. "As a fellow peripatetic traveller, I've found the overwhelming need to join a top-hole association called St Christopher – those good fellows are most frightfully generous with the old readies if a chap has the fearful misfortune to be deprived of his driving licence. If you – or your chums – wish to join our esoteric band of associates, please ring before luncheon, any weekday, at my Mayfair office..."

But Percy didn't bite. Instead he became less vague, as more and more plugs for the *Thrillington* album appeared in his notices. "Percy Thrillington is tickled pink by the spectacular display of his single and album recordings in the window of Chappell's Music Store in New Bond Street all this week," claimed one. In another, "Percy Thrillington wishes to inform all his friends that he will be taking an extended holiday in South America following the rigours of launching his first album 'Thrillington' and the single 'Admiral Halsey'. In his absence all enquiries should be directed to Miss Penelope Telfer Smallett." On other occasions, readers found that the album had been taken to "Newmarket ... for the enjoyment of his many friends within the racing fraternity" or to the "Berkely Dress Show." In the ongoing saga of the life and times of "Sir Percy", as Herbie Flowers would call him, Berkely met with rapture ("Percy Thrillington, delighted by the ecstatic reception afforded to his single 'Admiral Halsey' ... obliged the young beatuies by placing his moniker on the record sleeves clutched in their hands"), whereas at Newmarket the fictional character almost met his end.

■ Percy Thrillington's condition is causing grave concern following injuries sustained at Newmarket in a gallant attempt to pluck his latest single 'Admiral Halsey' from beneath the thundering hooves of runners in the 3.30. No grapes, by request.

The *Evening Standard*'s Stephen Clackson was by now on a mission, determined to track Thrillington down. He started off at the Kensington advertising agency Cream, which was placing the ads for McCartney, and then on to MPL (McCartney Productions Ltd) itself, where, despite the protestations of McCartney's assistant Tony Brainsby (they weren't ads for a record, he said, Thrillington "really just liked to keep in touch"), Clackson sussed the whole thing. "Aided by the efficient Penelope, he has slaved, between trips, over the last six years producing a long-playing record of some of McCartney's music. In case the picture isn't coming any clearer yet," Clackson reported, "the record – it's a pity it had to be something like that didn't it? – is due to be released soon." But McCartney had the last laugh, writing in a press release: "One reporter for a London publication claims he got hold of Percy Thrillington on the telephone once and asked him if he was really Paul McCartney. The writer says the answer was either 'Bah' or 'Baaa'." As McCartney acknowledged in 1992:

■ We started this whole business in the *Evening Standard* ad columns, which was the really fun thing, putting in things like 'Must get in touch with ... Thrillington', as a result of which the newspaper columns picked up on it – 'Has anyone seen this rubbish going on in the *Standard* about Percy Thrillington?' – and it was good publicity. It was one of our madcap publicity schemes, as if we were managing this character called Percy Thrillington. But it was really just an excuse to do a Big Band album ... now the truth can finally come out...

Mind games they may have been, but they didn't impress everyone. Not least the album's orchestrator Richard Hewson (the 'real' Thrillington). He was not in the slightest bit thrilled (excuse the pun) to see his work – which he had always thought was tour-worthy – become part of a fictitious smoke screen.

"The scam to my mind was a daft idea," Hewson told me. "I didn't get the point of all this fake bandleader thing and it didn't work anyway. I thought they should have just come out with the album in an upfront manner and marketed it properly. Indeed, I think in retrospect that this is one reason why it didn't do better since all the press knew it was a scam and thought that perhaps it was dreamt up to cover for a dodgy record." The Thrillington smoke screen was a particularly English affair. "I wasn't privy to any of the publicity upon the album's release," says Mike Keneally. "It barely had a ripple of impact in California, where I was at the time."

"You could say that Percy Thrillington was Richard Hewson, or just a fictitious leader of a band that never appeared anywhere," McCartney later decided. "We've put out some weird and wonderful things like that occasionally. We would put clues into songs about certain things, because if people are going to play mind games with our lyrics then we can play mind games with them. Thrillington was one of those."

From Percy 'Thrills' Thrillington to The Fireman and the artist-less front cover of *Liverpool Sound Collage*, both reviewed later in this book, McCartney has never had the confidence to release all his work under his own name. By the same token he's never tried to give his avant-garde experiments instant limelight by adding his famous brand-name, instead releasing them to succeed or fail on their own merits. The few pieces of McCartney avant-garde music that have been heard by a massive audience – *Strawberries Oceans Ships Forest* as the 1993 pre-concert tape, and the Riley-inspired minimalism of 'Church Mice' for the tours ten years before – were never given coverage or promotion.

Some McCartney pseudonyms were born out of necessity. When he wanted to record his eponymous debut outside the media glare of The Beatles' break-up, he booked all his Abbey Road studio time under the name Billy Martin. The fictional sleeve note author on *Wings Wild Life*, Clint Harrigan, put a certain distance between McCartney and the myriad of styles and roles he was trying to take on after The Beatles split. Hal Smith, meanwhile, was McCartney's farmyard DJ who presented a special version of the *Ram* album mailed only to radio stations.

Taking a break from the mainstream and the success of 1973's *Band on the Run*, McCartney travelled to Nashville. There, an extended Wings line-up including brass, piano, banjo, guitarist Chet Atkins (and Paul on washboard) recorded 'Walking in the Park with Eloise'. This instrumental, which was based on a melody fragment McCartney could remember his father humming, was later issued not as Wings but, appropriately enough, The Country Hams. This pseu-donym helped 'Walking in the Park with Eloise' avoid any sales when released as a single. But at that time Wings had only just established a name in their own right, *Red Rose Speedway* having had to be credited to Paul McCartney & Wings. But these and other off-shoot projects remain as close to McCartney's heart as any other. He chose The Country Hams' single as one of his Desert Island Discs on BBC Radio 2 in 1982.

McCartney's very first musical pseudonym, Paul Ramon, was a name he chose when The Silver Beatles toured Scotland. At the time John Lennon had become Long John Silver, George Harrison was Carl Harrison (in homage to Carl Perkins) and Stuart Sutcliffe became Stuart de Stael (after the painter Nicholas de Staehl). "It made us seem like great London showbiz guys," he remembered years later, "so that when we were in Fraserberg, instead of saying 'I'm just a kid from Liverpool' it suggested there was something more to us. It's an old trick."

Paul Ramon (which in turn inspired The Ramones) was one of many McCartney pseudonyms later used in his 1960s collaborations, many of which were dreamt up for contractual reasons. "Just put me down as anything!" McCartney told the Bonzo Dog Doo-Dah Band's Viv Stanshall after he produced their hit single 'I'm the Urban Spaceman'. Stanshall christened him Apollo C Vermouth. Ian Iachimoe was McCartney's experimental film alter-ego. As Iachimoe he placed an ad in the underground newspaper *Long Hair Times* in March 1966 looking for script ideas.

In his discussion of authorship, musicologist W Straw suggests that the con-tinually shifting pseudonyms of artists in the modern dance music field "are read as signs that the individual's origins in (or commitment to) any one style are not genuine, that the individual's participation in that genre's unfolding history is merely a momentary visit." Not so. McCartney's various pseudonyms covered here show not a lack of dedication to a particular genre but a desire to extend the creative process of its music into words, images, personae and contexts which, far more than just music alone, shape the modern world.

David Bowie and Peter Gabriel have dabbled in many fields of music – both pop, rock, dance music and avant-garde. They almost always release the results under their own name. But they are among only a handful of exceptions. In 2001, academic Roy Shuker cited Madonna as another absentee from the roster of postmodern artists who fail to let "each stylistic change add to [their] musical persona over time." But Madonna's work has always been in one particular field – dance music – even if she has explored various particular sub-genres and influ-ences. Shuker does point to UK producer Norman Cook, but as an artist who has successfully dodged preconceptions and had his work viewed on a level playing field by continually updating his alias. Freakpower, whose exotica anthem 'Turn On Tune In Cop Out', was mentioned earlier, was one such alias. And Fatboy Slim, whose groundbreaking remix of Cornershop's 'Brimful of Asha' is mentioned by Nitin Sawhney in Chapter Nine, was another. Just as McCartney has used pseudonyms for styles as diverse as country and avant-garde, Cook, according to Shuker, "has kept up a bewildering array of aliases … because he believes his musical past meant that some people would not approach his music with an open mind."

"More power to him to do something and not put it out under his own name," says Wings guitarist Laurence Juber of McCartney's avant-garde work as The Fireman. "Do it under a pseudonym, so that it just exists in its own space." Gruff Rhys from the Super Furry Animals agrees. "I suppose he doesn't need to," he says of the need to identify himself and promote all his work equally. "He has no need to prove himself to anybody."

McCartney first tried to let his music succeed on its own merits when he wrote the song 'Woman' for Peter & Gordon in 1966. The Beatles' music publisher Dick James was mortified when he found out that McCartney wanted it to be released without his name on it – or rather under the alias Bernard Webb. But the release went ahead and it became a hit. "I was a bit annoyed that anything by Lennon-McCartney was being a hit, particularly by Peter & Gordon," said McCartney. "I don't know, I just got an attack of the morals or something, but felt it was a bit much that automatically having our name on something made it do well, and I wanted to see if I could get around it."

The experiment worked and 'Woman' became a UK hit single, even though at number 28 it was the lowest chart placing the duo ever achieved: "The release suggested to me that my name didn't need to be on things – but then it wasn't as big a hit as some of their other singles so it sort of proved a point." That in itself is the dilemma of the pseudonym for McCartney: sales verses credibility. Even The Beatles took out cautionary full-page adverts in 1967, urging hazy-eyed acid fans to "Remember, *Sgt. Peppers Lonely Hearts Club Band* IS The Beatles." Of course, low sales are somewhat easier to justify in the avant-garde world as opposed to the pop world. As Brian Eno once noted, only about 1,000 people bought 1967's groundbreaking album *The Velvet Underground and Nico*. However, almost everyone who did went on to form their own, similarly influential rock group...

# EIGHT

# MUSIC MADE WITH RADIOS AND GIZMOTRONS

**W**ings Over America – 1976's triple live album – was final proof that McCartney had achieved his goal. The band that had started playing live at Nottingham University on 9 February 1972 returned to a former Beatles venue and played before thousands at San Francisco's Cow Palace on 13 June 1976. The success of this, 'Mull of Kintyre' and the *London Town* album, as well as the excitement of an upcoming new decade, gave McCartney the encouragement to diversify once more and break the mould a little.

While the *Wings Over America* film was being completed in London, McCartney relocated to Scotland in June 1978 to start recording what was to be the band's final album, *Back to the Egg*. It was also to be the band's most poorly received LP. The Wings nucleus of Paul, Linda and Denny Laine had been supplemented with drummer Steve Holly and guitarist Laurence Juber, who had joined Wings from David Essex's house band on the recommendation of Laine.

Holed up in a barn-cum-recording studio (nicknamed the Spirit of Ranachan) on McCartney's Cambletown estate, the new band played around. They recorded nine instrumentals for one of McCartney's many unissued and uncompleted films, this set being for the soundtrack for a Rupert the Bear animation. They played around with reggae jams and playwright Willy Russell visited for a time to talk about a screenplay featuring all the band members in another abortive cinematic whimsy, *Band on the Run*.

When recording for the album finally started, McCartney was being pulled in two opposing directions. On one side he had punk. 'Mull of Kintyre' may have been poles apart from the Sex Pistols, The Clash and most other singles in the chart when it sat at number one, but that didn't mean that punk wasn't an influence preying on McCartney's mind. On the other hand he had the less aggressive but equally mouldbreaking influence of progressive rock, with the likes of Pink Floyd and The Alan Parsons Project continuing to dominate longhaired bedsits and adult turntables.

Courageously (some would say stupidly), *Back to the Egg* attempted to combine both: a progressive concept rock album played out punk-style in as few takes as possible. 'We're Open Tonight', as the album was originally known, was based around the simple concept of life on the road. Its two avant-garde-inspired tracks, 'Reception' and 'The Broadcast', were bold experiments, at least by comparison to the rest of Wings' output. Looking back from his home in LA, Laurence Juber remembers:

> ■ There were a couple of things that went off into left field ...There was a track that never made it onto *Back to the Egg* called 'Cage'. It was basically two songs that got put together.There was a horn-type sound that ended up being done on a Mini-Moog, but I remember one day we were trying to record the horn on Paul's Rolls-Royce. There was another section that sounded almost like a calliope, where we basically got a bunch of four whiskey bottles and blew over the tops, and, in order to change the pitch, we had to drink some of the whiskey. If I recall we were kind of rolling drunk by the end of the session, but it actually turned out quite nice...

'Reception' is the sound of a listener tuning the dial of a radio, in search of something new. *The Lutheran Hour* (from Norway's Norea Radio), McCartney's new classical track 'The Broadcast', poetry recitals and the words of a Deputy Sheriff talking about a two-day chase to arrest a man for something "pretty desperate" can all be heard on the 'Radio', as the track was originally known. Right in the middle a funky one-take instrumental jam kicks in and the album's up and running. To judge from the bass playing on 'Reception', the dexterity of Holly and Juber, both accomplished musicians in their own right, was clearly bringing out the best in McCartney too.

Although edited down to just one-minute album intro status, 'Reception' was originally planned as a much longer piece. While radio noise, tuning and interference have since become commonplace in chill-out and modern electronic styles (cropping up on McCartney's later 1990s experimental track 'Trans Lunar Rising'), in 1978 it was still a pretty avant-garde form. The roots of radio-as-music can be traced back over 30 years before *Back to the Egg* to the composers McCartney was getting into in the late 1960s. In 1951, John Cage's 'Imaginary Landscapes No 4' was the sound of 12 radio sets being simultaneously tuned and retuned. In France in the late 1940s composers Pierre Schaeffer and Pierre Henry wrote the groundbreaking 'Symphonie pour un homme seul', which was made up of noise from many electronic sources. But the original radio collage spirit of 'Reception' was considered a little too way out for Wings buyers. When the track was retitled it was edited down from two minutes to one. Much dialogue and orchestral work was removed and the actual Wings rock jam was brought to the fore.

Experimental or self-indulgent, depending on how you look at it, Wings were not averse to recording in some odd locations. The previous year they had recorded much of *London Town* on a yacht off the Virgin Islands, and the early sessions for *Venus and Mars* had taken place in the thick of the New Orleans Mardi Gras. In 1978, McCartney set up Replica Studios, a painstaking recreation in his London offices of EMI's Abbey Road Studio Two, because the original was fully booked. Moving on from Spirit of Ranachan, Wings continued with *Back to the Egg* by installing recording gear in a 12th century castle in Lympne, Kent.

"This castle was pretty wild," says Laurence Juber. "12th century and Thomas a Becket slept there or something and it had ghosts and spiral staircases." The band incorporated many of the castle's features into the album, as on the track 'Million Miles'. "I have a picture of Paul recording that with a squeeze box sitting outside on this balcony at Lympne Castle," says Laurence Juber. "That was actually done outdoors. With the drum kit set up in the Lympne's great stone fireplace, it was quite a bizarre sight."

'We're Open Tonight', on the other hand, combined the natural sounds of Lympne with an accident of tuning (accidents – always the experimentalist's closest allies). "My acoustic guitar part on that was actually recorded in the spiral staircase using natural echo," Juber remembered. "That was an interesting one because I took the guitar out of its case, it was a 12-string and it wasn't tuned properly – the individual pairs of strings, instead of being tuned in unison or in octave, were actually tuned in different intervals. I didn't mess with it, I just started playing it and it fitted perfectly. There was actually some weird harmonica stuff going on inside there too."

During the recording of *Back to the Egg*, David Bowie made the trek to Kent to see what McCartney was up to and was impressed by what he heard, especially on 'The Broadcast', one of the most experimental tracks in the whole of Wings' output. "Bowie thought it should be the first single off the album," remembers Juber. 'The Broadcast' was a sweeping orchestral piece overlaid with random poetry readings. Rather than using a traditional orchestra, the backing was created using a Mellotron, piano and guitar with a special Gizmotron attached. The Gizmotron, invented by Godley and Creme, was one of the great 'might-have-beens' of 1970s musical experimentation. Pioneers of both sound and music, McCartney had first met Kevin Godley and Lol Creme when they comprised one half of 10cc. Wings had shared studio time with the band a few years before and McCartney would go on to write much of 1986's generally despised *Press to Play* album with 10cc's Eric Stewart. Godley and Creme had used the Gizmotron to achieve orchestral string sounds on the hit single 'I'm Not In Love', the unique atmosphere of which McCartney paid tribute to in the outro to 'Sweet Little Show' on his *Pipes of Peace* album).

Lol Creme has never been averse to technologically enhanced music – either through computers or handmade inventions. In conversation with him and his friend and musical collaborator Trevor Horn, we talked about the border between electronic and traditional music, which, since the days of Delia Derbyshire and 'Carnival of Light', had become increasingly blurred. "I've been Pro Tooled to death..." Creme said of Pro Tools, one of the most revolutionary pieces of software so far created for sound manipulation. "...To life actually. But also I enjoy playing the guitar. My fun is just having a little tinkle."

■ **Creme:** Well, it's amazing what the technology allows people to do. It's certainly opened the door for non-musicians.

**Horn:** It's difficult to imagine someone learning to play an instrument now because you look back to learning to play the guitar and I definitely remember spending a few months with sore fingers. You used to take it to the toilet with you.

**Creme:** That was the vibe. But now people will tire themselves out learning how to operate the computer so they can manipulate all the noises as opposed to just six strings.

**Horn:** Well, you can't blame people because it's a shit load more interesting, being realistic!

Back in 1977 the Gizmotron was bought by Musitronics, a company which specialised in manufacturing music effects and freaky foot pedals. Their products were loved by Frank Zappa, Jerry Garcia and all the luminaries of 1970s experimentalism. Musitronics planned to take the device into mass production. "The only problem was that Lol was the only person who could actually play the thing," Aaron Newman, the company's founder, later remembered. This, coupled with numerous production problems (Musitronics found that Gizmotrons made in winter would not work properly in summer!), was the end of the product and almost the end for Musitronics.

The vocals for 'The Broadcast' were provided, uncredited, by Dierdre and Harold Margary, the owners of Lympne Castle. "It's a bit hazy but the guy that owns the castle where we were recording, both he and his wife had these very plummy kind of voices," Juber told me. "I think it was like, 'Oh, wouldn't it be fun to have them read some classic English literature material and use the orchestral background to be just this kind of weird interlude.' And they were kind of game for it."

McCartney had selected random books from the vast castle library and had the Margarys recite sections in their most rounded of English accents. Mr Margary can be heard on the finished track reading from Ian Hay's *The Sport of Kings* and John Galsworthy's *The Little Man*, while Mrs Margary read from *The Poodle and the Pug*, a song from a 1946 light opera by Vivian Ellis (who famously wrote 'Spread a Little Happiness') called *Big Ben*. Her reading didn't make the final version but a few lines ("…with tufts of hair stuck here and there which one would like to tug…") were instead spliced into 'Reception'.

Despite coming from such a haphazard set of sources, the finished version of 'The Broadcast' (sections of which were also cut into the original version of 'The Reception') is stirring, emotional and impressively different from anything that had come out under the Wings moniker. "Paul had this Gizmo thing on his Telecaster," remembers Laurence Juber. "It had things that you pressed down, so you were basically bowing the strings on the guitar. So you could get all these kinds of orchestral sounds. We had that and I also had a guitar synth and an ARP Avatar, I think it was. It was cutting edge at the time but it had its limitations. A lot of the lead stuff on 'The Reception' part was played on that. I do remember Paul using the Gizmo thing when we did some fake orchestral stuff, which was pretty much what formed the background of all those speeches. I think that was the inspiration."

Juber continues to this day as a guitarist of both dexterity and experimental outlook. His unique tunings and finger-picking styles can be heard on various solo albums, while his 'straight' session work can be heard on albums by Ringo Starr, The Monkees and Belinda Carlisle as well as soundtracks like *The Big Chill*, *Ladyhawke* (produced by Alan Parsons), *Good Will Hunting* and George Harrison's *Shanghai Surprise*. His ambient track 'Liquid Amber' was released by New Age label Windham Hill, which in the 1980s was notorious for selling huge quantities of part Muzak/part minimalist chill-out albums. "My direction is going into this much more intricate kind of guitar stuff," he says. "More than different tunings, it's just like self-sufficiency. To be completely musical without having to rely on anybody else. It's very much at the kind of Jansch, Davy Graham end of things. But with Joe Pass thrown in and Hendrix too."

*Back to the Egg* won a Grammy for another off-the-wall idea – 'Rockestra'. The idea was quite straightforward – a simple rock melody played by as many musicians as possible, 'battle of the bands' style. McCartney attempted to gather a 'Who's Who' of 1970s rock musicians for a recording session at Abbey Road which Laurence Juber remembers well:

■ I have pretty vivid memories of that one because it was such a trip. Just looking down the guitar section and seeing Pete Townshend and Dave Gilmour and

Hank Marvin, players that I grew up being majorly inspired by. So that was a real trip for me just to be there. Doing 'Rockestra' was very much that kind of a session, where you just had a studio full of musicians. We got two tracks done in a three-hour session. There were no egos, everybody checked their egos at the door. Paul had had this 'Rockestra Theme' idea, and then we demoed it and played the demo to everybody and then just kind of did it. The thing that took more time than anything else was getting the two 24-track machines running in synch and marking everything up. There were six guitar amps, three drum kits ... It took a lot of logistics to do that, but it was a trip. That track won a Grammy. It apparently got used as a sports theme in France and it still comes up as being something that was actually just a very cool track.

'To You' was another guitar experiment which produced a unique, frenetic sound. The middle section of the song has a guitar solo by Juber, which he played through a harmoniser. McCartney, in the control room, could hear Juber's playback and fiddled with the harmoniser's settings live as he soloed. Juber, on the other hand, could only hear the completely altered harmonised output in his headphones as he improvised. According to the guitarist himself, "That was an interesting thing..."

■ That was actually the first solo that I played on the record. What happened was, we had it set up so I was playing in the studio, Paul was in the control room with my signal run through an Avonside harmoniser and he was screwing around with the pitch in real time while I was playing it. And I was hearing what I was doing and in the headphones I was hearing what he was doing, but I couldn't anticipate where he was going to go and he couldn't anticipate where I was going to go. So there was this cool, slightly random aeolotropic synergy that was going on. I've always been very pleased with that solo. Once in a while I'll find someone who figured out just how hip that really was ... There was more stuff on the end section but that got mixed into the background. Paul has never been into long guitar solos...

Among all the rock on *Back to the Egg*, there was a hint of the stripped-down, lighter, funkier approach that McCartney was considering on 'Arrow Through Me'. An overlooked McCartney classic, it's audibly inspired by Stevie Wonder and, according to Juber, has some clever intricacies in the instrumentation.

■ 'Arrow Through Me' is one of the great under-rated ones. There's no bass on that, the bottom end is all the left hand of the electric piano, the Fender Rhodes. I remember Paul Simon listening to a playback of it in the studio and just being wide-eyed at the sound that we got with this one Fender Rhodes. That's an interesting track because there are two drum tracks on that, one is regular and one is double speed. You have to look around to find other examples of two drum tracks on McCartney records. One them being I think 'Lady Madonna', I think that has two different drum kits on it.

Like any other McCartney album, there were various tracks left in the can, never to see the light of day. Juber remembers that these included a smattering of experimental items:

■ There were some other moments during that whole recording process where we did a couple of interesting things ... There was something called 'Robbers Ball' which was another one of the weird ones. Paul and I were jamming and ended up with just a guitar and drum kind of backing track and that got expanded upon and he wrote this kind of weird little opera that went on over the top of it. It kind of deserved to be on the album ... There was an outtake also of a tune of mine called 'Maisy', that was a little instrumental that had kind of like a Cajun feel to it. I was kind of disappointed that it didn't make it onto the record. There was a lot of variation ... Steve Holly and I both came from very diverse backgrounds and I always figured that one of the reasons that I got the gig was because I was versatile and so there were elements in there running the gamut from the weird, harmonised 'To You'-type things to this crazy 'Spin it On' stuff. There was a little more kind of mainstream and then stuff that was really kind of folky, like 'Love Awake' and stuff like that.

While *Back to the Egg* was being completed the music world was going through tumultuous change. The punk scene began to collapse when Sid Vicious was found dead in February 1979, while alternative synthesiser-based and new wave music began to come to the fore with groundbreaking releases in the same year by Talking Heads (*Fear of Music*) and Joy Division (*Atmosphere*). Both these developments rendered the final release of *Back to the Egg* pretty much redundant. The fervour that had greeted Wings' previous album, *London Town*, and the following hits package, *Wings Greatest*, was nowhere to be seen.

Sales weren't helped by the fact that McCartney refused to include that year's Wings hit single 'Goodnight Tonight' on the album. "I never quite understood why the one with all the speeches and everything ('The Broadcast') was on there," says Laurence Juber. "It was an oddball track and has its intrinsic interest, but they stalwartly refused to put 'Goodnight Tonight' on the album, which was the hit single and probably would have generated another three or four million sales. Paul has always been into this value-for-money thing. His argument was always that in England The Beatles never put the singles on the album, so he didn't want to do that." Released during the making of *Egg* to promote the *Wings Over America* film, 'Goodnight Tonight' had reached number five. By contrast, *Back to the Egg*'s 'Getting Closer', released just five months later, scraped in at number 60. But 'Goodnight Tonight' would have stood out like a sore thumb on *Back to the Egg* as it was McCartney's first – and wholly successful – attempt at disco, 12" remix and all.

"Wings was a great education," concludes Juber. As the 1980s began he left the band just as it started to disintegrate. "It ended up falling apart because Paul had a band that was too rock and roll for his lifestyle and for his musical intentions," he says. "The clear end for me was at the end of January 1981. I moved to New York. We had spent some time in January working on what they called *Cold Cuts* and at that point he went back to continue working on *Tug of War*, and my feeling was that, rather than hang around and kind of hope to be invited to play on that, I was just going to take off and go to New York. Then Wings officially disbanded in April of '81. It wasn't a definitive break-up, it wasn't a clear-cut ending, but after he got busted in Tokyo, things were pretty much winding down, because that cancelled the US tour; we were going to tour America that summer."

While *Back to the Egg* was receiving its critical mauling, McCartney spent the summer of 1979 holed up in Spirit of Ranachan and in a new ramshackle studio he'd set up at his home in East Sussex. Wanting to purge himself completely of the excessive blow-outs of 1970s rock – epitomised on the 'Rockestra' sessions – he went back into musical isolation. "It's like football," he told the press at the time. "You can be in a great team but sometimes you want to kick a ball about on your own." With this attitude he returned to the 'one man and his tape recorder' improvisation that characterised his eponymous post-Beatles debut ten years before. The end result was titled, appropriately enough, *McCartney II*, and it brought out further the experimental streak that had started to reappear that year with 'The Broadcast' and 'Reception'.

Having sampled the sound of Abbey Road's dripping taps for the *Thrillington* album, McCartney went back to the toilet and its unique acoustics to record the drums for many of the tracks on *McCartney II*. He used the kitchen as a giant echo chamber (audible on the ethereal Krishna-inspired 'One of These Days'). This wasn't the first time that different rooms had provided different atmospheres. Like the experiments at Lympne Castle, the B-side of 'Goodnight Tonight', 'Daytime Nightime Suffering', was recorded at Replica Studios with the drums in the kitchen and the organ in the basement.

*McCartney II* is basically a collection of demos and first takes recorded across a six-week period. In fact, if McCartney started recording anything that he didn't dig, he just wiped the tapes and moved on to the next song idea. There was little or no production, with all instruments being plugged, as they were for the *McCartney* album, straight into the tape machine. Surprisingly, especially given the public's reaction to *Back to the Egg*, it was a hit.

Over 20 tracks were recorded for *McCartney II* so a double-album was originally planned, although all this was merely theoretical. Before deciding exactly what to do with the tracks, Wings set out at the beginning of 1980 on what was to be their final UK tour. They then moved on to Japan with other new territories on the agenda. But, as has been documented on numerous occasions, McCartney was busted for possessing marijuana on arriving at Tokyo customs. Facing up to seven years in jail, he was released after nine days. Effectively marking the end of Wings as a band, McCartney's creative inspiration, direction and personal outlook received an even bigger blow 11 months later when, on 8 December 1980, John Lennon was shot dead.

---

Following the back-to-basics rock of his work with Laurence Juber, *McCartney II* marked a full-blown investigation into synthesisers, with much of the album based on the kind of heavily sequenced loops that were coming from the likes of Sparks. In the same year, Sparks, whom McCartney referenced in the video for the album's hit single 'Coming Up', released their *Terminal Jive* album, full of the same rhythms and instruments as *McCartney II* but all played out with rather more proficiency. Witness 'Stereo' or, more poignantly, 'Rock 'n' Roll People in a Disco World'. "The *McCartney II* album, that was his experimental stuff in that period, more than anything on *Back to the Egg*," Laurence Juber reckons. "That was where he basically locked himself in his studio all summer with a bunch of gear and fooled around ... I don't think that he was happy with his deal with Columbia. I got the impression that *McCartney II* was kind of, 'Let's do a quick album to get some of that contractual commitment fulfilled.' I could be wrong on that, but I got that impression..."

In ten years, electronic music had gone from being underground and avant-garde to the forefront of a new style of pop music, something McCartney was delighted to return to. Not that all of his experiments worked. 'Temporary Secretary' for one – which tried to evoke, of all things, a space-age typing pool – was an incessant, grating non-song and an absurd choice for release as a single. 'Front Parlour', on the other hand, was at least listenable. It was possibly the most non-McCartney McCartney track since 'Carnival of Light'. A driving, heavily compressed slap bassline bounces off a lightweight drum machine and a cheesy synthesiser melody that a young Jean-Michel Jarre would have been proud of. "I'll take a day every so often and I'll do stuff just for my own fun," McCartney once told Radio 1 of his private studio. "It's liberating for me because it says to me you don't have to be that Paul McCartney fellow that we expect all the time."

Another pure synthpop track on *McCartney II* was 'Frozen Japanese' (as it was known in Japan at least). Its beats were more rhythmic and its melodies more oriental, making for a more accomplished sound than he achieved on 'Front Parlour'. Although these three-minute bursts couldn't be called experimental or challenging – it was pure early synthpop – they were completely avant-garde compared to almost anything McCartney's rock and roll contemporaries were recording at the time.

The other tracks on *McCartney II*, the disco funk of 'Coming Up' aside, were standard rock and blues takes. Only 'Bogey Music' sounded any different from a Wings demo reel by ploughing the entire vocal track through a reverb unit – another of McCartney's new electronic purchases.

The most avant-garde of McCartney's recordings from these sessions were saved for B-sides. 'Secret Friend' was a mixture of laidback beats and plink-plonk sequencing. Its vocals were spaced out and repeated mantra-like. The timing of the vocals, too, is all over the place. One of the studio tricks McCartney played with during these sessions was vari-speeding – recording one track to a speeded-up or slowed-down version of the backing, the finished result sounding not of this earth. Running for over ten minutes, 'Secret Friend' would be the longest song McCartney issued until he returned to basing his music on technology as The Fireman in the mid-1990s.

The B-side of *McCartney II*'s 'Waterfalls' single was 'Check My Machine', recorded, unsurprisingly, to test out his synths, reverb units and other new-fangled devices bought for this second isolationist period. Combining a lazy seventies funk riff with sounds, samples, loops and backing vocals written specially to try out his echo unit, 'Check My Machine' is a hilarious six-minute (the original was even longer) tour of the possibilities new technology offered pop music at the dawn of the eighties. Even more avant-garde examples from this period remain unreleased, most notably the more ambient 'Blue Sway' and the new wave-oriented 'Mr H. Atom'.

The musical possibilities that were unearthed on 'Secret Friend' and *McCartney II* went back on ice for the rest of the 1980s. Just as the first eponymous McCartney album had started the seventies with an array of different ideas, the rest of the decade was built around traditional songs and albums. What experiments McCartney did make were in the form of remixes, rather than original tracks. Remixes offered the chance to play with new technology, rhythms, sounds and arrangements and are explored fully in the next chapter.

Saccharine singles like 'Ebony and Ivory' (with Stevie Wonder), 'Say Say Say' and 'The Girl is Mine' (both with Michael Jackson) and 'We All Stand Together' (with the Frog Chorus) combined to plant the solo McCartney right in the middle of the road, exactly as he had done as leader of Wings. But among all this unchallenging material, the eighties did throw up a few avant-garde(ish) surprises, if you dug deep enough.

The bookend albums of pain and absolution, *Tug of War* and *Pipes of Peace*, appeared in 1982 and 1983 respectively. *Tug of War* featured the Stevie Wonder funk work-out collaboration of 'What's That Your Doing?' and wistful, poetic songs like 'Wanderlust' and 'Here Today', a sweet homage to John Lennon. Both albums were produced by George Martin, who let some dark atmospheric ambience slip through into the openers of the albums' central tracks 'Tug of War' and 'Pipes of Peace'.

When *Give My Regards To Broad Street* hit cinemas in 1984, it did little to alter McCartney's image. It sits well in the big picture of 1980s mainstream movie-making – egocentric, thinly plotted, full of dance and music but more about playing with the budget than connecting with an audience. The film may have been the 1980s equivalent of a 'straight-to-cable' movie but the soundtrack was a McCartney highpoint, both in terms of songwriting and production. As a result it hit number one in the British album charts, a feat which he has failed to equal since.

By the mid-1980s the avant-garde was the last thing on McCartney's mind. He was vying for attention with Madonna, Prince, Michael Jackson and George Michael. He fought through with weighty ballads and pop tracks which were upbeat but lacked the opulent glamour that other mid-1980s megastars oozed. As a result, *Press To Play*, which appeared in September 1986, remains one of McCartney's most derided middle-of-the-road efforts. But it did contain the bizarre single 'Pretty Little Head'.

"Hillmen come down from the lava" chanted this outlandish synth-based piece, which had been inspired by the sci-fi film *Dune*. Personnel on 'Pretty Little Head' included drummer Jerry Marotta and producer Hugh Padgham, who between them had contributed to the leftfield sound of Peter Gabriel's third album a few years before. Originally titled 'Back to Pepperland', most likely due to its psychedelic throwback vibes, 'Pretty Little Head' was a brave choice when it was selected for release as McCartney's 38th single in October 1986. But with the album's other singles having only just scraped the Top 30, this wonderfully abstract 'song' failed to chart at all.

John 'Tokes' Potoker was brought in for the remix, a sound engineer who could handle well-known names like Peter Gabriel and Genesis but who had also worked with electronic explorers such as Paul Haig, New Order and Cabaret Voltaire. The black-and-white video for 'Pretty Little Head' was just as non-pop as the music. Images of McCartney were projected over a girl – played by the young Gabrielle Anwar – as she ran away from home. To set the scene for the story, McCartney sampled some of The Beatles' 'She's Leaving Home' over the opening of the video.

1987's *All the Best!* compilation put a full stop to McCartney's meandering mid-1980s output. He was determined to break away from the adult-oriented rock category that he had become trapped in, firstly releasing the *Choba B CCCP* album of rock and roll covers. For the next studio album, *Flowers in the Dirt* (perceived then as a return to form but pretty unlistenable these days), he brought in Phil Ramone as producer and Elvis Costello as songwriting partner. Under Costello's influence, McCartney was back on the musical map with one of his most warmly received and rockiest albums in years. It was just as well McCartney got back to guitars, melodies and rock and roll because in 1988 the pop world was going through the convulsions of acid house which, in its infancy at least, made no room for musicians from previous generations.

Of the many producers on *Flowers in the Dirt*, Trevor Horn did manage to coax McCartney back to playing with electronics if only for the album's bonus track. 'Ou est le soleil?' revolves around a nonsense, four-line French lyric on a bed of synths, in which Horn (and engineer Steve Lipson) basically recreate the sounds and feel of 'Lunar Bay' – a track they'd put together for their protégés Frankie Goes To Hollywood the previous year. While not avant-garde, it's certainly "wacko" (as McCartney described it) and proved that he was happy to venture away from the rock and roll sound Elvis Costello was famous for. And the everlasting life that 'Ou est le soleil?' received in remix studios – as investigated in the next chapter – was certainly forward thinking for the time.

The success of *Flowers in the Dirt* inspired McCartney to blow away the cobwebs and undertake his first major tour in ten years. He spent much of 1989 through 1991 on the road, playing over 100 enormously successful dates in Europe, the UK and several treks across the US before finally completing a string of dates in Japan. With guitarists Robbie McIntosh and Hamish Stuart and keyboard guru Wix (Paul Wickens), the band played Wings standards, *Flowers in the Dirt* and a good smattering of Beatles classics. Breaking concert attendance records in many of the countries and venues they played, various dates were taped and this period is well represented in the comprehensive if over-slick 1990 double live album *Tripping the Live Fantastic*. Surprisingly, this rock and retro tour also aired McCartney's first major piece of avant-garde music in the minimalism frame since 1970's 'Glasses': 'Church Mice'.

'Glasses' had adhered to the strict, almost academic principles of minimalism that Steve Reich had described. But by the time of *Flowers in the Dirt* minimalism as a genre had moved on, thanks to the amazing brains of Terry Riley, Philip Glass and others. In the early 1960s, the Californian Riley had played with

Daevid Allen in Paris, long before Allen talked about avant-garde music with Paul McCartney during the Roundhouse era. While in Paris, Riley invented a time-lag accumulator, a kind of infinite reverb device which was the inspiration for his classic minimalist piece 'In C'. It was the incessant, revered pulse of 'In C' that started to drive the genre forward. More followed on Riley's classic *A Rainbow in Curved Air* (1969), an album which had a massive impact on the US composer Philip Glass, who drove the art of minimalism further forward in the decades that followed.

'Pulse music', as minimalism could – after the impact of Riley and Glass – now be described, was what McCartney was aiming for with 'Church Mice'. He had listened intently to the work of both composers in Barry Miles' flat in the mid-1960s and was finally surrendering to its experimental beat. Bells and chimes ring constantly throughout this long (nine-minute), very upbeat (180 beats per minute) avant-garde track. Choral voices also chatter in and out of the pulse, with few, if any, individual words being audible.

While not exactly on a par with the minimalist pieces from Glass and his con-temporaries, 'Church Mice' was without doubt the most widely heard avant-garde piece of its type in the late 1980s. This was because, in what would become an ongoing outlet for McCartney's oddball tracks, 'Church Mice' was used as the pre-show warm-up tape for all McCartney's tours from 1988 to 1993. Sadly, if unsurprisingly, the piece was left off of the *Tripping the Live Fantastic* compendium and remains unreleased to this day.

After a decade that had begun with prison and death, McCartney ended the 1980s on a high. His new band played the last date of 1989 at Madison Square Garden in New York. Although his avant-garde output had been reduced in the last ten years, what work he had done – from the synthy experiments of *McCartney II*, the album tracks of *Back to the Egg*, and even the minimalism of 'Church Mice' – was put on a more public platform than anything he had done before. The persistent pulse of Riley/Glass-inspired minimalism boomed out through the PA of arenas around the world. An hour later each night, McCartney could be seen on stage playing his psychedelically painted piano during 'The Fool on the Hill'. This piano has become a trademark of his stage shows, sec-ond only to his Hofner violin bass. It's an exact replica of the one David Vaughan painted in 1966, when Vaughan was juggling painting with staging happenings like Carnival of Light. The reappearance of the piano, and the concerts' mini-malist opening, were just two indications that the next decade was to be McCartney's most prolific – and successful – experimental period yet.

# THE CHAPTER NINE REMIX

NINE

**B**eginning in the mid-1980s and evolving both creatively and commercial-ly ever since, remix culture has transformed the music industry. Paul McCartney hasn't shied away from this area but he hasn't been sucked into its more commercial machinations either – though not without a few close shaves. To trace the history of his involvement in this relatively new and often highly experimental area of music-making is to track the history, highs and lows of the genre itself. To say nothing of McCartney's head-on collisions with three of the most fundamental rhythmic revolutions in contemporary music – house, techno and drum & bass.

Mixing and remixing began to change from a chore into more of an art form when The Beatles gave up touring to become a full-time studio band in 1966. "We did this on the remix," John Lennon told Kenny Everett of 'I Am the Walrus' in 1967. "I notice on this one you've made a heck of a lot of editing. There's all voices and things," Everett said. "That's not editing," was John's explanation. "We had this track of electric piano, drums and things, and then we put on the bass and then we put the musicians on. And when we were remixing, we had all the voices, which we just brought in as we were doing it, sort of ad-lib. So it's not editing at all, it was all just going on."

Lennon was describing the end of editing as a predetermined, passive approach to music creation. He was using technology and a more 'live', active approach in spontaneously reworking and remixing existing material. When the psychedelic period ended, the individual Beatles retreated to more traditional recording techniques, and the style passed back into the underground until the dawn of dance culture 20 years later. Ironically, producer Youth would later explain how McCartney was intrigued at his modern-day version of "using the [mixing] desk as an instrument … and playing the desk" when remixing tracks from his 1987 *Off the Ground* album.

In the early 1980s, hip hop culture moved from the streets to the clubs to the mass media. Two turntables and a mixer became all that kids needed to make cutting-edge dance music. In the clubs, 12" singles were becoming common, providing extended versions of tracks, their popularity fuelled further by hip hop pioneers using the long-form format for lengthy musical experiments. By the mid-1980s, few singles were released without remixes either for club use or merely for filling the myriad extra formats – like cassette singles, picture discs etc – that had become available. At this time the artists (and/or their producers) themselves would often remix their own work, and Paul McCartney was no exception. Soon after, creative and commercial floodgates opened when master tapes began to be given out to third parties who had not been involved in the original recording process.

This new style of musical collaboration pushed the spirit of experimentation many miles further. It also stirred a massive debate over sampling – was it creativity, theft or plagiarism? "Samples are fragments of digitally recorded sound that are instantly played back via a computer trigger," explained Andrew Poppy in the speech which opened this book. "Digital sampling technology is the perfection of the collage technique. Any recordable moment can be stored and juxtaposed and modulated with any other moment. I record a small skin drum in a studio in north London and place it beside the sound of someone hitting an oil tanker on the Clyde … balancing them with the same sensibility as I would two orchestral instruments."

Theoretically at least, The Beatles were key defence witnesses in the debate over the legality of sampling, given recordings such as 'Revolution 9' and 'Tomorrow Never Knows'. The art of remixing then inspired a further backlash – in 1987, eight different versions (however original they were) of McCartney's 'Ou est le soleil?' brought forth cries of consumer exploitation. But following this, the media and the public began to accept remixes and multiple versions, allowing some truly creative results whereby a song would be recorded and finished, then handed to a remixer whose version would often become a completely new, retitled track in its own right. In this way McCartney's 'Hope of Deliverance' would be transformed via DJ Steve Anderson into the dance hit 'Deliverance', released in its own right with its own separate video.

In the 21st century, remixes have now become an essential marketing tool for artists of almost every pop genre. The thought of Wings being remixed by influential UK garage outfit Artful Dodger may have long-term McCartney fans reeling in anguish but it's proof that as an artist he is exercising creative control and using the remix to generate interesting results as well as promo kudos. The final twist to the history of remixing, almost bringing it full circle, is that technology has recently dropped so sharply in price that the tools only available to elite producers in the mid-1980s are now downloadable for next to nothing via the internet. As such anyone can become a remixer, and many people are, with the best of their work being bootlegged and automatically absorbed into the heritage of the artists they choose to remix.

McCartney's first 12" remixes appeared as part of the justifiably maligned *Give My Regards To Broad Street* project. The film certainly didn't live up to expectations but the accompanying soundtrack was full of new sounds and styles, and revisions of old ones. It was also McCartney's most significant flirtation with classical music since his soundtrack for *The Family Way*, when he re-recorded 'Eleanor Rigby' into the ten-minute reverie 'Eleanor's Dream'. The later film's main theme, 'No More Lonely Nights', existed in two different versions – the familiar ballad hit single and a radical, up-tempo re-recording for the end credits. To develop the up-tempo idea further, McCartney went straight to the top for his first major remix project – handing over the master tapes to house music God (and I don't use that description lightly), Arthur Baker. Bringing up the vocals and guitars in the mix, Baker's Special Dance Mix turned 'No More Lonely Nights' into pure mid-1980s disco funk. Far more experimental musically was McCartney's own seven-minute Extended Version. Random changes in tempo and a two-minute percussion-only breakdown made this a 12" aimed at the more daring club DJ.

At the same time as the promotional blitz launched to save the sinking ship of *Broad Street*, McCartney's music was evolving at a different promotional level, with other non-commercial versions of the film's title theme being remixed and pressed purely as promos under the guidance of Martin Freeland and his new division of McCartney's record label, Parlophone Club Promotions. Although they're unlikely ever to be released officially, further remixes by Arthur Baker and Warren Stanford took the track in completely new directions. Baker's Mole Mix was a slice of synthesiser-driven funk using a new melody while Stanford's Extended Edit has a misleadingly banal title. Also known as the DJ Edit, it placed a pulsating beat at the forefront and was furthest of all the remixes from the original version.

As an artist, J J Jeczalik of Art of Noise has seen remixing move from these early creative experiments to a commercial necessity. In the early eighties, most bands provided their own remixes and were unwilling to relinquish creative control (and master tapes) to a third party. But with the dawn of scratching and hip hop culture in the New York clubs, the music industry saw how DJs and producers could breathe new life into existing records. 'No More Lonely Nights' just happened to come out at this very moment. Jeczalik takes up the story:

■ Certainly, the remix adds value to the single, and it has now become a necessity ... In the pop area the time between singles has been compressed to an amazing extent. Besides, modern pop artists rarely write their own material, so it doesn't make creative sense for them to spend time remixing. And, as they are so busy promoting, it doesn't make commercial sense either. Also, there are lots of people out there who will work for nothing, and whilst that remains the case, it is to the artists' economic advantage to get someone else to do the work, especially when it's for free! Back in the 1980s things were similar, other than [the fact that] vinyl was still king, just. It was always interesting to hear what people did with a track and, once again, the commercial aspects have to be considered. So, yes, earlier on it was perhaps more of an interesting exercise but, as the dance scene developed, remixing became more of an absolute necessity.

Perhaps surprising given *Give My Regards to Broad Street*, McCartney's next project, which followed in 1986, was another film, although this time his contribution was only musical. *Spies Like Us* was the archetypal 1980s spoof thriller, a knockabout farce with Dan Ackroyd and Chevy Chase. McCartney's title theme was catchy and inoffensive but hasn't stood the test of time particularly well. The remixes, on the other hand, were blunt, in-your-face overhauls which abandoned the disco style of the 'No More Lonely Nights' remixes. For these he turned to Art of Noise.

In the mid-1980s, Art of Noise was a trio comprising session musician and latterly soundtrack artist Anne Dudley, producer and engineer Gary Langan and J J Jeczalik, artist, producer and one of the key early proponents of sampling. Dudley was attending various McCartney sessions at the time. She played keyboards on the original version of 'No More Lonely Nights' and provided the orchestral arrangement for 'However Absurd' from *Press To Play*. At the same time, Art of Noise were carving themselves a high-profile niche as one of the UK's most experimental and commercial production outfits. Early sample-driven instrumental singles like 'Close (To The Edit)' and 'Beatbox' had crossed over to the US dance charts as well as making the UK singles charts. 'Moments in Love' did the same, on the one hand becoming a cult classic chill-out anthem to this day, and on the other reaching a mass audience when Madonna used it for her wedding march with Sean Penn. These early releases were followed by a more commercial strain, which used vocals, of a sort, by the likes of Max Headroom and guitar lines from an Art of Noise-resuscitated Duane Eddy.

Jeczalik had been Trevor Horn's right-hand man during the making of albums by Malcolm McClaren, ABC and Frankie Goes To Hollywood. The production on these records was based around his use of the Fairlight sampler, the 'Computer Music Instrument' which could take any sound and replicate it across a whole keyboard. Such a varied CV is certainly based on a varied set of influences, with The Beatles as the foundation. "Just an amazing combination of sounds…" is JJ's first reaction to mention of their work. "Thinking of *Sgt. Pepper*, for example, really led one to think that anything was possible, as long as there was a tune in there somewhere."

"We were contacted directly by McCartney's office," remembers Jeczalik of the call to remix 'Spies Like Us'. "Gary Langan and I had done something for him before and this may have had some bearing on our being asked … I was not really aware of what McCartney was up to at the time; we were very busy in the studio ourselves and you can lose a grip on the outside world a bit!" The new, primitive sampling technology was the basis on which the trio deconstructed and then rebuilt the track. "Gary and I did most of the work on the basic track, sampling to create a new groove and attitude and so on," he remembers. "Gary's mixes were always brilliant … We would then put a structure together and Anne would come in and make sense of it all in a tuneful way. We would then deconstruct it again and do the final mix. The feedback was very good and everyone liked it…"

The results were alarmingly different from both the original and anything previously remixed for such a commercial 12". It wasn't a cover version, and it wasn't a disco mix. 'Spies Like Us' – the track least likely to – had been deconstructed, messed around and then deconstructed yet again into the Alternative Mix (Known To His Friends As Tom). Guitars, processed drums and burbled vocals crash through three minutes before Anne Dudley adds an improvised piano coda, reminiscent of the way the band closed their own tracks such as 'Beatbox' and 'Instruments of Darkness'. Amid all the sampling and resampling, Dudley provided the 'tune' that JJ knew any avant-garde piece should still retain.

With the track in the can, the hitherto anonymous Art of Noise (who had made a point of never showing their faces on record covers, instead using photos of spanners, cars and mask-wearing monks) managed to have their masks removed in a surprise visit to the studio by Linda McCartney. "She came to the studio and took some [as yet unpublished] photos of us," Jeczalik remembered, "which at the time were the only mug shots of us all!"

'Alternative' mixes like this bizarre take on 'Spies Like Us' were, at the time, the centre of a raging debate on the ethics of sampling. While collage was a respected visual art form, the musical equivalent – with the Fairlight and Art of Noise at its centre – was sending shock waves through the record industry. Some organisations, like the Canadian Recording Industry Association (CRIA) wasted no time negotiating. Based on a complaint by Michael Jackson, they seized and destroyed all known copies of the seminal release by composer John Oswald, *Plunderphonic*. This 1989 CD took samples and elements from such diverse artists as Jackson, The Beatles, Metallica and Stravinsky and blended them into something completely new. Unlike The Beatles' work on 'Revolution 9', *Plunderphonic* was not seen by the recording industry as a strange one-off but as part of a new wave of copyright-infringing piracy.

Sample-driven collage music was the next logical chapter in a story which starts with musique concrète composers such as Pierre Henry and Pierre Schaeffer and their work with tapes of environmental sounds in the 1940s and 1950s. But this jarred head-on with the dollar-worshipping 1980s, as Oswald himself remarked:

■ The hit parade promenades the aural flotsam of pop on public display, and as curious tourists should we not be able to take our own snapshots through the crowd, rather than be restricted to the official souvenir postcards and pro-grammes? Listening to pop music isn't a matter of choice. Asked for or not, we're bombarded by it. In its most insidious state, filtered to an incessant bass line, it seeps through apartment walls and out of the heads of walk people [sic]. Although people in general are making more noise than ever before, fewer people are making more of the total noise. Difficult to ignore, pointlessly redundant to imitate, how does one not become a passive recipient?

Another group at the centre of this debate took their name from one of the original bands to take looping and sampling to a mass audience. The Tape-Beatles' *Music With Sound* was a 30-track album made purely from sampled voices and beats from other records, something *EST* magazine summarised as "a powerful, compelling album: a trawl through the info-swamp, an attempt to invoke meaning from apparently random data."

Few artists could be so influential as to inspire a whole band from just one song. But without 'Revolution 9' and The Beatles' tape-loop experiments there would have been no Tape-Beatles. And without the Tape-Beatles there would have been no logical full stop placed on the spiralling sampling-is-collage-is-copyright-is-theft debate. In their own manifesto, the Tape-Beatles described *Music With Sound* as:

■ An appropriately entitled recording and complete practical guide to the current copyright controversy. Not only does it include detailed examples of unregistered, transcontextualised, and copyright protected works, it also describes a world where ideas and their consequences are not ownable. The Tape-Beatles compose others' output with cost-effective wit, desperately edged. They share with you traditional-classic style music, folk, rock, pop, musique concrète, 'third stream' and styles so far out there that copywriters wouldn't dare touch it with a ten-foot version of the constitution. Hence it is

a very useful disc for anyone with copyright questions – and far more listenable than any copyright office whining about protection for 'artist's' creative
or business interests.

If the sampling debate was getting out of hand, it took The KLF – the anarchic
art/dance production house aka Kopyright Liberation Front – to bring things
back down to earth and remind us why remixes had arrived in the first place. In
1988, The KLF were pushing 12" singles and remixing further than ever before,
with sample-heavy epics like 'Last Train to Trancentral 'and 'What Time Is Love?'
that were as at home on the dancefloor as they were in the charts. In their book
*The Manual (Have to Have a Number One the Easy Way)*, the band recommended a process for creating the ultimate 12" remix, "where the only con-
straints are that the physical and sexual elements of the track are left naked and
the dancer should never be let free from the grip of the groove".

■ Take risks. Have him [the engineer] drop all sorts of things out and stick repeat
echoes on everything. Don't stop the beat. Don't lose the beat. Don't mistreat
the beat. If you have time to do another mix that is radically different, do it.
Don't be afraid to have next to nothing in it. Worship at the feet of the
primeval goddess of Groove.

What The KLF had in mind were dub-heavy remixes which plundered like any
other sampling pioneer on the one hand but never forgot why they were there
on the other, which was to move people physically as opposed to intellectually.
It was this style which was the basis for a stack of McCartney remixes... but a
backlash was just around the corner.

Remixing was pop music's evolution into areas that were part of the heritage
of jazz and classical. In jazz, multiple cover versions are a staple part of how any
artist develops. To say nothing of the classical world, which is built on influence
and interpretation. But before it could become an accepted form in the pop
world, a knee-jerk reaction was to be expected. In McCartney's case it came from
the old guard, 'first generation' Beatles fans, with author Mark Lewisohn declar-
ing 12" singles "a hazard." In a 1987 article for *Record Collector* titled 'Paul
McCartney – Too Many Versions?', Lewisohn was incensed, stating that
McCartney's "most dedicated fans, the ones who have stood by him through
thick and thin, have had enough."

So much for moving with the times. "At a time when Paul McCartney needs
his most loyal and dedicated fans more then ever before," commented Lewisohn
on the poor sales of *Press To Play*, "it really does seem rather odd that he is risk-
ing their alienation on such a grand scale." Though McCartney's collaboration

with Arthur Baker could have been looked upon as one of the most inspired of any 1960s artist, journalists like *Record Collector* editor Peter Doggett didn't get the point, deciding that "McCartney isn't the only performer who has flooded the market with remixes, rehashes and gimmicks, but he is a perfect example." Today, magazines like *Record Collector* and, in the US, *Goldmine* celebrate remixing and the wildly different worlds of the 12" and 7" singles. But back in 1987 they were the first to come up with the classic 1980s gag, to quote Lewisohn himself: "Why didn't the artist get the mix right in the first place?"

Fortunately McCartney answered these critics by diving even further into remix culture, most notably with the track 'Ou est le soleil?' from the *Flowers in the Dirt* sessions. The song was effectively a studio jam – created by fusing song fragments and playing with samplers and sequencers to find the groove. It was made in collaboration with Trevor Horn, who had been brought in as one of the first (of many) producers to work on different *Flowers in the Dirt* tracks. One of the UK's most successful and creative producers, Horn follows a lineage that begins with Jo Meek and George Martin. He had been one of the main forces behind remix culture, notoriously producing countless different 12" mixes (all of which pushed the boundaries) for Frankie Goes To Hollywood and Propaganda's early hits, and bringing Anne Dudley, J J Jeczalik and Gary Langan together to form Art of Noise. Epic isn't a strong enough word for the music and remixes Horn was producing at the time, and it was, as McCartney put it, a "Paul Goes To Hollywood" sound that McCartney wanted to try out for himself.

"If in the '60s, Phil Spector created a wall of sound," wrote author and lateral thinker Paul Morley, "by the middle of the '80s Horn had already established his sound, a whole room of sound, the walls, floors, ceilings, doors, windows, decorated with absolute flourish. As an architect of sound, Horn was unashamedly an exhibitionist, an utter show off … Early work with ABC and Malcolm McLaren set out his credentials for mixing experimentation with studio perfection, for mixing the wonderful with the weird, for mixing the grandiose with the subtle, for just great mixing."

With 'Ou est le soleil?' in the can, the masters were handed to renowned US producer Shep Pettibone (who had made a name for himself with early remixes for Pet Shop Boys and then Madonna). Four tracks were delivered from his studio, including standard Extended and 7" mixes for release on the B-side of the 'Figure of Eight' single, and a much more leftfield Tub Dub mix which was created by Pettibone's engineer Goh Hotoda. This loose, percussive 120-BPM track finally transplanted McCartney's work from the US clubs to the UK dancefloors, with the 'Ou est le soleil?' creating a buzz in dance magazines like *Record Mirror*. This is one track which is derided by McCartney purists – but solely thanks to a feeling of alienation from the scene it became a part of. Baggage aside, this is one McCartney track that stands up in its own right as an effortlessly confident slice of late-1980s dance.

'Ou est le soleil?' may have fitted with the acid/dance explosion of 1988, and in mainland Europe the track's Shep Pettibone remixes got a single release in their own right. But McCartney held off from any further dance-oriented releases until 1992, when he took the remix idea even further with the 'Deliverance' project.

'Deliverance' was a one-off dance release which came out solely on 12". It began life traditionally enough as 'Hope of Deliverance', one of McCartney's most chart-friendly songs for some time and the lead track from 1993's *Off the Ground* album. It was classic middle-of-the-road McCartney, cemented with a campfire singalong video. When it came to single releases from *Off the Ground*, McCartney took the more traditional route of adding b-sides and unreleased songs. But remix culture wasn't ignored; in fact, it was embraced when hot UK producer Steve Anderson was brought in to create a piece of his own, taking elements from various tracks on the album and using 'Hope of Deliverance' as its base.

The early 1990s were a pivotal time for UK house music. Clubs like Renaissance and artists like Brothers In Rhythm lead the way with a sound known as progressive house. Theoretically, this was yet another genre-within-a-genre subdivision of dance music. Practically speaking, it meant long, epic 12" tracks with build-ups, breakdowns, Italio piano and anthemic strings. Brothers In Rhythm, a duo of DJ and journalist Dave Seaman and producer Steve Anderson, released the single 'Such a Good Feeling' to critical and commercial acclaim and followed it with both original productions (notably 'Peace & Harmony' and 'Forever and a Day') and many years as some of the UK's most in-demand remixers. They put their stamp on work by just about every pop artist needing to find dancefloor credibility, while at the same time sticking to their roots with remixes for Judy Cheeks, Dina Carroll and Billie Ray Martin.

These days, Brothers In Rhythm takes a back seat for Steve Anderson, who has been an integral part of Kylie Minogue's sound and style since 'Confide in Me', a track he co-wrote which took her out of bubble gum and into the credible record racks. In May 2002, while McCartney was in the middle of his Driving USA tour, Anderson was in the middle of producing Kylie's Fever tour, but was happy to cast his mind back. As an artist he's a passionate authority on remix culture, affirming that "remixing in one way or another has been my life for 15 years."

■ At the time I was working for a company called DMC which operated a DJ-only mix album service. This is how I was able to learn my craft remixing artists that I would never have got access to at that point in my career. My boss was Tony Prince, who was a legendary radio DJ on Luxembourg and knew Paul and Linda from this and his work on the Buddy Holly stuff (Holly being one of

McCartney's many music publishing interests). I think the chance to remix 'Hope of Deliverance' just came out of a conversation with Tony and Paul and as you can imagine I was gobsmacked when I found out.

Like other prominent remix outfits, at their height Brothers In Rhythm would be drafted in by record companies for 'career-resuscitation' duties. They managed to get Heaven 17 back to the top of the charts with a remix of 'Temptation' ten years after the original version. To say nothing of the oxygen-style blast of dance credibility they gave Michael Jackson, just as he was going off the boil with 'You Are Not Alone'. All these mixes took elements of the originals and scattered them across Brothers In Rhythm's own unique sounds and structures. McCartney, however, wanted Anderson to take a new approach:

■ It was the norm at that time to get remixers to create unrecognisable versions of seemingly un-credible artists using very little of the original, sometimes just a tiny cut-up vocal sample. I never saw the point in this but was really intrigued and inspired when the plot was explained to me for 'Deliverance'. Paul had the idea that the 'Deliverance' remix should only contain sounds sourced from the album multi-tracks. I could use anything providing it existed in one of the songs. Also, all work was to be done at his studio in Rye and with his engineer Bob Kraushaar. Any additional playing or material had to be done by either him or his band, who were rehearsing at the time. This really clinched it for me as it was such a challenge and I could absolutely not revert back to tried and tested sounds.

With these rules in place, Anderson journeyed to the McCartney family home-cum-studio in Sussex. "Any nerves were totally calmed," he remembers, "when I first arrived as I met Linda, who was wonderful. And then Paul chirped up 'Cup of tea?' which, after my nod, was followed up with 'Well, there's the kettle.' Great family, really down to earth..."

'Deliverance' is certainly the most unashamedly hedonistic of all McCartney's remixes. But it was backed by a darker, Dub version from the same sessions. All the Steve Anderson/Brothers In Rhythm trademarks are there: the Italio-piano, the one-minute intro of piano and percussion, minimal vocals and single-note strings hanging across almost nine minutes of 140-BPM house music.

■ It was structured like a journey with a recurring theme and obviously some manipulation of samples, in particular the main vocal sample which had to be stretched considerably (a process that today is a button push but then was much more tricky). The bass sample was Paul's Hofner, which I couldn't get clean so he played it. Also all the vocals which ended up gated on the mix were him just larking about in the studio, even going into a bit of Jamaican toasting at one point. In the end we had so much stuff that we decided to do two mixes, one very up and happy and the other being the Dub, which was a lot darker and minimal. Due to the unique approach, the first few days were literally spent trawling through the multi-tracks sourcing sounds. In those days it was two Akai samplers and a Cubase Sequencer, so everything had to be done in stages then recorded to multi-track. It really was like layering with sections that had very little in them but were left in the template until we found something to fill them up with. The whole process took about three weeks, including recalls for things Paul or I wanted to change.

'Deliverance' "really pushed the boundaries" says Anderson, who noted that although "Paul had of course done this before with 'Ou est le soleil?' and 'Party'," their collaboration "remains one of my most cherished experiences."

The track was the first step in a concerted effort by McCartney to embrace the elements of modern dance music he could relate to, and which excited him. Its roots – sampling and sound collage – went right back to The Beatles, the avant-garde and before; only the beats per minute had changed. With the 'Deliverance' promos working the clubs, the project was taken a stage further when director Richard Heslop was commissioned to make a new video for the track. McCartney had tried this previously when a performance video for the Playout Version of 'No More Lonely Nights' was shot in the mid-1980s.

With a new video in the can, 'Hope of Deliverance' had become 'Deliverance', not a remix but a completely unique track with an official release in its own right. Combined with other experiments of the time, it proved how the remix had grown from a promotional tool into a true creative art form. In Sweden, Dot Records then took the process one stage further with "the world's first never-ending remix race" and their album, *Endlessnessism*. Released in 1997 this 16-track compilation featured some of the UK and Europe's most avant-garde artists, such as Nonplace Urban Field and Bedouin Ascent. "*Endlessnessism* could be described as the musical equivalent of Chinese whispers or an Olympic relay race," read the liner notes.

■ One track is taken as a starting point and then remixed by each artist in succession until all artists have completed their tracks. The last track will then become the starting track for the next *Endlessnessism* (Volume 2). There is only one rule that participating artists must follow; that the remixer should utilise at least one element of the track they receive and incorporate it into their remix. The listener will then hopefully be able to trace the link between each track and so the evolution from one into the next.

"The technology we use today allows anything to become anything else, literally," Steve Anderson told me. "I still admire it when someone crafts a remix as opposed to applying a well-worn formula to every track because it works. My absolute favourite remix of all time is the Civilles and Cole version of 'Black and White' [Michael Jackson] as it took it to such a different place. David Cole was my absolute role model. I was so upset when he died."

*Endlessnessism* was the avant-garde world's discovery that remixes could become tracks in their own right. Several years later, this had become the norm in the commercial pop world. "It is now very common for the version to be an entirely new production or even song," says Anderson, citing Jennifer Lopez's 'Aint It Funny' and Mariah Carey's 'Dream Lover' as examples. "There is even a Grammy for it, which was won in 2002 by Deep Dish for their mix of Dido's 'Thank You', which is a perfect example of remixers treating the song and the vocal with the respect it deserves."

Another of McCartney's remixers, Nitin Sawhney, agrees:

■ I think things have changed a lot. A lot of people, their record will only do well because of the remix. It will be the remix of a track that'll do well. If you take Cornershop with the Fatboy Slim remix of 'Brimful of Asha' – that got to number one because Norman Cook did the remix. I think even Daniel Bedingfield [his 'Get Through This' was a UK number one in 2001] – that track wasn't the original thing that he did. From what I understand, from inside sources, what he did was not a garage mix, somebody else did the garage mix and then it became the main single. Or you have Gorrillaz with a garage version and that was the thing that got played a lot, the garage version.

As an artist in his own right, choosing other remixers to work on his original material, Sawhney has experienced first-hand how an original musical mood can be reworked into something completely different. "I did [a track called] 'Sunset' last year. That was actually MJ Cole's mix, which got played a lot in Ibiza. Trevor Nelson was playing it and loads of people like that. Whereas the version that I did was actually quite down-tempo, so you can change the vibe, the energy, the BPM and everything so it can work in a completely different context from the original intention. That's the power of a remix."

From *Endlessnessism* to 'Sunrise', remixing had become a truly interactive art form. 'Deliverance' had been just a spoke in the wheel of transition. And projects like Thurston Moore's *Root* (in which the Sonic Youth guitarist mailed 30-second audio lumps to both musical and graphic artists, including Damien Hirst and Yoko Ono, to be curated later for exhibition and album release) and Sprawl's *Chinese Whispers* continued to push the boundaries. *Chinese Whispers* appeared the year after *Endlessnessism*, calling itself "The remix album with no composer... The track with no name..." Featuring a UK roster of avant-garde luminaries (among them Ultramarine, Mike Paradinas and Stereolab), it was the brainchild of Sprawl label founder Douglas Benford. "Unlike other remix albums, Chinese Whispers is a hermetically sealed cyclical recording remix project, but with no original track to begin with," he explained. "All the artists participating had no idea who they were remixing. They were working in the dark, samples arriving anonymously. All they were aware of was who was involved, who these audio snippets *might* be from." This process wasn't lost on McCartney, who worked to similar principles for his *Liverpool Sound Collage* album.

At the same time as it reached this creative peak, the remix also became a complete commercial necessity. Steve Anderson describes its "unique power" and says "It is important to remember that before Todd Terry remixed 'Dreams' by The Corrs they were really struggling to sell records. [Remixes are] absolutely a necessity, especially within pop music as the labels want their song or artist to be played as much as possible. The obligatory 'Almighty' mix on a pop record means it will be played in all the more commercial clubs even if the original is a ballad or a bouncy pop tune. But at the same point it can totally lose the integrity of the artist for the sake of a hit (like Tori Amos' 'Professional Widow' and Cornershop's 'Brimful Of Asha')."

Buoyed by its results, McCartney decided to repeat the 'Deliverance' process, this time replacing swapping Steve Anderson with Youth, to take *Off the Ground* and compound it into a contemporary dance track. But Youth's results – *Strawberries Oceans Ships Forest* – deserve a chapter of their own...

By the mid-1990s producers were remixers were artists. The boundaries had blurred to the point that some of the best remixers were artists and producers in their own right and vice versa. Tracks created purely in the studio, a la 'Ou est le soleil?', were the norm. As such, when it came to choosing remixers for his next project, 'Fluid' by his experimental alter-ego The Fireman, McCartney chose one of his favourite contemporary artists, Nitin Sawhney. "He's really cool," McCartney had said of Sawhney in an interview on French TV in December 2001. "I love him."

In the late 1990s Nitin Sawhney became the leading light in Asian dance music, with his third album *Displacing the Priest* (1996) being described as "a polyglot groove that traverses decades, genres and continents in the space of ten tracks". Born in London in 1964, the Hindu Punjabi played with the James Taylor Quartet and Talvin Singh (as the Tihai Trio) before moving on to film and TV soundtracks and a solo career. Sawhney's sound is a pure global mixture, with influences and elements as varied as drum & bass and flamenco. While recording this extensive, experimental early work, Sawhney was working from a small PC-based set-up in a London bedsit which saw a parade of unlikely visitors, including Sinead O'Connor, Massive Attack, Brian Eno and film director John Schlesinger.

"The whole thing I'm trying to do is show there are no barriers, it's just about checking other cultures and finding where they meet up," Sawhney told Sarah Davis of *Music Week* in one of his first interviews. "For example, flamenco music came from India originally, it's fusion music and I'm simply developing those kind of roots. Asians born here have the same influences as white people plus another set of reference points from our parents and our heritage, so I feel it's an advantageous thing. We have more to say and a stronger vocabulary."

His early work spearheaded Outcaste, a UK record label set up to exclusively showcase the pioneers of a new breed of Asian pop. Outcaste compilations such as *New Breed, Untouchable Outcaste Beats 1* and *Outcaste Presents: The First Five Years* are vital listening, the latter catching the ear of Paul McCartney. "Who loves Outcaste?" read the label's *First Five Years* press release. "Madonna, Paul McCartney, Robbie Williams, Massive Attack..."

"Paul McCartney? Robbie Williams? Hmm, maybe they've more taste than we give them credit for," wrote one reviewer, Rosie Wild of the *Big Blue Spot*, who declared: "*The First Five Years* is a fine, fine thing and certainly gives a bloody good impression of the label if you've not heard 'em before ... You get Thievery Corporation's splendidly soulful 'Lebanese Blonde', new Ninja Tune bod Bonobo's sex'n'tablas slow-burner 'Terrapin', and – best of all – late sitar god Ananda Shankar's extraordinary take on the Doors' 'Light My Fire'."

"Years ago," Nitin Sawhney told me, "McCartney's company, MPL, called up my manager of the time and said 'Would Nitin be interested in doing a remix of a project that Paul was doing called The Fireman?' I said, 'Yeah, you know, wow.' It was an amazing thing because Paul McCartney is *Paul McCartney*, that's pretty cool." Sawhney then met up with Youth, McCartney's collaborator as The Fireman, and became one of the first people to hear their secret avant-garde album, *Rushes*. "I liked it a lot," he told me. "He played everything and I thought, 'This is nice.' It had a kind of Floyd-y vibe to it in some ways. I thought it had something ... It was great, it was all so analogue, but it was played live. And I thought 'Wow, this is cool.' It also had some sampling things going on and sounds that you could really play about with, so I created a load of kits and just a load of weird little vibes..." 'Fluid' was the track Sawhney decided to work on, taking Youth's master tapes back to his bedsit with some degree of trepidation:

■ I got all the parts for a track called 'Fluid', which was the one that I thought worked for me. I checked out a few things and they sent me the parts to 'Fluid' and I thought, 'OK, this is cool.' It was quite a long time ago, a few years back, so I was working on a little PC at the time. So I was up in my little bedsit, up in this room working, that's how I did a lot of things. It was just a PC and a sampler and a tiny little disc. It was a real bedroom job. I thought, 'OK, well, I'll give this a shot and hopefully Paul McCartney is gonna think it's all right.'

I was commissioned to do it and I was sitting at home just staring at the computer thinking, 'How do I approach this?' [Later on…] I get this call from McCartney's manager or whoever, who suddenly says, 'Paul would like to come by this evening and see how you're doing.' I was living in Tooting in this tiny little bedsit and sharing with four other people. I came down the stairs and I said, 'Listen guys, Paul McCartney's coming round at seven o'clock this evening!' They're looking at me like 'Yeah, right,' and I said, 'No, Paul McCartney is coming here at seven o'clock this evening.' Everyone started running round tidying the place up, getting rid of beer stains on sofas that had been there for a long time.

He came round and came upstairs and it was such a weird moment. At first I kind of looked at him and thought 'That's Paul McCartney!' I suddenly realised that, although I'd never met him, I knew a lot about him. I've never been a major Beatles fan or anything like that, though I think they wrote some beautiful songs, so I've never really focused on The Beatles or on Paul McCartney. So it was a weird thing, but then at the same time I realised that this is somebody that I know. I know that his wife died, and when he picked up my guitar to play about I thought, of course, he's left-handed. And then he started talking about clubs and I thought he might be talking about The Cavern…

As I was talking to him, I thought how he's really down-to-earth and not an arsehole. In a way I kind of half expected him to be an arsehole. You think if someone's worth half a billion pounds they've *got* to be an arsehole, but I thought he was very easy to talk to, I thought, 'I could go for a drink with this bloke.' He was just kind of chatty, and he was talking a lot. The thing that freaked me out, though, was when he goes 'Maybe I could put down a bit of guitar on this mix that you've done now.' I went 'All right.'

OK, I've got to now record Paul McCartney in my room in my piddly little studio that doesn't really work that well. It was kind of set up for me, and that was about it. I thought, 'Shit, I've got my guitar here, I've got to set up all the mics', and I was shaking like a fucking leaf. But it was great. What was nice was that he played me a bit of 'Yesterday' on my guitar and he was going 'I wrote that in a little bedsit a bit like this', and I think he called it 'Scrambled Eggs' or something. He was talking about the whole vibe of how he did it and he showed me all the original chord structures and I was sitting there thinking 'Fucking hell!' It was a bit of a mindblowing thing as he's like part of world history.

More poignantly, Sawhney was meeting McCartney in the aftermath of his wife's death. "I also think that it [the 'Fluid' remix session] was almost the first creative thing he did after his wife died really," he recalled. "He hadn't, publicly anyway, done anything creative since. I think he wanted to keep himself busy, I got that impression. I think that's probably part of the reason why he took such an active, proactive interest in something that he maybe wouldn't do normally."

In Sawhney's 'Out of Body & Mind' mix of 'Fluid', he took the familiar elements from McCartney and Youth's finished version – backwards and forwards piano phrases, the sampled vocals ("Have you ever had an out of body experience? … What does the concept of time mean to you?") – and laid them across a drum & bass groove. Drum & bass, an urban rhythm that defined late-1990s UK street culture, was second nature to Nitin Sawhney but was entirely new to Paul McCartney. He first heard it in Sawhney's bedroom. "I was talking him through the thing and I said, 'I've done a few different versions of the remix' (cos I'd just worked my arse off all day until he got there!), and he said 'Oh, I like that.' I said, 'Right, *that's* called drum & bass!' I was talking to him about it and he said 'I really like that, it sounds great.'" McCartney's avant-grade streak was fine with drum & bass, and he was enthusiastic enough to let Sawhney continue down that path, turning the atmospheric, mellow original into a high-voltage (almost 180 BPM), experimental dance track.

> ■ He was saying, 'Oh, you've got to make sure that all the parts are what I originally played.' What I had to work with was everything that he did, so what I had to do was cut up his parts to make it work in the drum & bass thing, so all the parts are played by him. But I cut them up in such a way that I created a completely different beat and completely different thing, but I made sure that everything was played by him. It was all derived from his sounds … He was probably quite surprised that I could get that out of the same piece of music, by cutting things up differently, or editing differently or whatever. It's just kind of recreating the beats, so like the kick [drum] would be his kick but I'd place it in a different point and EQ it differently and all the rest of it. So I didn't want to take away from the integrity of the fact that he'd played everything. And I didn't want to augment it with my own playing. In this way I wanted to literally be a remixer, so I stuck to the principle of remixing, keeping all the original material and not adding or taking away anything, but trying to give it a completely different slant.

At a single-friendly 3'44", Sawhney's drum & bass version was possibly the most commercial Fireman track to date, although it remained purely at promo status for club use. More leftfield was his 'Out of Body' mix and its almost identical partner, the self-explanatorily titled 'Out of Body with Sitar' mix. The idea for a sitar part had come up when McCartney visited Sawhney's bedsit studio and listened to his work in progress. "He kind of went, 'Oh yeah, I really like that,'" he told me, "so I said OK and I kind of mucked around a bit when he was there and he said, 'Do you want me to play some sitar?' I said, 'Yeah, if you want, that'd be good.' So he went off and played a bit of sitar and sent that to me a couple of days later." The finished 'Out of Body' mix dispensed with the drum & bass beat (save for the odd filtered fill and riff) to create a very ambient four and half minutes, most of which are completely beat-less. McCartney's sitar part jams with further female vocals to create what is quite simply classic chill-out. "There's a few different versions, one with sitar and one without," remembers Sawhney. "It's a bit trippy – I liked that about it."

'Fluid' and its 'Out of Body with Sitar' mix was one of McCartney's more recent Indian-influenced experiments. 'Arizona Sky' on *Strawberries Oceans Ships Forests* was also based around a sitar performance, followed more prominently by 'Riding into Jaipur', which was based lyrically as well as musically around his Indian experiences on the *Driving Rain* album. This follows a lineage which goes back to The Beatles' 'Norwegian Wood'. Released on *Rubber Soul* in 1965, it was the first time a sitar had been heard on a pop record. (The song came full circle when covered by Cornershop, one of the UK's most progressive Indian bands, on their 1997 album *When I Was Born for the 7th Time*.) The next year brought more – on the *Revolver* track 'Tomorrow Never Knows' – and the year after, further Indian influences appeared on The Rolling Stones' 'Paint It Black'.

In an essay entitled 'The Beatles, India, and the Counterculture', Neal Sawhney (no relation) traces The Beatles' Indian influence back even further. "The actual inception came from Ringo Starr's predecessor, Pete Best," he says. "Half Indian, Best was actually born in Madras, India. The Beatles were also well aware of other cultures while growing up. They described their thriving hometown port of Liverpool as 'colourful neighbourhoods of immigrant ethnic minorities'. These associations provided The Beatles with the foundation for their keen interest in Indian music and culture…"

Some may have seen The Beatles' dabblings in Indian music as a fad, but Nitin Sawhney disagrees. "A lot of people in the Indian classical community are a bit dismissive of The Beatles' Indian experiments," he said in an interview at the time of 'Fluid'. "Ravi Shankar has totally disconnected himself from all that. McCartney impressed me, as he was hugely knowledgeable about Indian music, past and present, both here and in India. So for him, it wasn't just a fad."

2001 saw the release of *Wingspan*, a double album retrospective of tracks hand-picked by McCartney from the Wings era. Although the accompanying film and DVD were accused of almost reworking history, or at least of telling it entirely from McCartney's side, it succeeded in placing a mach-maligned musical force firmly back on the map. While the media promotion was fearsome, the musical promotion – in terms of accompanying promo-only club remixes – was by contrast surprisingly restrained. The sight of promotional *Wingspan* ladies' underpants (no joke) on the official website set off warning bells. What next? *Wings – The Remix Album*? Fortunately, McCartney and EMI showed a great deal more taste in selecting collaborators to put Wings back on the dancefloor. And they made sure the results stayed firmly in that arena, with the 2001 revisions of Wings tracks pressed purely for club promotion and not for general release.

Artful Dodger, the UK duo who lead the way in the early 2000s in transforming 2-step garage from underground sensation into commercial force, were chosen to remix 'Silly Love Songs'. The duo made few radical changes save for a stronger rhythm track and bringing out parts of McCartney's vocal which had hitherto been hidden. 'Silly Love Songs' keeps recurring on the remix front – fortunately, though, this version was saved any of the 'breakdance version' hype that the *Give My Regards to Broad Street* mix received. Loop Da Loop took things further with their own bass and string arrangements for remixes of 'Silly Love Songs' and a Vocoder-led 'Goodnight Tonight'. But the most out-there of the *Wingspan* remixes were Different Gear's very leftfield nine-minute version of 'Let 'em In' and the JSM/Alessi Bros Mix of, believe it or not, 'No More Lonely Nights', which included random studio talk and new guitar parts.

In the past 20 years, the story of remxing has come full circle. Technology is now in the hands of the masses, allowing anyone with an interesting idea to create their own version of an existing track. And, as already noted, these are becoming absorbed into the original artists' heritage by the relentless bootlegging industry. On the black market, Yellow Dog and Vigotone are two of the most legendary bootleg brands. Between them they have pressed up and released hundreds of hours of Beatles music with has yet to find a legitimate release. While some defend bootleggers as curious mavericks robbing from the rich to give to the poor, recent releases on these labels have proved just how they are driven 99 per cent by the fast buck and maybe one per cent by some kind of curator-type approach to music. How else would a new breed of McCartney homemade remixes go from being posted on the worldwide web for other fans' enjoyment to appearing on a full run of market stall CDs without the artists (of course) or even the remixer having any knowledge of it?

'cb70' is one McCartney fan who has seen the remix story come full circle. Tinkering at home with the samples and sequences that PC technology now puts in the hands of the masses, he has become a prolific amateur and bases his art on the work of Paul McCartney. The internet and MP3 allow him to share – as opposed to selling – his new mixes for other fans to enjoy. But now a pattern has emerged. No sooner has cb70 posted some new experiments on-line but

Yellow Dog are selling CD compilations of his work across the world's bootleg market stalls. "This is the second CD I've seen booted of the CDs I sent out to people in September. Except this time Yellow Dog, a pretty big name, booted me," he told other McCartney fans on-line. "At least my remixes are spreading around," commented a flattered cb70, "but I hope they're not passing them off as 'legit' remixes."

Legit or not, it's proof of the ever-spinning wheel of influence that an artist can set in motion. In this case McCartney is at the centre of the spokes and factors completely outside his control are reworking his material, while factors outside *those* artists' control are packaging and releasing that work. Nitin Sawhney agrees that in 2002 remixing is very much a creative art form in its own right. "When you remixed something [in the 1980s] you just got the original parts and you actually just changed the volumes or the EQs of various parts in the mix," he remembers. "I think that Paul McCartney was kind of half expecting that with 'Fluid'. When I met him I think I changed this ... It was like he hadn't seen it from this perspective and I was impressed by how open he was to it."

TEN

# "A LONG WAY OFF THE FROG CHORUS..."

**"I**t's a long way off the Frog Chorus..." was the first and not altogether unexpected reaction of Will Hodgekinson on first hearing *Strawberries Oceans Ships Forest*. The *Guardian* journalist was listening to Paul McCartney's first full-length album of leftfield techno, released in November 1993 under the guise of The Fireman.

Seven years later, in November 2000, Hodgekinson was visiting the Notting Hill flat of The Stranglers' founder Hugh Cornwell for a browse through his record collection. The obvious rock influences were there – Dylan, John Wesley Harding, Led Zeppelin, Dr John – as well as some more psychedelic albums by the likes of Captain Beefheart, Frank Zappa, Love and The Byrds. "Me and my producer grew up with psychedelic music," said Cornwell, "and I've ended up listening to the music that excited me when I was a kid." Which is possibly why "one very experimental, sample-heavy CD, *Strawberries Oceans Ships Forest*," was unearthed in his alphabetically filed drawer. "This is Stella [McCartney]'s copy. We used to hang out together a few years ago," Cornwell explained. "It's a product of the producer Youth teaming up with Paul McCartney. Youth went to McCartney's house, got stoned for two days, took away the 24-track tapes of McCartney's latest album and remixed them. There's no singing on it, it's just noises, and it was McCartney's idea. It sold about ten copies."

That, in a nutshell courtesy of a punk icon, is the story of *Strawberries Oceans Ships Forest*. The full story is of how McCartney's interest in remix culture led to a meeting with one of dance music's most quietly accomplished figures and the creation of The Fireman, his longest-lived and most unexpected experimental sideline.

When *Strawberries Oceans Ships* Forest is described in the press it's almost always referred to as 'ambient house', possibly because McCartney's musical partner for The Fireman, Youth, was once a pioneer of this genre. But in reality the album is a million miles away from ambient house, and is much more in tune with the early 1990s 'Teutonic beats' techno sound. All these connections, genres and sub-genres are best traced through the story of the other Fireman, Youth. McCartney's songwriting collaborations with John Lennon and Elvis Costello have been more than adequately covered in print. But little or nothing has been written about Youth, a collaborator who has pushed McCartney's vision as far as any.

Born in Africa in 1960, Martin Glover is one of the UK's most consistent, credible producers and musicians. Originally the bass player in the notorious punk band Killing Joke, it was there he earned the nickname Youth and met their roadie Alex Paterson, who would later become one of the 1990s' most influential figures in experimental music. When Killing Joke disbanded in the mid-1980s, Youth began seamlessly merging dance and rock music with experimentation. McCartney and The Beatles had a 'massive' influence on Youth. "I grew up with The Beatles," he told me.

> ■ I was born in 1960 so The Beatles were up until I was about ten. So I was a
> bit young to be fanatical about them when they were flying, but I remember
> my dad getting *Sgt. Pepper*. I was cutting out the sergeant badges and patch-
> es and sticking them on my jumper with Sellotape. I didn't really get locked
> into The Beatles until I started playing in bands, although I liked them. They
> were the yardstick for songs basically. In my youth, I got into more '70s bands
> when I got into music. I got into glam first, then I got into Led Zeppelin and
> Floyd and progressive.

Following Killing Joke, Youth formed Brilliant with June Montana and Jimmy Cauty. One of the first bands to merge club sensibilities and rock attitude, Brilliant were way ahead of their time and suffered commercially as a result. When it was over, Youth and Cauty began working with Alex Paterson as The Orb and cooked up the first ever chill-out and ambient house music. DJ Paul Oakenfold had asked Paterson to oversee the chill-out room for his Land of Oz night at London's Heaven nightclub. The music he and Youth provided with was a never-before-heard, largely beat-less collage of 12" singles and found sounds. It was far from classical avant-garde in that these long-form soundscapes were not predetermined or planned but DJ'd and improvised. "It's all the fault of The Orb, of course," said US music/tech journal *EST* of the birth of ambient house and chill-out. "Fannying around in the studio late at night, trying to get the drum-track on their second single to work properly, they suddenly decided to do the unthinkable: they took the drums off altogether."

Paterson later described how they would use "an eight-track mixer with four or five record decks" to produce ambient house soundtracks where "we'd loop the intro of 808 State's 'Pacific State' minus the drums into parts of The Beloved's 'The Sun Rising'." Using this approach, they even managed to radically rework Chapter Eight's Gizmotron classic: "a version of 10cc's 'I'm Not In Love' that went on for two whole hours!"

When Cauty moved on to form The KLF, Youth and Paterson worked together to create 'Little Fluffy Clouds', the track which would define the genres of ambient house and chill-out. 'Little Fluffy Clouds' blended samples from Ennio Morricone, Steve Reich and Pat Metheny with engine noises and dialogue from a US country singer. It set the tone for the debut Orb album, *Adventures Beyond the Ultraworld*. "Bookended by 'Little Fluffy Clouds'," remarked Mark Prendergast in *The Ambient Century*, "the album's contents not only pushed house music into another dimension but set new standards for ambient sound production."

System 7 also sprang up at this time, a collective featuring Youth, Paterson and others, all overseen by experimental guitarist Steve Hillage. Hillage had previously worked with one of Paul McCartney's early avant-garde collaborators, Daevid Allen, when he joined Gong in 1972. System 7's '777 Expansion', 'Mektoub' and 'Sunburst' (all co-produced and co-written by Youth) are classics of their time. By the time the next Orb album, 1993's *U.F.Orb* appeared, Youth had begun winning awards for production in his own right and was even the subject of a notable press article headlined 'Can This Man Save Pop Music?' *U.F.Orb* got into the front window of Woolworths; dance music – even experimental ambient house – was being sucked into the mainstream.

In the early 1990s dance culture and indie guitar rock were coming together to form an exciting, credible and – fortunately for the record companies – hugeselling blend. And Youth was at the forefront. His 12" remixes for Siouxsie and The Banshees, The Sugarcubes, Stereo MCs, The Wonderstuff, World of Twist and Sunsonic are all classics of the period. As one of the few dance producers who could also work with guitar music, Youth was more in demand than most – from both the press and record industry, which had been resistant to dance music up to that point. As Simon Napier-Bell would note, "The traditional rock-loving music press decided that if they were going to have to deal with hordes of knob-twiddling electronic musicians, they might as well support ones … who injected rock into their dance tracks."

As such, Youth was roped into remixing everyone from INXS, Sting and U2 to posthumous post-production on Jimi Hendrix. The remix spiral extended further still when Youth spent a mammoth studio session editing the mellow highlights of several albums' worth of McCartney's most creative remixers, Art of Noise, into a single-track album entitled *The Ambient Collection* for release in 1992. Over the next ten years he got this down to a fine art – producing tracks for Dido and all of The Verve's number one album *Urban Hymns*. Verve tracks such as 'The Drugs Don't Work' and 'Bitter Sweet Symphony' earned him a 1998 Brit award for Best Producer, having previously been nominated in 1991, 1992 and 1994.

Ambient house was a quintessentially English notion. But it was pushed one stage further by German musicians such as Time Unlimited, Sun Electric and Thomas Fehlman. They brought stronger techno influences into play, using pulses and more relentless rhythms to create the Teutonic or Berlin Beats sound. Youth happily embraced this new approach, as his remixes of Marathon's classic 'Movin'' and ST Melody's 'QTopia' proved.

"The Orb was a crucial part of house music's genesis," *The Ambient Century* concludes, "a unit who did more than any other to prove that sampling technology could produce startlingly creative new music." The Youth collective also had a clear connection to late 1960s and early '70s avant-garde rock, not only via the Hillage collaborations but even from parodying Pink Floyd images for their album sleeves. These factors combined to make Paul McCartney decide upon Youth as an interesting collaborator, initially to remix tracks from *Off the Ground...*

"I originally got in touch with Youth so I could ask him to do a couple of dance mixes from the *Off the Ground* project," remarked McCartney in 1993. "He's a 'buzzy' character so I was glad when he agreed to do it. The brief from me was that he should only use stuff from our recordings, because dance mixes often feature a kick-drum sample or a James Brown snare sound and, as a consequence, the record ends up sounding a bit like someone else's. So I told Youth that I'd prefer any sound he might select to come off our recordings, mainly *Off the Ground*." Youth vividly remembers taking the call from McCartney:

> ■ He wanted to do some experimental music, some ambient stuff. He didn't say the word ambient, but ... I think he'd read an interview I'd done and he liked what I said in it. He said, "I've been recording pots and weird things and I want to collage them together somehow." And I said OK and we went down there. He said "It's still a collaboration basically, where we go anonymously under the name The Fireman." That's what he wanted it to be called because his dad was a fireman, he liked that. And I liked it.

Youth took up the gauntlet and prepared to take McCartney's music in completely new directions. He hadn't heard *Thrillington* but McCartney had told him about 'Carnival of Light' and how he wanted to return to that avant-garde spirit. "I think that [Carnival Of Light] was a direct influence for him to do The Fireman," remembers Youth. Youth also had the influence of The Beatles weighing in. Not only avant-garde tracks like 'Tomorrow Never Knows', but also a more spiritual influence.

■ I rediscovered The Beatles when I started going to India in the late eighties/early nineties. I started listening to *Revolver* and *Rubber Soul*. I remember taking *Revolver* around the country. It just made total sense. And I didn't really get it before then. Also, I think by the end of the acid house thing I started appreciating how big an influence they were on everything, from 'Tomorrow Never Knows', and all their psychedelia and all that.

It was in this spirit that Youth arrived at McCartney's private home studio in October 1992 to begin work. Studio engineer Chris Potter and programmer Matt Austin were in tow. Youth abandoned the original 'remix' idea in favour of creating totally new music, albeit made up from samples from *Off the Ground*. Paul gave him the green light and so the first day of the session was spent breaking down the source tracks into interesting, recyclable components. They then drafted McCartney back into the studio to add some original content. In a short five-hour session, Youth recorded McCartney playing banjo, flute and whispering. He also improvised some parts on Bill Black's 'Heartbreak Hotel' double bass, which Linda McCartney had bought him for a birthday present. The most traditional of rock and roll artefacts, McCartney also surprisingly used the Bill Black bass on his avant-garde work with Yoko Ono, explored in Chapter 11.

■ Basically we spent a few days with me getting him to do something in the studio live, looping it up, taking a few loops, and then getting him to play over it with some other things. And then we'd start jamming over it, us playing different things. Him playing most of it and I'd occasionally get on the bass or something like that. He's got an amazing studio. He's got a lot of the original Abbey Road kit in it and a lot of the original early Wings, late Beatles gear, Mellotrons ... So we just worked our way through all of it basically. He's got Bill Black's, Elvis Presley's bass player's, double bass. So we'd just go: "Let's put some of that on and let's do some of this."

McCartney loved Youth's free-form approach, just playing, recording, and letting the producer take the experiments away to mix into a finished track. "Normally these are the bits that producers try to get me to shut up about – they usually say, 'Stop messing around, Paul, sing the song properly'," he remembered. "But Youth wanted all the messing around. It was an interesting release for me." Other material for the album was 'found' on tapes and disks in the studio. A bass riff here, a vocal track there (most noticeably from *Off the Ground*'s 'Cosmically Conscious').

In an interview with the *Good Day Sunshine* Beatles fanzine, studio engineer Tony Clark once described "a spirit of energy" that lasted throughout the *Thrillington* album's 24-hour mixdown. "Paul used to live in St John's Wood then," Clark recalled, "and he'd pop home with Linda and then come back again. Which was great, because if I was flagging a bit in the night, he'd help put a bit of energy back into it." Uncannily, what Clark described was mirrored 21 years later when Youth was working on *Strawberries Oceans Ships Forest*. "I put all the ingredients together," remembered Youth in 1993, "told Paul I was going to mix it on the last night and suggested he pop down to have a look. So he came down with Linda and their children after attending the opening of Linda's photographic exhibition in Bath, and they all really got into what we were doing. Paul was blown away because he was hearing his album in a totally new context. And he also saw how we mixed – using the desk as an instrument and playing the desk. After I'd done one mix he asked 'Is that it?' and I said 'No, we're going to do a lot!' He ended up staying until about four in the morning, and got totally into it. It was a very special night."

By the end of that night, not one but nine remixes had been completed all with titles given to them there and then by Youth as he mixed. Each track sounded very similar, building on the previous one and adding elements to the next. Track titles like 'Transpiritual Stomp' are classic Youth – "I could imagine a caveman kicking up the dust to it," he said at the time. "It still sounds good I think," he says, looking back, agreeing that it's "a bit harder" than ambient house, fitting more with the Teutonic Beats and techno sounds of the time. "Also it was pre-audio, it was still Akais and samplers," he recalls. "It was pre-Pro Tools, so you couldn't put audio in and treat it. Technology was pretty limited, pretty basic then. When I listen to it now, it sounds pretty basic."

'Transpiritual Stomp's opening nine-minute burst sets the tone for the entire album. It's led by a throbbing analogue bassline, supported not by the 'stomping' techno drums you'd expect but by a light rhythm track, leaving room for the lead – not vocals but a banjo loop which trades with guitar and keyboards. The only vocals present aren't singing but a selection of whoops and exclamations – the likes of which had not been heard on a McCartney recording since 'Carnival of Light'. They're complemented by a single phrase – "I sense the situation" – mixed very low in the music which, when looped, takes on an ethereal quality.

Messing about in the studio, Youth had opened up the sample disks of McCartney's Chamberlain – one of the original samplers – and found a poetry reading of John Galsworthy's 'The Little Man'. Youth didn't realise it at the time, but McCartney had used this recording he'd made of Harold Margary almost 15 years previously for 'The Broadcast', Wings' vocal tape and funk jam interlude on *Back to the Egg*.

As techno and even Teutonic Beats go, 'Transpiritual Stomp' is slow. At 85 beats per minute, it's positively laidback before reaching a completely rhythmless, ambient breakdown at the end, which uses only a shaker and the processed vocal sample. Building on the 'broadcast' concept, the track moves into the next – 'Trans Lunar Rising' – via the sounds of Youth tuning through stations and interference on a transistor radio. This was another avant-garde musical idea which began with John Cage and had last been heard on *Back to the Egg*'s 'Reception'. Tiny bursts of random pop music can be heard on the radio – so trainspotters should listen out for a chance appearance of Chris Rea and also 'Boys Boys Boys' by Sabrina popping up 32 seconds in! But again, this is mixed very low because for this track the guitar has even more overdrive, while Youth has also developed the trade-off between rhythm track and sampled vocal cries.

'Trans Lunar Rising' moves into 'Transcrystaline' via another ambient break-down, this time using classical violins and Indian melodies. This is the first piece to be heavy on rhythm and drums and features much of McCartney's original contribution – a (heavily reverbed) whispered vocal track and a flute solo. 'Pure Trance' comes from a slightly different standpoint to those heard so far. It's a consolidation of themes and ideas from previous mixes, but with speech from 'The Broadcast' plundered a little further. As such the title is appropriate – 'Pure Trance' was often used as a mix title for Orb and off-shoot projects. 'Arizona Light Mix', on the other hand, takes the experiment much further. Percussion (of the sampled oil tank variety) and ethereal, eastern guitar combine to make this one of the album's highlights.

'Celtic Stomp' doesn't stand up as well, majoring as it does on McCartney's banjo loop. Perhaps someone with Youth's abilities should have realised that the paths of the banjo and house beats were never meant to cross. The Grid's 'Texas Cowboy' singles from the same era are testament to this. The title track is anoth-er stand-out, taking a mellower approach with less overdrive but more of 'Arizona Light Mix's percussion track. Echo-chambered percussion, an incessant bass drone and a true feel of live mixing takes *Strawberries Oceans Ships Forest* in a completely new direction on the track '4-4-4' before the album – and the session that produced it – reaches a climax with 'Sunrise'. Shouts of "Beautiful!", random replays of vocal tracks and washes of sitars make a fitting finale.

On listening to the nine finished remixes, McCartney heard a full album's worth of material. Youth's plans to either edit them down to one single version or leave them as separate tracks (to be issued alongside McCartney's own B-sides on the 12" singles for *Off the Ground*) were abandoned. McCartney decided to release the full set in one go. Even the titles Youth had given them remained, although somewhere between the studio and the pressing plant 'Arizona Light Mix' became 'Arizona Light', 'Sunrise' became 'Sunrise Mix' and other grammat-ical changes were made to the titles Youth had noted down that night ('4-4-4' became '4 4 4' and the title track, 'Strawberries, Ocean, Ship and Forests' became 'Strawberries Oceans Ships Forest').

"I wasn't really thinking too much about [the titles]," Youth remembered. "They came spontaneously – it was a full moon that night so I was getting quite esoteric ... 'Sunrise Mix' was the last one of the night, done as the sun was creeping up over the horizon." He and McCartney named their project The Fireman and the 77 minutes of techno beats were collectively christened *Strawberries Oceans Ships Forest*.

"It started off as two 12 inches that became an album," recalls Youth, "We just did it as two vinyl 12 inches at first and then he put all the mixes together as an album. I was a little disappointed with that because I thought it could have been a bit more of an album really, rather than two 12 inches. But I was still really glad that he wanted to put them out." He was pleased that the next Fireman album, *Rushes* (explored in Chapter 13), was approached a little differently. "We had a few more sessions to work on and I then had the luxury of, once we'd done the mixes, bringing them all back here to my studio and spending a couple of weeks editing them," he told me, "which I'd had to do there [for *Strawberries*], which is always a bit intense because you're staying down there and there's a limited amount of time."

But Youth was cautious. "I was planning to edit them into one single mix, but [McCartney] said he wanted them as an album," he said at the time. "I had slight reservations because if I had known it was going to be an album I would have done them slightly differently. As a bunch of 12" mixes they're excellent, very spontaneous and, though I don't want to get bogged down in the dogma of conceptual music, they have a charming naïvete. But, to be honest, as an album it may fall a little short. But all due respect to Paul, though, he felt it was valid as an album and was saying, 'I don't care, I think it's great! I want it like this!'"

With *Off the Ground*, and *Flowers in the Dirt* before it, McCartney was rebuilding a strong solo profile and leaving behind his more directionless 1980s material. Little wonder then that this most experimental of albums was put out under an alias, rather than as either Paul McCartney or McCartney & Youth. As noted, McCartney's father had been a fireman and this became the inspiration for a new fictional artist (complete with odd doodles of his antics on record sleeves) to follow Percy Thrillington. "For various reasons it just seemed appropriate," McCartney said of this reference to his father's work, which came a decade before his salute to the New York firemen at the Freedom concert of 2002.

But the pseudonym smoke-screen didn't hold up as long as Thrillington. "When the mysterious Fireman album came out, it was largely ignored," noted Stewart Mason for RollingStone.com, "until rumours started floating that somehow Paul McCartney was involved with the project, à la Percy 'Thrills' Thrillington's easy listening version of *Ram* in 1977." As *Rolling Stone's* John Bush reported, "A bout of rumor-mongering reminiscent of the 1977 Beatles-are-Klaatu scam quickly gave way to the fact that McCartney had indeed been a part of the project."

Not only the name but even the initial distribution method kept McCartney's involvement hidden. He had entered the promo age. Promo or demonstration copies of records had been in existence since the dawn of vinyl – test pressings of material already set for release, made up in short runs for band members, promotion and others involved. But by 1992, they had taken on a new purpose and music lived on promos as a new medium. Musicians used promos (12" singles or even tapes) to take their music straight from the studio to clubbers, their audience, free of record labels or publishing contracts, in order to gauge their reaction before either remixing, releasing or abandoning.

Graham Massey of 808 State remembered the freedom that this afforded musicians in the 1989 book *The Haçienda Must Be Built*. "I remember me and (A Guy Called) Gerald used to spend all day in the studio, make a tape, jump in a taxi, go down the Hacienda and be able to get played a 20-minute track we'd just done," Massey said. The track that Youth and Alex Paterson would later remix in their original chill-out room was first played to an unknowing crowd by its nervous creators. "That seemed really exciting at the time because that interactive culture is dead rare now," recalled Massey. "'Pacific State' was played off cassette down there for weeks before we got the acetates – the first time it was played was quite terrifying, waiting to see if people were going to go for it or not." Another famous example is Fatboy Slim, who tested many tracks from his million-selling *You've Come a Long Way Baby* album months before they saw the light of day in shops, pressing up promos to DJ at his Brighton club night, the Big Beat Boutique.

What for the musician was a heightened audience interaction was, for the major labels and the music industry in general, an opportunity to become complacent (becoming "more interested in marketing music than in recording it," noted Simon Napier-Bell), leading to the form's complete overhaul and, some may say, breakdown. On reaching the DJs, though, the promos for *Strawberries Oceans Ships Forest* did stand out a little more than the standard handwritten white label. The double LP was issued on clear vinyl as a numbered edition. Later Fireman issues would have holograms and giant posters.

With the catalogue number FIRE 1, the only clue that the promos had anything to do with McCartney was the fact that they appeared on Parlophone Records, plus the reference to Juggler Music (the juggler being the logo of his company, MPL). The finished CD was equally anonymous – plain red with just part of the album title across the top. An early, withdrawn alternative version featuring illustrations of Paul and Linda McCartney and Youth sampling various drugs is also rumoured to exist. By 2002, ten years after *Strawberries Oceans Ships Forest*, the promo 12" is a major force in the music industry, with many (if not the majority) of major labels entering into bidding wars to sign the artists whose promos have caused most reaction in the clubs.

The overall impact of *Strawberries Oceans Ships Forest* was encouraging, but many reviewers couldn't get over the fact that something so unashamedly repetitive had come from Paul McCartney. "Youth may as well have had Morrison and Clapton aboard for all the tunesmanship injected by his mature new pal," said *Q* magazine. "77 minutes of techno/ambient music, with a disco beat and not much melody," was the judgment of Randy Krbechek for *Metronews*. "Riff and Variations," wrote an uninspired Robert Christgau (*Esquire/Playboy/Village Voice*), or "techno for seniors", when it appeared on Capitol Records in the US two years later.

*Q* magazine may not have registered much McCrartney input but they were genuinely impressed by the finished album, as it had something to offer listeners from the present as well as McCartney's past. "Conveniently enough for the fretting hipster, Macca's presence is difficult to detect (and both parties remain nameless)," remarked Andrew Collins. "The sprawling nine-track melange relies on a palette of throbbing electronics, Aboriginal chants, sampled babble and clattering beats, very much the tricks of Youth's trade as a hep knobmonger. Perhaps McCartney supplied the overall title from an old shopping list. As an infectious, first-gear, instrumental dance album, it's fine..."

As dance music it was strong, and as artistic development, *Strawberries Oceans Ships Forest* was a giant leap for Paul McCartney. The reviews may not have had the album flying off the shelves, but was that ever the point? More appropriately, the album did make it into the musical drug cabinet of organisations like the Biocybernaut Institute (BcI) in California. The BcI was founded in the late 1970s by psychologist Dr James V Hardt, who for over 30 hears has researched "neurofeedback brainwave enhancement"...

"Peak performance, being in the zone, and operating at a higher level, are all descriptions of an optimised mental state which most of us rarely experience," reads the BcI's brochure. "Although these levels of consciousness are highly productive and enjoyable, they have remained fleeting and often just outside our abilities to control; until now. The Biocybernaut Institute training programs can dramatically improve your brainwave control through state of the art training with Neurofeedback." Neurofeedback displays the patient's brainwaves – via the BcI's "patented electronic technology" of course – as 'live' sounds and lights. The theory being that, the more the patient sees these live interpretations, the more they can control them.

"Neurofeedback training has demonstrated success in improving creativity, mental clarity, physical and emotional well-being, athletic performance, and work productivity, as well as clinical applications including treating alcohol and chemical dependency, attention deficit disorder, personality therapy, and relieving stress and anxiety," the Institute proclaims. Visit their Mountain View centre and they can "gently guide you to your own self-discovery through the process of enhancing your skill with your brainwaves." It's closer to Zen than to Yoga, apparently.

Curiously, the only commercial application of such theories, outside alternative medicine, has been in clubland, when in 2002 Hewlett Packard announced the 'HP DJ'. Created by the international computer company's artificial intelligence team in Bristol, the HP DJ is mixing software which, as Dave Cliff from HP's laboratory told the *New Scientist* in December 2001, "monitors the way dancers respond to the music and composes new tracks according to how animated the crowd becomes." As yet unavailable commercially, the system has been used in clubs, so far managing to convince only a minority of the audience that a human being is providing the music.

*Strawberries Oceans Ships Forest* is listed with others on the Biocybernaut Institute's list of "CDs that you might enjoy", which, for those interested in trying neurofeedback training at home, is given here in full:

- Darol Anger/Barbara Higbie – Tideline
  Astralasia – The Space Between
  Blink Twice – Demon Haunted Hour
  Cocteau Twins – Treasure
  Deep Forest (Mouquet/Souchez) – Deep Forest
  Brian Eno, David Byrne – My Life in the Bush of Ghosts
  Bill Evans – Moon Beams
  The Fireman – Strawberries Oceans Ships Forest
  Philip Glass – Glassworks
  Heptones – Party Time
  Inti-Illimani – Imagination
  Kraftwerk – Autobahn
  k d lang – Ingenue
  Pat Matheny – Offramp
  Sarah McLachlan – Surfacing
  Michael McNabb – DreamSong
  Moodswings – Mood Food
  Pink Floyd – Meddle
  Steve Reich – Drumming; Music for Mallet Instruments, Voices, Organ; Six Pianos
  Return to Forever – Romantic Warrior
  Roxy Music – Avalon
  Shakti, with John McLaughlin – Shakti
  Tangerine Dream – Phaedra
  Joe Walsh – But Seriously Folks ...

Glass and Pink Floyd – both floating in the sea of influences explored in Chapter Two – are notable inclusions in this list. Many others are pretty classic examples of the many genres of music – leftfield, ambient, chill-out, electronica, trance, etc – which are pretty impossible to 'dance' to yet are still squeezed by the mainstream into that already overflowing pigeonhole. Maybe it's all dance music for sitting down. Or lying down. "It's time to lay down and be counted," sloganeered The Irresistible Force on the release of their 1994 album *Global Chillage*, a call to arms for the ambient masses.

Back at the Roundhouse in 1968, Roger Waters of Pink Floyd had pointed out that some dance music could make such an impact it left you standing, rather than gyrating. Especially if combined with drugs. "It's definitely a complete realisation of the aims of psychedelia," he argued. "But if you take LSD, what you experience depends entirely on who you are. Our music may give you the screaming horrors or throw you into screaming ecstasy. Mostly it's the latter. We find our audiences stop dancing now. We tend to get them standing there totally grooved with their mouths open." If Richard Hewson had moved from Mary Hopkin via *Thrillington* to charting in *Mixmag* as Key West, why couldn't Paul McCartney – and other 1960s luminaries – make a similar leap?

This was a question that was asked several years later when, in 1997, 'electronica' was the new buzz for both rock and dance musicians, spurred on by the rebirth of Madonna's career thanks to her *Ray of Light* album (effectively a 50/50 collaboration with UK electronic guru William Orbit). As Alex Paterson's post-Youth line-up of The Orb rolled into Denver that year, on tour with his *Cydonia* album, he tried to point out that 'eclectronica' was nothing more than record company hype designed to shift units, and that music of the type found pasteurised on *Ray of Light* had been out there for years. "The most absurd side of it is that this music has been under your noses since 1985," he told Denver's *Westword*. "All it does is show you the power of the media and the music industry. And it is no reflection whatsoever about what's really going on musically in America." Paterson was talking to journalist Michael Roberts, who was disillusioned with rock's most recent forays into dance territory, calling David Bowie's *Earthling* "a shallow excursion into jungle grooves that tanked almost immediately" and dismissing U2's *Pop* as "layers of electronic textures atop yet another recycling of its trademark sound".

As with *Thrillington*, McCartney had again masked his involvement in one of his pivotal albums. The press release talked only of two famous, unnamed musicians who had never worked together before. Unlike *Thrillington* though, it didn't take long for the secret to come out. "No time for silly guessing games, The Fireman comprises Paul McCartney and Youth," said *Q* magazine. They were still surprised, though, when they observed: "That the jolly ex-Beatle and reinvented

Killing Joke bassman should collaborate at all is noteworthy, but to have conceived this perfectly usable ambient album beggars belief."

McCartney's new alias lasted long enough to fool some of the dance press into giving unbiased reviews of the record, but he was certainly not the first to use the industry's system of faceless promo releases as a means to shed preconceptions and be treated equally based on music alone. The Thompson Twins were seen as redundant 1980s haircuts by the mid-1990s, until 12" promos by an unknown Feedback Max (a secret Twins alter ego) began receiving rave reviews in the dance press. OMD pulled it off too. Having been revered in the late 1970s (as Orchestral Manoeuvres in the Dark), ten years later they were accused of having sold out, but by the early 1990s they proved detractors wrong with an impressive dance promo under the guise of Liberator.

But The Fireman, and 'Deliverance' before it, were musical projects as opposed to an effort to prove a point, or reinvent a career. As 'Deliverance' remixer Steve Anderson remembered, "I loved the idea that cool house DJs would be playing a Paul McCartney record which usually they stop when they find out the scam, but on this one they continued. I would have never created something like this if I hadn't been challenged with the approach and so inspired by Paul's enthusiasm for doing something different."

McCartney appeared to have succeeded in circumnavigating preconceptions and delivering the goods – unlike his 1960s contemporaries when they tried the same thing. "These efforts (*Pop*, *Earthling*, etc) are works of genius compared with *Retail Therapy*, a CD credited to T.D.F., an aggregation built around well-known technophile Eric Clapton," argued Michael Roberts. "The onetime God of guitar is not the first performer from his era to anonymously dip his toe into electronic waters; Paul McCartney did so – to surprisingly good effect – with *Strawberries Oceans Ships Forest*, a 1994 release credited to The Fireman. But Clapton's offering, which is dominated by somnolent, quasi-new-age picking decorated with undeniably slack dance beats, is so jarringly tepid that even Grammy voters might accuse him of being a dilettante. Keeping his name off the liner was the smartest move he could have made."

Despite being an intentionally lowkey release, *Strawberries Oceans Ships Forest* did reach an audience of millions, albeit unawares, when McCartney edited excerpts into the pre-show music for his 1993 New World tour. Certainly one of the biggest tours of the time, New World reached 19 countries across 79 dates. It was also the first Paul McCartney tour to feature live renditions of Beatles hits. For McCartney, the pre-show tape was a chance to surprise the audience as well as getting them in the mood before the band took to the stage. Alongside cover versions ('Let 'Em In' by Shinehead and Guns N' Roses' 'Live and Let Die' among them) were rare McCartney jam sessions and a variety of styles, from classical

('Vespers of the Blessed Virgin' by Montiverdi) to industrial (Laibach). It was also a chance to put his new dance efforts in front of his audience, with tracks from *Strawberries Oceans Ships Forest* and 'Deliverance' getting an airing.

Regardless of Youth's caution, or even Hugh Cornwell's dismissiveness, *Strawberries Oceans Ships Forest* was a successful experiment. In Youth, McCartney had found the first collaborator since John Lennon to truly take his music and ideas in new, avant-garde directions. But Youth doesn't particularly see The Fireman as a duo.

> ■ It doesn't seem to be either one of our personalities per se, but something else kind of comes into the equation when we do it. We both kind of navigate to that to a degree and are both surprised by what happens at the end. I think he's loose and confident enough to allow that to come and happen and also loose enough for me to say, "What do you think? What do you want to do?" He'll let me produce it.

Via his collaborations with Steve Anderson and Youth, McCartney managed to save his music from the tacky end of the remix process – the James Brown kick drums which he had warned of at the start of the project – in favour of creating a brand new and wholly original set of tracks. Two very different producers remixing the same material also proved what a spectrum of sounds can come from this creative process. "The thing is, if you listen to Youth's interpretation of the same sounds you will hear how completely differently a project can be approached," agrees Steve Anderson.

"I like it very much as a record and I think Youth did really good work on it," McCartney concluded, "even though we didn't realise we were making an album and it's all really the same track remixed nine times. But it was good fun and we kept our integrity because although the sounds were speeded up, slowed down or whatever, it's still us: the ingredients on The Fireman are still us. Not everyone will enjoy it, and I admit that your taste has to be in that direction for you to enjoy it, but I really like it as a record. I think it's a very interesting album."

McCartney was right – not everyone did enjoy it. It couldn't have been more different from his other album of that period, *Paul is Live*, which was released on the same day. But Youth was unfazed.

> ■ I think *Strawberries* was like the worst-selling result of anything he'd ever done ever and I was like "Yeah!" I thought it was quite an achievement! I think he really appreciates being able to do that stuff when he knows what it's like to be in a creative *prison* of sorts from your own success and other people's expectations. I think for him it must be very hard to find people to work with

who are going to give him challenging feedback and not just go with whatever. Despite that, just because he is who he is, there's obvious limitations around what you can and can't do, timespan and things like that. But those don't seem to really kind of enter into that Fireman world for some reason. It's got a kind of nice energy, you know. It's a whole other side of him that's quite mystical I think. He's got stones on the land where he lives and with the Fireman stuff, there's kind of a weird vibe around that when we do it..."

ELEVEN

# IN THE STUDIO WITH ꟾ YOKO ONO

**B**ells ring in an echo chamber. Silence. A voice emerges. "John, we're here now together. Bless you. Peace on earth. And Strawberry Fields forever." This from the recording session few could have dreamt possible. One of Paul McCartney's most avant-garde works was recorded in collaboration with none other than Yoko Ono, the high priestess of freak-out and his media nemesis.

It was at the time of the *Beatles Anthology* sessions. McCartney had met up with Ono in New York when John Lennon was honoured by the Rock & Roll Hall of Fame. It was at this gala event, on 19 January 1994, that Ono gave McCartney the Lennon demo tapes that would form the basis for the 'new' Beatles tracks recorded that year – 'Free as a Bird' and 'Real Love'. McCartney also used the event to invite Ono and son Sean Lennon to the McCartney family home; they joined him there soon afterwards.

"I knew what I was doing when I gave them 'Free as a Bird' and 'Real Love'," Ono said a couple of years later, "because I thought it was a great thing to happen. I think this world is so depressed and a lot of people are feeling directionless and everything, that for them to have an 'up' feeling is great, even if it's just three minutes."

McCartney had worked on an avant-garde collaboration with Ono, albeit in a very minor way, some 30 years before. Although she had been recording, performing and exhibiting long before she met John Lennon, Ono's avant-garde music only became world famous with 1968's *Two Virgins* album of sound collage and twisted performance. Perhaps better known for its naked cover shot than for the music it contained, it is nonetheless a startling and unsettling voyage, showing a mid-sixties audience the extremes that music could be pushed to. McCartney contributed its sleeve note. In an act of randomness inspired by the music on the record, he clipped a piece of newspaper text, typed it up and handed it over. "When two great Saints meet it is a humbling experience," it read. "The long battles to prove he was a Saint."

Ono and Lennon followed *Two Virgins* with two more albums of scathing, emotional sound trickery – *Life with the Lions* and *The Wedding Album*. From then on their music took a more conventional route, Lennon sticking to his rock roots and Ono pre-empting punk and then new wave with albums such as *Plastic Ono Band* and *Fly*. She threw herself into music on Lennon's death in 1980. *Heart Play*, *Season of Glass* and, as her first positive steps were taken, *It's Alright (I See Rainbows)* all appeared in the years immediately following the tragedy.

The late 1990s saw a massive re-evaluation of Ono's music triggered by the *Onobox* box set and CD re-release of her entire output. Critics are quick to mock her extreme vocalisations and radical instrumentation but, in the 30 years since *Two Virgins*, it's possible to look back and see how visionary some of her music was and the debt owed to her by musicians ranging from David Bowie to Sonic Youth.

It was March 1994 and the Ono Lennons were in residence at the McCartneys'. Paul spoke later of how odd it was in the mornings to see Yoko Ono in her dressing gown, but things were to get odder still.

McCartney gave his visitors a tour of Hog Hill Mill, his home recording studio where much of his songwriting and recording takes place. 'Pretty Little Head' and much of *Press to Play* was recorded at Hog Hill, as were both of the Fireman albums. Everyone was in high spirits and Sean Ono Lennon was fascinated by some of the instruments he found there, just as Youth was on a similar visit described in the previous chapter. The harmonium The Beatles used on 'We Can Work It Out' is there, as is the early Mellotron synthesiser which provided the distinctive opening chords on 'Strawberry Fields Forever' and an electric spinet which had been used on 'Because'.

Sean wasted no time in trying out the spinet and playing it for himself. In 1994 he was fast becoming an accomplished musician in his own right. Having appeared as a child on Ono's 'healing albums' in the 1980s, he guested on albums for artists as diverse as Motoharu Sanu, Stuntman and Lenny Kravitz. Lennon co-wrote and played on 'All I Ever Wanted' from Kravitz's 1991 *Mama Said*. In the same year he assembled a choir of famous musos for a re-recording of 'Give Peace a Chance' as an anti-Gulf War anthem. He continues to plough his own musical furrow, sitting somewhere between Japanese punk and US pop. As well as releasing *Into the Sun*, a 1998 solo album for the Beastie Boys' Grand Royal label, he and his band IMA (Japanese for 'now') have been a key part of Yoko's more recent work, acting as musical partners in a way that transcends their mother/son relationship.

"I was always kind of deterred from playing music," Sean Lennon said in 1996. "I was always asked by people, 'When's your record coming out?' when I was like six. So it kinda made me not want to do that, and I kind of denied my musical inclination for a long time." Until then he had struggled with the weight of his father's legacy. "I'm intimidated by everything," he said, "let alone the Lennon legacy. But I'm not trying to overcome my father or fill his shoes or reach any kind of level that he did. We're talking about a Mozart of rock music. I don't think of it in those terms. If I can communicate something creatively and artistically to a small number of people who are actually listening, I will feel like I've succeeded in life."

With Sean, then 25, playing the original Beatles spinet, McCartney suggested they made a track together, he and Yoko and Sean. Rather than re-record something from the days of 'Because', Yoko suggested they recorded 'Hiroshima Sky is Always Blue', a song she had recently written in New York for a stage play. Ron Destro's *Hiroshima* follows the stories of 20 victims of the atomic bombing in August 1945. Based largely on first person, historical accounts, the play would premiere on 9 October 1997 at the Joyce and Seward Johnson Theatre of the New City. Its music featured various Ono tracks, some live, others (including 'Hiroshima Sky') played via backing tapes. Writing for *Village Voice*, Randy Gener called the play "stunning." The *New York Times* called it "epic", describing a "lyrical, harrowing meditation of the effects of Hiroshima on Japanese peasants and soldiers." Small wonder that *Hiroshima* earned Ron Destro the 1997 Kennedy Center New American Play Award.

The writing of the score coincided with the production of Yoko Ono's *Rising* album. Acclaimed on release in 1995, it was her first record for almost ten years. At the time, she wrote of *Hiroshima*:

> ■ A playwright, Ron Destro, came to me in 1994 and asked me to write a few songs for his play *Hiroshima*. He reminded me that 1995 was the 50th anniversary of the Hiroshima tragedy. In his script there's a scene where a little girl tries to fold 1000 paper cranes. In Japan there is a tradition of folding 1000 paper cranes to make a wish. The little girl dies before she is able to fold all 1000 cranes. I was particularly touched by this scene, and went into the studio.

Once in the studio, Ono drew on her own memories of evacuating Tokyo as a small child while the city was bring bombed. The image of the sky over Hiroshima had been ingrained on her memory, as she waited in desperation as a refugee. "I was very, very young and it was quite simply alarming," she told the French magazine *Yellow Submarine*. "Somebody came to see us saying that the war was over, that was in August. Then a farmer explained to me that a strange bomb had been dropped on Hiroshima. We took refuge in the mountains. A great number of children had been taken there because of the bombings over Tokyo. I remember that we were dying of hunger. Some were desperate and were eating poisonous mushrooms. Whole families would die of poisoning. The hunger had made me very weak. I spent my days laying looking at the sky."

Ono had been living in the US before World War II had begun and, like many Japanese families, was then forced to move back to Japan. The pressure to move back came not from the US government but from a culture of racism that, although aged only seven, she was all too aware of. "I remember going to see films when I was a little girl," she later told *Hot Wired* magazine in 1996, "and the baddies were always the Japanese – Oriental – you know, and everyone would be booing. And then the lights would go up, and I would look at myself, and go, 'Oh no, I'm one of them! What am I going to do?' I was just a little girl."

Alienation awaited her in Tokyo. She had left behind the racism of America, but also her friends – she had been in the US since the Ono family emigrated there for her father's job in finance. She never quite settled back into life in Japan, always feeling different to the other children who had been there all their lives.

So although the song 'Hiroshima Sky is Always Blue' tackled issues of a global scale, it was also an intensely personal, family-oriented piece. When McCartney suggested they record together that day at Hog Hill and they agreed on the song, "I said," remembered Ono, "since it was a song for Hiroshima and world peace, we should have his whole family involved." So for the first time ever, all members of the McCartney family could be heard on one record. Paul took backing vocals and picked up Bill Black's 'Heartbreak Hotel' double bass once again. Linda McCartney played a Hammond B-3 organ and son James (plus a friend of his who was also reportedly at the session) played guitar. James' sisters Mary, Heather and Stella all joined in too, adding percussion and backing vocals to the live, free-form jam. Yoko, of course, handled lead vocal and Sean Lennon played guitar.

As Linda hits an endless E-minor chord into the organ, McCartney clunks in with single bass notes. Ono murmurs briefly before moving into a threatening rattle-snake-style vocal. As her singing begins to involve words (variations on the title), the childrens' percussion creeps in, sounding like the cracks and pops of wood on a fire. Soon after, Linda and Ono begin jamming – the keyboards and vocals playing off each other. With Ono rapping Japanese poetry, the others throw in abrupt cries and yelps as McCartney puts in runs and fills on the double bass. The music is, on one hand, classic Yoko Ono. On the other, it's the most extreme avant-garde performance McCartney has ever been involved in.

"The first take we did was just the right thing," Ono later told *Rolling Stone* magazine. "It was in the tradition of the old Plastic Ono Band – what happens in that moment is what's important." Sean was equally enthusiastic about collaborating with McCartney. "It was incredible working with Paul," he said. "Regardless of my heritage, I am a total Beatles fan. And he organised everything incredibly. Here were these people who had never played together actually making music."

'Hiroshima Sky' follows a tradition of McCartney producing songs for or with members of his family. Odes to Linda McCartney are scattered throughout his solo albums, beginning with 'The Lovely Linda', track one side one on his debut, *McCartney* (1970). There were private recordings too, such as the track 'Linda', which McCartney recorded and pressed as a one-off single for his wife's birthday in 1986. In 1996 he followed this with a Christmas present of 'Ingrained Funkiness', recorded with daughters Stella and Heather. Stella, Mary and James had provided backing vocals for a track recorded during the *Press to Play* sessions, 'Simple As That'. More recently, on 2001's *Driving Rain*, McCartney wrote a song with James which followed their previous collaboration on Linda McCartney's final, cathartic *Wide Prairie* sessions, just months before she died early in 1998.

The finished 'Hiroshima Sky' tape – recorded in just one take – was taken back to New York by Ono, where she added an overdub of Sean playing chimes. Paul McCartney was keen to see the track released but told Ono he was happy for her to decide when and how it should see the light of day, if at all. Ono, for one, was thrilled with the result. "It was a marvellous moment," she said afterwards. "Musically, the result was excellent. Paul had told me that he wanted to release this song. He knew that I was working on *Rising* and he was happy for the track to appear on my album. But I decided that, because the children had taken part in the recording, I didn't feel that you could use them for commercial purposes." But that didn't mean she knew what to do with this most unlikely of collaborations. "It will be put in a different way," she concluded, "not on a commercial base. But it's hard to do it, it's very difficult, just one track."

Even if the recording – dubbed the "Ono-McCartney Reconciliation Tape" by the *Los Angeles Times* – may never get released, it did represent an end to the bad feeling that had grown between the two families ever since The Beatles began breaking up. The reconciliation, which had begun with the handing over of the Lennon demos for McCartney, Harrison and Starr to build on, was cemented in Hog Hill studio with this recording. At the time, McCartney, who described the impromptu session as "Quite strange, lovely strange," said it was "a very cool way to cement our friendship ... We've been through so much shit over the years that inevitably people look at these things and suspect some ulterior motive. It isn't like that any more." Sean Ono Lennon was more direct, telling *Rolling Stone*'s David Fricke that 'Hiroshima Sky' "was more the result of our reconciliation after 20 years of bitterness and feuding bullshit."

But this peace wasn't destined to last. By the time McCartney toured the USA in 2002, the *New York Daily News* was running headlines like "A Love Song for Yoko? Don't Be Silly," reporting comments McCartney made when asked if he planned to invite Ono to one of his concerts when he visited her home city. "We're not friends," he reportedly told them. Although "I don't hold a grudge," he continued, "I don't intend to invite her. I don't mean it as a snub [but] life is short, and if I throw a party, I just invite who I wanna have there, people you're gonna have a laugh with." The blue sky over Hiroshima appears to have been blighted this time by Ono's refusal to allow the writing credits for McCartney's song 'Yesterday' to be changed from Lennon/McCartney (as was used on all Beatles songs, including pure Lennon compositions such as 'Give Peace a Chance') to either McCartney/Lennon or just McCartney.

Stir in the unending media need for conflict and the peace that descended over Hog Hill in March 1994 looks more like a momentary truce than an ending. Yoko Ono, however, remains apart from any public wars of words. "Bless him," she replied in the *New York Daily News*. "He is still family. I wish him great success on his concert."

In the years between Ono's first meeting with Ron Destro in 1994 and the premiere of the play in 1997, she, Sean Lennon and IMA performed 'Hiroshima Sky' at an acoustic outdoor concert in Japan. This was a special event – the 50th Commemoration of the Hiroshima Atomic Disaster – held at the Itsukushima Shrine on 10 August 1995.

Four days earlier – on the exact date of the 50th anniversary – as part of a television tribute to those who died in the bombing, the Ono/McCartney version of 'Hiroshima Sky' received its only public airing to date. NHK, Japan's national public radio and TV network, began a day of commemoration with their breakfast show *Ohayou Nippon* (Good Morning Japan). Just after 7.00 am they featured a special interview with Yoko Ono and a broadcast of 'Hiroshima Sky' from a DAT she had given them. "'Hiroshima's Sky is Always Blue' is a prayer," Yoko told them, "and I hope that human society will be beautiful like a blue sky in the future." In a 1996 interview with Jody Denberg for *Approximately Infinite Universe*, the definitive Yoko Ono website, Ono recalled:

■ IMA and I recorded it first and then when I went to London we recorded it again with the McCartney family, and they were great about it. In fact, the result of that is very good. The original idea was for the 50th anniversary of Hiroshima, and we were just doing it for Hiroshima city. I just wanted to do it that way – NHK Radio played it nationwide in Japan on the anniversary day. That's how it was meant to be, in my mind. I think this album [*Rising*] has the same kind of feel about it, without 'Hiroshima Sky is Always Blue'. It made its point anyway.

Although McCartney's avant-garde releases such as *Strawberries Oceans Ships Forest*, *Rushes* and *Liverpool Sound Collage* are all readily available, other recordings covered in this book are much more difficult to obtain, never having been officially released. As a result, until McCartney or his collaborators decide otherwise the likes of 'Hiroshima Sky is Always Blue', 'Stella May Day' (covered in Chapter 14), the *Rushes* Webcast soundtrack and the various remixes described in Chapter Ten all remain in the murky world of the bootlegger. Vigotone and the other labels mentioned at the end of Chapter Nine have made vast sums of money over the years by obtaining (through various less-than-legal means) tapes of unreleased Beatles-related music and distributing them worldwide.

But, as of 2002, these operations look set to face extinction with the proliferation of the internet, and new technology becoming cheaper and cheaper. For less than the price of a few bootleg CDs, an avid record collector can get on-line and start sharing music as MP3s. Of course, the artists and record labels aren't willing to tolerate this any more than they did the companies who had been distributing illegal recordings off-line; in fact, on the internet it's even more difficult to keep track of. Napster may be dead but internet tools such as IRC and FTP (both of which were around before the dawn of the www) remain hotbeds of unreleased material for music traders. The Napster court cases of 2000 (when bands such as Megadeth joined together to shut down a net-based file-sharing system) made it clear what some bands thought of MP3 and bootlegging. Other artists remain a little calmer, however. "I heard that somebody picked it ['Hiroshima Sky is Always Blue'] up on the radio and put it on some internet stuff," commented Yoko Ono to Jody Denberg, "so I said 'whoops, ok!'"

"Hiroshima sky is always blue; Hiroshima sky is always beautiful" sings Ono in a track which unites the extremes of both the avant-garde and the emotions. At times the result of Ono and McCartney's collaboration is disturbing and haunting. At others it's comforting and playful. Proof positive that the last thing avant-garde music should be is cold, inhuman and soulless.

# Postscript

In writing this book, Yoko Ono supplied background notes and articles but, considering the time that had passed since the recording, felt that a full interview would not be helpful. Instead we exchanged word play.

John Lennon and Yoko Ono had subtitled their final album together, 1980s's *Double Fantasy, A Heart Play*. She followed this in 1983 with *Heart Play (Unfinished Dialogue)*, an album of interview material and candid tape recordings of Ono and Lennon in conversation.

To Yoko Ono, words have always been the most effective weapons in her artistic arsenal. She rewrote the idea of the visual arts in the 1960s with her Instruction Paintings series. *Painting for the Skies* (1961), from the legendary book *Grapefruit*, read: "Drill a hole in the sky. Cut out a paper the same size as the hole. Burn the paper. The sky should be pure blue." Another Instruction Painting, *A Piece for Orchestra* from the following year, read,

■ Count all the stars of that night by heart. The piece ends when all the orchestra members finish counting the stars, or when it dawns. This can be done with windows instead of stars.

According to an oft-cited scientific study, the average person has over 40,000 thoughts per day. I took five of Yoko Ono's on 6 June 2002 for a new Heart Play, based on a free-form word association inspired by 'Hiroshima Sky is Always Blue'. I passed her five words, related in some way or another to the track, in the hope that these inspired five words in answer. The ones I suggested were family, Hiroshima, Beatles, experimentation, privacy. "Hi, Ian," she emailed in reply. "This is my word-per-word reply to your five questions."

**1)** Family: Love
**2)** Hiroshima: Healing
**3)** Beatles: Innocence
**4)** Experimentation: Courage
**5)** Privacy: Need

**yoko ono NYC**
**June 6th, 2002**

# TWELVE
# ON STAGE WITH
# ALLEN GINSBERG

I n the mid-1990s, Youth, The Orb and The Fireman were part of a re-emerging post-psychedelic counterculture in the UK. Clubs like Return To The Source, The Big Chill and Megatripolis became platforms for more than music, hosting speakers, debates, and technology sessions as well as DJs and live bands. Megatripolis was at the forefront and scored a major coup when, in 1997, Lee Harris – founder of London's oldest culture shop, Alchemy, and original publisher of *Homegrown* (Europe's first cannabis-oriented magazine) – organised groundbreaking poet Allen Ginsberg's first major London performance since the 1960s. Harris had been inspired by Ginsberg's arrival in London in 1965, recalling:

■ It was on the eleventh of June that I first heard Allen Ginsberg at the International Poetry Reading at the Royal Albert Hall in London. We turned up in our thousands to hear some of the best poets of the Beat Generation. When Allen Ginsberg stood up to read his poems you could feel an electric charge in the air. There he was, like an Old Testament prophet, with his long dark hair and bushy beard, his voice reverberating with emotional intensity. Never before in that hallowed hall had such outrageous and colourful language been heard. Hearing Allen that first time was a revelatory and illuminating experience. That event and his presence in London that summer, helped kindle the spark that set the underground movement alight in the mid-sixties.

"Tonite let's all make love in London as if it were 2001, the years of thrilling god," read Ginsberg at the Albert Hall from his poem 'Who Be Kind To'. The flowerpowered crowd that listened had been hearing about Ginsberg since 1955, when he read his seminal 'Howl' poem in San Francisco. A work which led to an obscenity trial, 'Howl' was a landmark collision of homosexual, psychedelic and Buddhist experiences portrayed through words. According to poet Michael McClure, this saw Ginsberg's "metamorphosis from a quiet brilliant burning bohemian scholar, trapped by his flames and repressions, to epic vocal bard."

A leading light of the Beat movement, Ginsberg had attended Columbia University in the forties with other leading lights such as Jack Kerouac and William Burroughs. He returned to Britain in 1967, appearing at the Roundhouse months after The Beatles' 'Carnival of Light' soundtrack had been aired, for an event called The Congress of the Dialectics of Liberation, followed by Hyde Park's Legalise Pot rally. Ginsberg was "one of the few older people the hippies thought they could trust," Lee Harris recalled.

Although The Beatles had not attended these events, Allen Ginsberg had still made a great impact on them. McCartney had spent an evening in the company of Ginsberg, Mick Jagger, Marianne Faithfull and Barry Miles discussing Eastern mysticism and the Beat poets. While they talked through clouds of smoke and pot-induced hyperbole, McCartney painted a shirt which he presented to Ginsberg on leaving. The poet was seen wearing it the next day at the Legalise Pot rally. John Lennon later referred to Allen Ginsberg as the "elementary penguin" chanting Hare Krishna in his 1967 song 'I Am The Walrus' from *Magical Mystery Tour*. Ginsberg, who later described *Sgt. Pepper's Lonely Hearts Club Band* as "a towering modern opera", was an icebreaker when all four Beatles uncomfortably and embarrassedly met their hero Bob Dylan after a concert at the Royal Albert Hall. Lennon kept in touch with him until he died, with the poet making occasional visits to Lennon and Ono's New York apartment.

Intermittently, Ginsberg met socially with Paul and Linda McCartney during the 1990s. They shared an interest in haikus, naturalistic mini-poetry, and Ginsberg would look over the McCartneys' writings and offer advice. Linda had an especially strong rapport with Ginsberg. Both New Yorkers, Linda wrote haikus until she died, several of which Paul recorded for the avant-garde project *Rushes*, explored in the next chapter. During his New World Tour of 1993, McCartney was in New York filming sketches (with host Alec Baldwin) and live tracks ('Get Out of My Way' and 'Biker Like an Icon') for the *Saturday Night Live* TV show. While there he met up with Ginsberg again and made a point of inviting him back to his family home the next time he was in England.

This came round when Ginsberg joined Anne Waldman and Tom Picard at the Albert Hall for the Return Of The Forgotten poetry festival in 1995. He planned to use the event to perform a new piece called 'Ballad of the Skeletons', which he described as "A political poem, with very definite political statements about the far right, and the monotheist theocratic Stalinists." The poem had recently gone through a name change after Ginsberg was interviewed by US journalist

Steve Silberman. "The original title of Allen's poem was 'Skeleton Key'," Silberman told me. "About a month before Ginsberg wrote it, I had given him my 1993 book on the Grateful Dead, 'Skeleton Key: A Dictionary for Deadheads.' He told me he changed the title to avoid confusion!"

Ginsberg read 'Ballad of the Skeletons' to McCartney when he visited his home and McCartney was impressed enough to film the recital with one of his daughters, using an old eight-millimetre camera. Ginsberg's plan was to perform at the Albert Hall with a live band and he asked McCartney to suggest some possible players. A couple of years later he continued the story with Steve Silberman:

■ I asked McCartney for advice for a young guitarist who's a quick pick-up – a quick study – and he gave me some names. They sounded like older guys, like Jeff Beck. And he said, "But as you're not fixed up with a guitarist, why don't you try me, I love the poem...." and I said, "Sure, it's a date." So he showed up for the sound check. Actually, we rehearsed one night at his place. He showed up at five pm for the sound check, and he bought a box for his family. Got all his kids together, four of them, and his wife, and he sat through the whole evening of poetry, and we didn't say who my accompanist was going to be. We introduced him at the end of the evening, and then the roar went up on the floor of the Albert Hall, and we knocked out the song.

Long-time Ginsberg collaborator David Mansfield remembers the performance from a cassette tape of it which Ginsberg played him when he returned to the US. Having signed his first record deal at age 16, Mansfield spent four years as part of Bob Dylan's band by joining the legendary Rolling Thunder Revue tour. Later, as one of the founding members of Bruce Hornsby and the Range, he won a Grammy for 'The Way It Is'. Today, Mansfield writes and produces film soundtracks, excerpts from which have been performed at both the Royal Albert Hall and the Carnegie Hall.

Mansfield first met Ginsberg on the Rolling Thunder tour and the pair collaborated off and on thereafter. The poet was impressed by Mansfield's dextrous, multi-instrumental skills. "He's a really good all-around vibraphone, guitar, fiddle, dobro, pedal steel [player]. He knows everything. He can play almost anything – the mandolin – exquisite," he once said of him. Mansfield, who has described Ginsberg as "the sweetest revolutionary-queer-Buddhist-maniac I've ever met," told me more about their relationship.

■ It's a long story... I met Allen on the Rolling Thunder Revue when I was about 19. In fact, he wrote about me on the liner notes to Dylan's *Desire* album (even though I wasn't on it). I participated in the sessions produced by John

Hammond Sr around that time, which John eventually released on his own label, as they were too risqué politically (and sexually, in places) for CBS. There was a long period where I didn't see Allen much or play with him, but in the last few years of his life we reconnected and I played on various concerts with him, mostly at The Poetry Project in NYC.

Ginsberg told Mansfield about the Albert Hall concert – and Paul McCartney's involvement – and gave him as noted, a cassette of the performance from that night. "Allen and Paul had performed the song live at the Albert Hall with Paul playing electric guitar – sort of a reggae groove," he remembered. "I think that may have been its first public performance with music. Allen, Lenny Kaye and I then played it live at a benefit for Tibet House at Carnegie Hall (NYC) on 19 February '96, and Lenny and Allen performed it again in Ann Arbor on 5 April 5 '96. Allen always recorded and kept everything, so there were tapes of all these versions."

Lenny Kaye entered into the history books of experimental and alternative music as soon as he stepped on stage with Patti Smith at St Mark's Church in New York in 1971. He laid down raw guitar noise as Smith delivered a spoken word performance. Four albums with Patti Smith and his own band The Lenny Kaye Connection made for important vinyl across the 1970s. To say nothing of Nuggets, the revered double album of 1960s psychedelic garage bands which Kaye devised and curated. Since then he has juggled musical production (Suzanne Vega, James, Soul Asylum and Throwing Muses) with academia (teaching a university course in rock history).

■ I met Allen a couple of times through Patti Smith and became more friendly with him at a benefit for Tibet House at Carnegie Hall in February of 1996. At that, which is an annual benefit, Allen asked me to play bass with him on 'Ballad of the Skeletons', which was a lengthy poem of his which I was, of course, more than happy to do. It was very exciting to play and it went down quite well and Allen particularly seemed to enjoy himself.

Kaye's performance came after 'Ballad of the Skeletons' had been aired with Paul McCartney at the Royal Albert Hall and he told me how Ginsberg was keen at that time to merge rock music with his readings. "It was something I think he liked to do," he told me, "and if there were musicians he knew, and he knew a lot of musicians, then perhaps they would accompany him..."

■ In the audience at Carnegie Hall was Danny Goldberg who, at that time, was the head of Mercury Records in New York and they had a kind of poetry off-shoot called Mouth Almighty. He was very impressed with the performance and thought it would make a good single. He asked me to gather the people together and produce it, though of course it was not specifically a production since my respect for Allen would make it more [like] helping him to achieve his art ... I think it was around May 1996, we went into Kampo Studios on Bond Street in New York City, which was a local studio. I had done some work there, it was a Japanese-run studio and so I thought the atmosphere was good. They were very happy to have Allen there. We went in in May and basically did the tracks.

Although McCartney didn't join Kaye and Mansfield in the recording, Ginsberg was convinced he should add something special to the final disc. "He [McCartney] said if I ever got around to recording it, let him know," Ginsberg told Steve Silberman in one of his last interviews. "So he volunteered, and we made a basic track and sent it to him, on 24 tracks, and he added maracas and drums, which it needed. It gave it a skeleton, gave it a shape. And also organ, he was trying to get that effect of Al Kooper on the early Dylan. And guitar, so he put a lot of work in on that. And then we got it back just in time for Philip Glass to fill in his arpeggios on piano."

Replacing McCartney's live guitar part for the studio version of 'Ballad of the Skeletons' was David Mansfield, who told me more about how the basic tracks were set up. "Mark Ribot, Lenny Kaye, Allen and I recorded the original tracks (mostly 'live') at the Kampo Cultural Center in downtown Manhattan on 23 May 1996. I played guitar and violin. We also recorded 'Amazing Grace' with new lyrics by Allen, and re-recorded one of his older songs 'Don't Smoke' (which I had played on about 20 years earlier as well). Phil Glass and McCartney overdubbed their parts on 'Ballad of the Skeletons' later."

"Allen, I believe, suggested the guitar players," says Kaye of Mansfield and Ribot. "The idea was just to kind of create the settings. I used as my template the music that Allen suggested. I played bass, David and Mark played guitar and Allen recorded his vocals. We did it pretty much live in the studio although, at one point, after Allen did his vocal, we went back over it and made some adjustments to a couple of the lines he felt he hadn't delivered [properly] and so we were able to approach it as you would a standard vocal on a record, where you'd be in the studio and we'd kind of punch in a few words, or something..."

■ It was just a great experience for me to sit there in the control room and say, well, let's try to get this line a little better, and we'd work on it. Allen was very into working on his delivery. There was a very nice feeling in the studio ... I remember at one point he came out and showed us how to do the Buddhist walk, in which you walk in a way that your feet become one with the curvature of the Earth and you move within the Earth's orbit. It was a very beautiful thing ... It was a nice insight into him.

According to David Mansfield, Lenny Kaye was the perfect record producer. "I think he's wonderful on both counts," he told me. "He knows when to leap in with conviction and when to get out of the way and let it happen."

As avant-garde composer and organiser of the Tibet House benefits, Philip Glass was a natural choice to play piano. He and Ginsberg shared the same Buddhist teacher and adviser, Gelek Rinpoche. Twice a year they would decamp to Rinpoche's large meditation retreat, where they would often play and write music together. "Philip Glass came in after and overdubbed his piano part," Kaye remembers. "He was a very good friend of Allen's and actually performed behind Allen on several occasions, playing one of his piano pieces as Allen read."

"Philip was easy," says Lenny Kaye, "he just sat down and improvised and created his part and then we sent the tapes to Paul in England..." For McCartney's part, "He added drums and keyboard and sent them back. I believe he also added some percussion as well. I did take great amusement in the fact that I'm playing bass to Paul's drum. We were a rhythm section even though we were divided by an ocean..."

Crediting the track to all four lead players – Ginsberg, McCartney, Glass and Kaye – Mouth Almighty released 'Ballad of the Skeletons', describing it as "a contemporary protest song that rails against today's heartless global political establishment." For the *New York Times* it was "basically a diatribe against [Ginsberg's] familiar enemies, the military-industrial complex, politicians, homophobes and censorship." It became a surprise hit – enough for MTV to request a video from Mouth Almighty. In a resurgence of acclaim for Ginsberg he was interviewed by *People* magazine, which wondered how a poet interacted with rock musicians. But to him there was no difference. "McCartney is a poet, Lennon was a poet, Dylan is a supreme poet," he told them.

On a modest budget (by the standards of most MTV videos), a film was produced for $14000 with the help of Ginsberg's friend, director Gus Van Sant (*Drugstore Cowboy, My Own Private Idaho*). MTV viewers lapped it up and the song and video became a 'buzz clip' and received a showing at the Sundance Film Festival. America's youth had a new subversive anthem and Ginsberg had a hit record at age 70. "It was quite a cool video," remembers Kaye. "Whether you could call it a hit, I'm not sure. It was chosen as one of 100 best records in Australia, by some magazine..."

■ Basically it got out there and showed a kind of direction that Allen, unfortunately, was never able to follow up because he started getting sick the following year. There was no hint of it at the sessions. Certainly he seemed to have his energy, drive and inspiration intact. For myself I was particularly saddened. Because of this record we were starting to develop a very nice working relationship and a friendship and who knows where it all might have gone to. One of the great might-have-beens...

I spoke to Lenny Kaye at his home in New York City where he was finishing a book on "the crooners of the 1930s" ("a very interesting saga of a pre-rock 'n' roll time...") and playing music at a more relaxed pace. "I just work with Patti and do some stuff of my own and play guitar for my friends basically," he told me.

> ■ 'Ballad of the Skeletons' was a good time ... I think maybe we might have spent two days doing the recording and fixing-ups. Maybe another day for mixing. It was one of the most valuable and appreciated experiences of my life, getting to see how Allen works. Someone like myself, who looked at the Beat poets and took an inspiration for lifestyle, it was a great honour to be able to be in the same room with him and work on his vocals with him ... It's always nice to talk about this moment in time, because it's very special to me.

As mentioned in Chapter Two, the UK's Black Dog avant-garde outfit have often been at the cutting edge of electronics and the music/Beat poetry overlap. In recent years they've been driven by Keir Jens-Smith, who devised their 2002 album *Unsavoury Products*, a collaboration with William Burroughs released on a record label named after Allen Ginsberg and Philip Glass' 1993 album *Hydrogen Jukebox*. "While today's critics discuss, vote and evaluate the literary and musical offerings of the late 20th century, it is the Beat writers and The Beatles that history is proving to be the most original, socially aware, inspirational and groundbreaking artists," Jens-Smith told me. "Specifically, in Allen Ginsberg and Paul McCartney you have two artists that embody a vision and a cultural criticism shared and expressed through their art."

> ■ Ginsberg and McCartney both found inspiration and peace in Eastern thought and philosophies in the late sixties, practising and preaching this thinking from China and India; Ginsberg with Buddhism and The Beatles with Krishna. Both shared joyous views of human nature and their unique expression and practice of empathy. This only goes to further highlight both men's alternative thinking and unconventional minds, giving them a voice to showcase their lack of mental satisfaction with the doctrines and dogmas of the west...
>
> These two men have in turn been key figures involved in redefining their art forms. Ginsberg (together with the rest of the Beats) vastly helped in developing a new interpretation of popular literature and poetry, and how it was perceived and accepted, bringing it to a new audience desperate to hear a voice they didn't know was missing. The work of the Beats from the 1950s

onwards subconsciously paved the way for the hippie movement in the '60s, with their heartfelt belief in peace and love and their active support of all things anti-corporate, anti-war, anti-propaganda and anti-hate.

McCartney and The Beatles helped redefine what music could be in the '60s, sitting on the fringe of popular music yet swiftly embraced by the masses and subsequently granted worldwide acceptance. Being a member of what, to this day, is still cited as the most influential band on contemporary music culture. Like the Beats, McCartney is never afraid of pushing the boundaries of his artistic talent, as a genuine multimedia artist.

For Jens-Smith, McCartney and Ginsberg were perfect collaborators, even if it did take place over 30 years after their first meeting. "What is also interesting is that both men's work is still as valid, important and popular today as it was during conception," he remarked on browsing the McCartney back catalogue with me.

■ They both shared a unique vision and drove a vehicle for free minds and alternative thinkers to ride upon. Key to the work of Ginsberg has been his poetry. His melodic approach owed a lot to the inspiration of the jazz and bop scene of America in the late '50s and the readings they all gave in San Francisco's jazz clubs. To the untrained mind his words appear and sound as if written to imaginary melodies, with their own stanzas and rhythms. This makes his work and his performance the perfect compliment to music.

Lenny Kaye, on the other hand, experienced the fusion of music with Ginsberg's poetry first-hand. "He had often done musical things," he told me…

■ He was not unfamiliar with the song form. I believe at one point there was an album mooted with him and Bob Dylan. But who knows exactly how these things develop … I believe that the same year [as 'Ballad of the Skeletons'] he had his collected works released, and he had a celebration at St Mark's Church in which the producer Hal Wilner gathered together musicians from all stripes of New York and gave them each a poem of Allen's, in which he wanted to construct a musical setting. As Allen read through the poems each one would come up and perform his piece with them… He did enjoy blending music. I know that he would sometimes accompany himself on the harmonium and he always liked the concept of music embracing poetry, I'm sure back from the old Beat days when little jazz combos would play behind the Beat poets. Allen also liked it when things got kind of a little wild. I remember we also played 'Ballad of the Skeletons' at a Buddhist benefit in Ann Arbor, Michigan that same year [1996], in the fall. He wanted me to play on guitar with an MXR fade

> shifter and in the middle break he kept encouraging me to get wilder and
> wilder and wilder until it kind of sharded off into noise. He just really liked the
> excitement of sound.

The success of 'Ballad of the Skeletons' led Mercury to request a full album from
Ginsberg and MTV planned an *Unplugged* special. Both would have featured
Paul McCartney, playing alongside Bob Dylan, Beck and Philip Glass for
*Unplugged*. But none of these projects came to fruition. Ginsberg died of cancer
on 5 April 1997. As Bob Holman from Mouth Almighty records remarked, "His
death, like his life, was a defining, orchestrated moment: a beautifully choreo-
graphed departure reminiscent of the final lines of 'Ballad of the Skeletons,' his
venture into rock stardom at the age of 70."

"He was a very gentle, sweet soul as far as I'm concerned," remembered
David Mansfield, "and I miss him greatly..."

# THIRTEEN

# CROSSING THE BRIDGE TO PALO VERDE

In 1998 Paul McCartney teamed up with Youth again for a second experimental album as The Fireman. They left behind the Teutonic techno of *Strawberries Oceans Ships Forest* to record McCartney's first work in subliminal, ambient territory. An album which dubs post-rock, horse tapes, phone sex, poetry readings and sitars across a chill-out soundscape. As such they took a whole new approach to recording and delivered McCartney's most spaced-out, yet most melodic and listenable, avant-garde work to date.

McCartney and Youth again used their Fireman pseudonym, in order to put this second collaboration, *Rushes*, and its new ambient direction on a level playing field with its peers. But this is one album that would be impossible to categorise as an 'off-shoot' or 'side-project'. *Rushes* was written, collaged and recorded during the most turbulent and emotional period in McCartney's life to date – his wife's final battle against cancer.

"I think in hindsight you can hear the emotions of what was going on in his life," says Youth when he listens back to *Rushes*, "or what was going on in our lives, and it becomes quite poignant. It was while Linda was going through the cancer and, towards the end, dying." Linda McCartney had been involved in the making of both Fireman albums. "We got her to do some spoken word on it and she was quite involved in the first one as well," Youth reveals, "just encouraging and playing percussion."

But throughout the making of *Rushes*, Linda's cancer was never talked about or dwelled on, certainly not in the studio. "It was quite relaxed, as I remember it," recalls Youth, "and I remember they were quite calm. I certainly wasn't aware of how seriously ill she was..."

Ambient music was born in 1978 when experimental musician and producer

Brian Eno first described a new form of music that a listener might "swim in… float in… get lost inside." Such environmental music had hit a mass market in the 1950s, thanks to the Muzak corporation – their 'easy listening' versions of well-known hits were the first ever mass-produced examples of ambient music. No small inspiration for McCartney's *Thrillington* album, the music of Muzak quickly hit the bottom end of listening quality. Thanks also to a backlash against piped music of any kind it was soon consigned to the history books. Although originally designed, like Muzak, as an element of modern living spaces, the music Eno was devising would sound completely different.

He called it ambient music to separate it from Muzak's canned varieties and described how it was a genre "intended to induce calm and a space to think." These revolutionary thoughts first appeared on the sleeve of 1978's *Music for Airports*, the first ever ambient album (although Eno had refined his style on the preceding *Discreet Music*). A conscious decision to create a new form of music that was both meditational and highly integrated into the pace of modern living, it was one of four key releases on Eno's own Ambient Records label, complimented by Harold Budd's *The Plateaux of Mirrors*, Laraaji's *Day of Radiance* and his own *On Land*.

The almost subliminal sound and highbrow concept of *Music for Airports* was initially treated as something of a joke by critics. But it caught the imagination of avant-garde composers and eccentric pop bands, and the 1980s saw ambient music develop further with key releases by Robert Fripp, Laurie Anderson, Michael Brook and others. *Music for Airports* was created before the synthesiser revolutionised experimental pop. At the same time Eno was moving into a production capacity, defining a unique sound on record for Talking Heads and U2 thanks to the use of ambient textures. Fripp also furthered ambient production, both in collaboration with Peter Gabriel (himself one of rock's key exponents of the form) and solo.

In the first half of the eighties, Kraftwerk, Jean-Michel Jarre and other synthesiser pioneers pushed ambient music even further. Having spent the middle part of that decade dovetailing alarmingly with 'new age' and relaxational music, ambient received a huge boost from the late 1980s' acid house, rave and techno scenes. 'Ambient house' was born, and the story of this unique genre catches up with the work of Youth detailed in Chapter Ten.

By the mid-1990s, ambient house was coexisting quite happily with the more intellectual, original ambient artists, under the loose umbrella of chill-out. That is, until the corporate record industry's thirst for the 'Next Big Thing' came along. Fuelled by the commercial exploitation of Ibiza and anything remotely connected with Balearic dance music, chill-out became pushed into every supermarket compilation until eventually there were no true chill-out tracks left to put on further compilations. But a genre that has influenced so many aspects of music cannot help but evolve further, with Eno himself describing its spin-offs, developments and influence as "like Chinese Whispers – unrecognisable but intriguing."

It was at that late 1990s stage, with ambient music on the cusp of chill-out, when Paul McCartney decided to start experimenting with the genre. Perhaps he and Youth wanted to record the definitive Fireman album, following the first's mere collection of remixes. Their finished work is an exemplary 70s minutes of ambient – environmental and organic, compelling and personal. At the same time it is, quite literally, wallpaper music. Many trademarks of the genre are scattered across its eight tracks. Mantra-like piano and guitar lines, vocal fragments buried deep in the mix. Simplicity. Sound effects. Recurring themes. Ethereal melody.

McCartney had left the *Strawberries Oceans Ships Forest* session for the acoustic rock of *Flaming Pie* and The Beatles' Anthologies. Meanwhile, Youth remained heavily involved in the dance scene, juggling this with mainstream musical activities too. In the latter he produced (and won a Best Producer Brit Award for) The Verve's *Urban Hymns* album. In the former he continued with his trance label Dragonfly (which would celebrate its tenth anniversary in 2002) and set up three other small labels, each with a distinct musical direction. For one, his psychedelic/Goa trance outlet Liquid Sound Design, he started with an 11-point manifesto. It could equally be read as a manifesto for *Rushes*, The Fireman or any of Youth's other experimental work in the 1990s.

■ **1.** Transform sound as a medium to envelope the senses.
   **2.** Undermining conditions of meaning.
   **3.** Define the difference between source and copy.
   **4.** To express that which we know rather than that which we see.
   **5.** Displace, translate and repossess.
   **6.** Reinvestigate, experiment, create.
   **7.** Sound drawing and visual fidelity.
   **8.** To facilitate the process of research and design of the creative idea.
   **9.** Fetishise snapshots of apparent reality.
   **10.** Create structures that facilitate and allow social function and
       free expression.
   **11.** Make a better world.

The music may be poles apart, but the similarities between the recording of *Rushes* and *Thrillington* are strong: McCartney handing over control to a producer, dropping in and out of the sessions, and recording it all in a very short space of time. "We only did about seven days' recording," says Youth, "maybe six days, not even that. We didn't spend a lot of time on it but that's Paul's vibe.

He likes to work fast and keep it spontaneous and keep the momentum going and not get too kind of intellectual or stuck in the mud on something." The only tracks that remained in the mud were 'Plum Jam' and 'Through the Marshes', two now legendary unreleased Fireman tracks.

For *Rushes*, McCartney finally let his avant-garde ideas run free and Youth channelled them onto tape. "He'd keep coming up with these mad things that they'd done," he remembers. "Or that he'd heard someone had done, because he's a big fan of things. And we'd just say, 'OK, well, let's try that'. Whenever he worked we worked really fast and really fluidly. And nothing ever got to the point where we were sitting around not doing much."

The finished double-album is McCartney's most accomplished and confident avant-garde work to date. It starts with an 18-minute epic split into two tracks. 'Palo Verde' has its main guitar line pulled out to the front for the six-minute intro, 'Watercolour Guitars'. 'Watercolour Guitars' is an ethereal McCartney guitar line, with Youth's trademark spacey bleeps coming in and out.

Pink Floyd's influence on the McCartney/Youth partnership is clear. McCartney's melody is highly reminiscent of Floyd's Dave Gilmour. In fact, Laurence Juber was sure when he first heard *Rushes* that it wasn't McCartney playing at all. Gilmour would actually crop up later that year on the cathartic *Run Devil Run* album of rock and roll covers. And Youth later followed his love of Pink Floyd through to its natural conclusion with his *Orchestral Pink Floyd* album. Another obvious reference in McCartney's guitar work across 'Watercolour Guitars' is 'Sentinel' and Mike Oldfield's *Tubular Bells*.

In 2001, UK music industry svengali Simon Napier-Bell wrote *Black Vinyl White Powder*, his personal history of English pop music, from rock and roll to the present day. He made some pertinent points about the more experimental forms of dance music, name-checking The Orb and also acts like Massive Attack, Underworld and Goldie. "Working with keyboards and computers, painting with sound and rhythm," he said, "they could create an aural collage that could be considered on a par with the best contemporary art of all sorts." And, as Napier-Bell concluded, "Like all seriously considered art, the imagery contained in it was often obsessive and personal."

"I think there's a lot of emotion in a lot of ambient music," agrees Youth, "even the sort of really minimal darker stuff like Biosphere. Especially Aphex Twin. But when I think of things like The Orb, there's a lot of emotional depth in that. I think it's because it's kind of spatial and it's sort of atmospheric, it allows you to get into a kind of different... Quite often a lot of it's jolly, but I mean The Fireman stuff has always been quite dark."

'Palo Verde' is a prime piece of emotional ambient music and is one of McCartney's most poignant paeans to his late wife. In March 1998, doctors found that Linda's cancer had spread to her liver, but the family tried to carry on living as normally as possible. For Paul, this meant juggling two musical projects – *Rushes* with Youth and a collection of Linda's own recordings called *Wide Prairie*.

*Wide Prairie*'s 16 songs were eventually released posthumously in October. It gathered the highlights of Linda's on-off recording career, which dated back to 'Seaside Woman', a reggae-inspired number from a McCartney family holiday to Jamaica at the time of *Wings Wild Life*. Although her recordings were directionless and patchy (often only existing as moral support for Paul), in the later years she found an energy through the influence of both haiku and her fight for animal rights.

A Japanese form of poetry, haiku was a love of both Paul and Linda as well as Allen Ginsberg. As Ginsberg mentioned during the making of 'Ballad of the Skeletons', haiku would be a main topic of conversation during the evenings he shared with the McCartneys. By 1998, haiku rivalled photography as Linda's main creative outlet. Her work formed the lyrical basis for some of the *Wide Prairie* songs and were printed in their own right in a retrospective of her photojournalism. Entitled *Light from Within* (which she also used as the title of an emotionally charged rocker on *Wide Prairie*), the book was compiled by her daughter Mary and featured portraits of Ginsberg, the Grateful Dead and others. Alongside the more experimental *Sun Prints*, its 155 pictures stand as testimony to her skill as a photographer. Various haikus were scattered amongst the pictures.

Haiku dates back over 700 years. As one of the most popular forms of poetry in the world, it is characterised by its simple, brief and non-rhyming verse. Famously simple to read, haiku is difficult to write. Although popular in schools, the haiku masters in history – most notably Basho from the 1600s – would train for decades before producing their best work.

Writers of this form follow a set of rules. But none of these are set in stone, and academics have been trying to pin down haiku's true essence for some years, most notably Blyth (1949) and Higginson (1985).

■ Poetry that, although only a few lines long, can convey a sense of awe or transcendental wonder; observations of both nature and human nature; distinct images from any of the five senses in favour of generalisations; always presented in the present tense.

These are the main 'rules' of writing English haiku that Linda McCartney followed. It's a style that's also apparent in Paul McCartney's mainstream lyric writing, most notably the chorus on *Driving Rain*'s 'Rinse the Raindrops'.

The narration that floats in and out of 'Palo Verde' is made up of three of Linda's haikus, all of which are reprinted in *Light from Within*. One paints an evocative picture, summed up in just ten lines, of climbing the high, hot plains of her Arizona reserve on one of her beloved horses. From this, Youth sampled Linda reading the first line, which also formed the basis for the album's title: "The adrenaline rushes through you…" In another, truly psychedelic, poem Linda describes a spectacular sunset. Perfect chill-out poetry. Extracts like "So amazing that you think you're on drugs" are mixed almost subliminally into the music.

Linda McCartney summed up much of her love of, and philosophy of, life in her haikus. For *Rushes*, Paul recorded his wife reciting these pieces and Youth blended them into the soundscape they were producing together. The end result is dreamlike and touching at the same time. Beneath organic analogue synths, Linda's contribution is juxtaposed by an ethereal bass solo from her husband. It was Brian Wilson who inspired McCartney's bass-playing to fly off on melodies of its own, as it does here, and not just follow the root note of the song. This is as close to a duet as chill-out has ever come.

Aside from Linda's readings the only other voice on 'Palo Verde' is a melodic vocal line – "Let me love you, always" – which weaves in and out of the music. Sticking to the rule he gave Youth of only sampling from original material, this is taken from a track of the same name recorded as a demo during McCartney's year 'off' for songwriting in 1995. Aside from the glimpses used in 'Palo Verde' it remains unreleased. But the inclusion of McCartney's distinct vocals certainly fuelled speculation that The Fireman was his work.

'Auraveda' is similarly epic in length and full of McCartney's sitar-playing, something he saves entirely for avant-garde projects. The track builds with sitar backed by tablas and shakers for over five minutes. From there other instruments come in to play – harmonium, flutes and a strange, over-processed guitar/vocal hybrid noise. Well past the seven-minute mark, 'Auraveda' breaks down completely to a mixture of eastern bells and classic Youth synthesiser pads. Keyboard arpeggios replace the sitar-playing for a dubby piece of slow (126 beats per minute), completely instrumental trance. The track closes with distorted sub-bass meanderings and playful, discordant guitar – a taste of things to come.

If 'Palo Verde' was the ambient love song, 'Fluid' was the ambient sex song. It even included recordings McCartney and Youth made by dialling a phone sex line from their studio. Before the album was even in the shops, the *Rushes* press release dropped the phone sex reference. At the same time as name-dropping Apple Records' Derek Taylor, it still attempted to deny McCartney's involvement.

■ It would be massively incorrect to assert that Sir P McC has anything whatso-ever to do with the fact one track on the *Rushes* album (called 'Fluid') features the quite obvious sounds of a woman engaged in what the late and great Derek Taylor called "charvering." On the same (wildly speculative) fact, Sir P McC's publicist could not, of course, possibly comment on documented affidavits from DJs all over Europe who – when asked to fill in the record company's DJ Reaction forms – voted The Fireman's *Rushes* to be great music to charver to."

"Like the bastard offspring of Moby and Ash Ra Tempel," was how one journalist described this track in a somewhat astounded review of *Rushes*, which they called "a record worth listening to (if you're taking a hefty amount of drugs)." 'Fluid' was taken as the lead track from the finished album, with a 12" and CD promo of remixes provided by Nitin Sawhney, as well as appearing on a promotional album sampler with an unused take of another track, 'Bison'.

'Fluid' is classic Fireman. Pure Youth chill-out techniques mixed with McCartney's ear for melody. As such the opening minutes are a simple-scape of a heavily reverbed, evolving five-note piano refrain and hypnotic recordings of a woman asking intermittently "Have you ever had an out of body experience?" and "What does the concept of time mean to you?" The whole track is on a bed of tapes of running water, like an intravenous recording of fluids coursing through the body.

Elsewhere, bass counter-melodies and guitar counter-counter are mixed in and, although the track remains at a meditational tempo, it is made up of layers upon layers of sound. Some of these layers are voices, not from Linda McCartney or anyone connected with Youth and McCartney, but taken from a variety of sources. The "ooh, yeah" female vocals, which the pair had sampled from a phone sex line, come in to the track at one of its quieter, more atmospheric moments.

The lyrics, if they can be called such, come from a recording of a young woman describing a UFO encounter. A familiar source of ethereal words in Youth's early work with The Orb, the woman describes a "white light, but not like a plane. It was... too bright for that. It was, um... travelling quite slowly and then became really bright, brighter than any star I'd have seen, and then... faded away and then became bright again and then travelled away at the same speed... It had me convinced anyway."

'Fluid' builds and builds and, just before the rhythm breaks in (after over ten minutes of beat-less ambience), a looped voice from an astrology phone line can be heard deep in the mix. "When you least expect it, things are going to start changing," says the psychic.

When the beat breaks in, the track mixes into the next, 'Appletree Cinnabar Amber'. The 'Fluid' elements remain but are overlaid with a dirty, Ry Cooder-esque guitar line and a rhythm track. It's clearly McCartney on drums but playing – surprise! – a classic hip hop loop. Another odd sound in the 'Appletree Cinnabar Amber' extension of 'Fluid' is a subtle, almost spy theme-style, harpsichord counterpoint. *Thrillington* fan Mike Keneally would have been proud.

Track six on *Rushes*, 'Bison', is an oddity. A rambling, shambling, freeform punk jam for bass, drums and guitar, it couldn't be less ambient. Reminiscent, perhaps, of Wings' 1971 New York play-around, 'The Great Cock and Seagull Race', it's totally discordant in the 'verse' but has a razor-sharp melody with familiar elements from 'Auraveda' acting as a 'chorus'. 'Bison' actually saw Youth coming out of the production booth and playing live bass.

> ■ That was a jam. McCarney's a good drummer, you see. Bonham used to really like his drumming, apparently, and was an admirer. He played all the drums on *Band on the Run*, and he is a good drummer. So we said, "OK, let's have a jam and I'll play bass." But it was quite intense because I had all his team there, and they were all like guys who go back to the '60s and they were all like "Oh, you're going to play bass on a Paul McCartney record are you?!" And they all stood there with their arms crossed while McCartney presented me with a bass. But it was a good laugh… I didn't even think anything of it at the time, I just thought I would jam along. I knew that he liked dub and so it was a bit of mutant, dubby, tribal stomp thing. And we did a live take to get the drums and then afterwards he said "Go on, have another go at doing your bass as an over-dub" and I went through all that. I don't think he's precious at all, he's often saying, "Oh go on, you have a go."

Youth was happy to step in on bass but found the most rewarding part of *Rushes* was drawing out McCartney's avant-garde streak. "I'm more interested, actually, to sort of get him to do everything and then let me play around with it," he told me. "But I do step in occasionally, but not very often. I think it's much more interesting for the music if it's him, to be honest, because I think I fire him off in different ways. But to use his musicality is a good idea."

In 'Bison', McCartney and Youth ventured – if only briefly – away from chill-out and ambient into post-rock territory. Post-rock was rock's last fight for life and a new direction before the last century folded. Balanced between Chicago and England, at its worst it was freeform jazz meets grunge for beard-stroking intellectuals. At its best it was a breath of fresh air for rock music, replacing attitude with something truly alternative. Bands like Tortoise, Laika, Fridge, Labradford and Ui all – for a brief period, which coincided with the making of *Rushes* – gave new life to the alternative rock scene.

Simon Reynolds, a journalist for *The Wire* magazine, is believed to have first coined the term, which was summed up rather well (in a review of Tortoise's second album *Millions Now Living Will Never Die* (1996) by Sheryl Scott of Sister Ray Records) as "Dub, Kraut, free jazz, avant-electronica and classical minimalism played by veterans of the punk circuit." While *Rushes* was being finished off,

I reviewed Ui's *Lifelife* album in April 1998 for *DJ* magazine, in which the band presented "a melting pot of real instruments and electronic vibes in a mix-down of phat, beat-driven sound-lumps. This is far too loose and far too damn funky to be called fusion…"

The full, glorious seven-minute thrash of 'Bison' remains unreleased. Instead McCartney and Youth edited it down to a compact two-minute wake-up call, which comes in as the blissful *Rushes* is about to wind down. '7AM', the album's penultimate track, is an otherworldly trio of the analogue arpeggios from 'Auraveda', classical strings and, when percussion does appear, clinks and clanks from McCartney's tin-pot sample session.

Six minutes in, a few McCartney vocals slip in. They're from another unreleased demo tape for a song called 'Hey Now (What are you looking at me for?)', which, like 'Let Me Love You Always', had been penned in 1995. With 'Watercolour Rush', a two-minute coda to the opening track, *Rushes* comes full circle.

Although word as to who exactly The Fireman was had leaked out with the release of *Strawberries Oceans Ships Forest*, *Rushes* was again released almost completely anonymously. The names Youth and McCartney appeared nowhere on the sleeves. "I was very impressed that he played everything himself," Nitin Sawhney recalled of the first time he heard *Rushes*. "He didn't want to sing on it, he didn't want his vocal identity stamped all over it. He wanted it to be heard for what it was. That was what was nice about it, it wasn't about glitz."

As if to further distance McCartney's traditional image from *Rushes*, some odd photographs from the family archives were scattered across the otherwise mini-malist packaging. McCartney's backside, a fireman ornament, a holiday beach snap (McCartney's back with the word "fire" written across it in sun-tan lotion), and so on. Record collectors had a field day with promo versions including posters, holographic labels and secret Arabic messages. The main image that threw people off the McCartney trail was used on the LP's inner sleeve – a nude woman sitting on a bed, gazing out of a window. Completely full frontal, although with strategically placed Fireman logos on the poster version and with a Celtic dial overlaid, reminiscent of images from *Back to the Egg*. Precisely who the young woman is, remains a mystery.

This "incognito ambient dance album," as *Billboard* described it, appeared on Hydra Records. An imprint of EMI used solely for McCartney's experimental out-put, Hydra is the closest McCartney has come to Zapple since the sixties. He also used it to release the *Liverpool Sound Collage* album two years later.

The Fireman's 70-minute chill-out soundtrack – with naked female co-star – was released on an unsuspecting public on 20 October 1998. In retrospect it's no wonder the public had difficult believing this was the work of Paul McCartney, especially as the album was 'announced' with typical Fireman flair. Suitably obscure adverts were accompanied by a press release signed "Rudely, 7am." Which read as follows (complete with eccentric spelling and punctuation)…

■ The Fireman brings bison for trancing in the streets.
   The Fireman gives a watercolour rush, fluid.
   The Fireman understands darsh walls and emerdeen sky. Do you?
   The Fireman know's a lemon's peal.
   And the powers of the equinox.
   The Fireman heard a girl's snatch-talk of a saucer flying.
   The Fireman likes the sound of mud.
   The Fireman plays it all; Bass. Watercolour Guitar. Keyboards. Cymbal.
   And the fool.
   The Fireman looped a shadow's clipclop. And made auraveda.
   The Fireman taped the talk of sex.
   The Moon is right. So The Fireman comes.
   The Moon is right. So The Fireman comes.

*Rushes* was such an accomplished ambient album that, if released as Youth & McCartney, it could have been highly successful (and a turning point in the popular view of McCartney). But Youth was happy for it to remain 'unknown'. "I've always seen it as quite avant-garde fringe music," he told me. "I never saw it as a chart contender. Mind you, I always thought The Orb was like that. A lot of music I've done I thought was like that and then it's become popular, to a degree. I wouldn't have expected them to have done a big number on it. I quite like the way it was kind of low-key and anonymous."

Nitin Sawhney agrees. He sensed the emotional nature of the second Fireman album when McCartney visited him in his bedsit studio. "In a way he couldn't have avoided being as huge as he is and as rich as he is," he remembered, "but he's much more about expression, he's still a great artist."

■ He's somebody who has a side to him which he wants to express. I think The Fireman project… in a way, what was going on was very much the first expression since his wife died. It was a very genuine thing and he didn't want it to be a big commercial thing. It was much more of an expression that was coming from his playing and not from the concept of, "Well, this has got to do well commercially." He does think commercially and he said, "Normally I would be thanking you now because this is going to do well, but with this I don't want to think like that, I want it to be just what it is and it should work and make sense and be creatively exciting for people." That was what I liked about his approach to it.

When the secret did get out, McCartney's involvement in The Fireman put ambient music in front of a whole new audience. And his songwriting skill, however transformed by Youth and the new devices and rules of ambience, meant that listeners found it unexpectedly accessible. Few ambient albums had ever appeared in the pages of the *Sunday Philadelphia Inquirer* but they loved it, describing 'Watercolour Guitars' in particular as "disarmingly pretty." "An interesting thing happens when pop songwriters ditch their identities, don experimental gear, and set off for unknown destinations in the ambient realm," wrote the *Inquirer*'s Tom Moon. "They often find more melodic stuff than the techno knob-turners who live there."

Outside the mainstream, *Rushes* was also welcomed by the more unorthodox music press. The *Weekly Wire* likened *Rushes* to "half-ambient, half-pop artists like American Analog Set, Flying Saucer Attack or the folks on Darla Records' Bliss-Out Series." (But they also knew where to draw the line, calling *Strawberries Oceans Ships Forest* "a rather tiresome collection of remixes of a rather tiresome song.") *Aural Innovations*, known as 'The Global Source for SpaceRock Exploration', thought *Rushes* stood out from other ambient records of the time as "dreamy ambient music that mixes lots of wild space sounds, making it a bit more adventurous than most..." They liked the relaxation elements but warned listeners not to get too relaxed and miss out on some of its intricacies and subtle, subliminal moments. "It's a pleasure to know that Paul McCartney is still interested in sound and pure musical possibilities not having left all that behind in the '60s," wrote *Aural Innovations*' Jerry Kranitz.

But it would be wrong to say that *Rushes* was universally acclaimed. Far from it. *Q* magazine in the UK was scathing, with Ian Cranna calling the tracks "aimless doodles" which "exhibit no particular imagination, tunefulness or evocative qualities, and barely hold the attention at times." Some reviewers, meanwhile, still had one foot painfully stuck in the past. Reminiscent of *Rolling Stone*'s take on the Siegen exhibition described in the next chapter, Ryan Schreiber ended his review of *Rushes* by asking, "How much better could a collaboration between John Lennon and The Orb's Dr Alex Paterson have been? It'd have beat the shit out of *Flaming Pie*, that's for damn sure." Oh dear.

McCartney and Youth decided to name their first 'proper' collaboration *Rushes*. Beatle-ologists have long believed that the name was a 'Penny Lane' reference, partly because McCartney was on the cusp of beginning his avant-garde works when he wrote 'Penny Lane' (working on it in the same month as 'Carnival of Light') and partly because of the lyrics from the seventh verse, where The Fireman (a reference to McCartney's father) "rushes in" from the pouring rain. But – more obviously – the reference also appears in the first line of the first haiku that Linda McCartney recites in Palo Verde – "The adrenaline rushes through you..."

Emotionally, *Rushes* had provided an outlet for McCartney's turbulent feelings of 1998. Musically it was a rock-solid ambient album which, with Youth's expertise, also offered something to the genre itself. With McCartney's name attached, it put a challenging avant-garde genre in front of a new audience. *Rushes* also showed signs that McCartney might start to embrace his avant-garde side and include it in his overall work. "It's ironic that it took an alias for Paul McCartney to make his most interesting, listenable album since ... geez, probably *Venus and Mars* in 1975," wrote Michael Henningsen. "But perhaps he should apply this newfound experimentalism to his next 'real' album..."

Youth was thrilled with the finished result. "I was much happier with *Rushes*," he said, comparing it to the previous Fireman album. "And I hear *Rushes* when I play at festivals that I'm doing trance at. Last year in Africa I heard Mixmaster Morris spinning it. And I've heard it in other places. People mention it to me as being something they've got a lot from. It sounded beautiful in context in those places. It really worked."

In the third of Linda McCartney's haikus sampled by Youth at Hog Hill for 'Palo Verde', she talks of flowers, aromas, skies and poppies. An almost addictive evening air. The poem, which begins "The flowers turn into fruit," is full of haiku-style references to nature and the revitalising blasts of wonder and inspiration it clearly gave her. From this poetry it's clear that the vast plains of Arizona were calling her and in March 1998 she relocated there with her family. In April she died, aged 56.

# FOURTEEN

# FROM STEEL
# TOWERS TO SIEGEN
## (AND BALACLAVAS)

**P**aul McCartney's avant-garde work hasn't been confined to the "shameless construction" of the "vinyl environment", as Andrew Poppy of Chapter One would put it. Many experimental musicians stick purely to recorded sound as it would be impossible to recreate their work in live performance. But in 1998, as a platform for his two most eccentric recordings to date – *Rushes* and *Feedback*, McCartney embarked on his two most wildly avant-garde performances ever.

For *Rushes* he and Youth created an hour's worth of live remixes and word play in a primitive but psychedelic webcast. For *Feedback* he created a Stonehenge-like installation of video screens set in steel monoliths, each one overlapping music and video on the other. Both these psychedelic, 'generative' performances have pushed against an age in which technology promotes repetition rather than spontaneity in music.

Some of McCartney's most extreme (and most 'unknown') musical experiments have not been on record, but performed live. If *Rushes* had surprised McCartney fans with just how far his music could extend into experimental areas, he was about to surprise them even further. His first public appearance after Linda's death was in October 1998 for the Fireman webcast, one hour of kaleidoscopic visuals, subliminal messages and extended, live renditions of the album. An unlikely return to the public eye was made stranger still by the fact that McCartney was still trying to shroud his involvement in The Fireman in mystery – and so spent the entire performance in disguise. "We'd done *Rushes* and, although he didn't want to tour it, he wanted to do something to promote it," Youth explains. "But because we were anonymous it was tricky!"

■ He came up with the idea of doing a live gig at Abbey Road that we could broadcast over the web. I think it was one of the first ones. McCartney was in disguise, he had these mad masks and things. There were these kind of mad oil wheels and lightshows going on which they were filming. It was just us, no audience, but he had a big team of guys there. There were about 15 guys just doing the web thing, there were roadies and all sorts, you know. So it was pretty mad in there. It just managed to fly, we took off and it sounded great. I thought it was brilliant…

Broadcasting live sound and vision via the internet had been a reality since June 1994, when California garage heads Severe Tire Damage became the first band ever to webcast a live concert. But ease and speed of use for broadcasters and, more importantly, viewers had only recently become a reality when *Rushes* was released in 1998. Back in 1994, when The Rolling Stones became the first name band to stage such an event, I wrote in my book *Music & The Internet* that "you may need hardware of military proportions and software that would take weeks to download" in order to view a webcast. By 1999 the most basic computer was capable of viewing what McCartney planned for *Rushes* with no major upgrades. This rapid technological progress had opened up a whole new performance 'environment'.

McCartney had first dallied with internet broadcasting for his famed Town Hall Meeting of 17 May 1997. This was a simple 'meet the fans' question-and-answer session held in conjunction with VH-1 at London's Bishopsgate Memorial Hall as a *Flaming Pie* album promo. Even with this most mainstream of interviews, the webcast version went a little off the wall. It continued for a further half an hour after VH-1 stopped broadcasting by relocating to the pub around the corner. The Fireman webcast was actually one of two that McCartney staged in 1998. In December of that year, he recorded an 80-minute special for Linda's posthumous *Wide Prairie* album, in which he cooked some of her recipes, sang some of her songs, and played archive footage of his late wife.

McCartney thought The Fireman webcast "was really good fun," according to Youth, "and he really enjoyed that because it did actually reach quite a few people, even though it was an early one. He thought 'That's a great way of doing a gig.'"

A year later McCartney would make webcasting history with a much more mainstream performance. A live relay was set up for his historic return to the Cavern Club in Liverpool. "I think they got it a bit more fine-tuned for that one," said Youth of an event which sent ripples around the internet, beating all previous records by attracting over three million viewers.

Ever since 1973's *James Paul McCartney* TV special, McCartney had often prepared long-form films and TV shows to promote his albums. But with no station likely to broadcast anything as avant-garde as The Fireman, Youth and McCartney decided to broadcast through the worldwide web for one hour on 2 October

1998. Unlike any other webcast of its time, and most since, this was not an average concert. A special set was created in Abbey Road's Studio Two, recreating a psychedelic '60s vibe – all dimly lit with candles and crystals. Only intermittent images of McCartney were broadcast, and when he could be seen he was in total disguise. To announce the event, McCartney issued a press statement which – in abstract terms – tried to perpetuate the "Is he really The Fireman?" hype.

■ As you probably know, there have been persistent rumours of late, that an occasionally-erotic CD of ambient chill-out music, called *Rushes* by The Fireman, is not the work of The Fireman at all, but is rumoured in fact to be the music of Paul McCartney – collaborating with that renowned producer of ambience, Youth. This rumour is, of course, quite untrue. The documented fact that some years back (1993) Sir P McC and Youth released another album (*Strawberries Oceans Ships Forest*) under the *nom de guerre* The Fireman has nothing whatsoever to do with it … The muted publicist is completely unable to confirm talk that The Fireman will be going on the internet to explain (a) himself and (b) his complete and utter lack of association with Sir P McC.

As a result, that Friday in October 1998 saw several thousand bemused and intrigued web surfers – and various EMI staff and hangers-on in the actual studio – witness one of McCartney's most avant-garde performances. Photojournalist Jorie Gracen was one of the curious McCartney fans who managed to log in to the webcast. "This was one of the most bizarre, avant-garde things I have ever seen," she said afterwards. "All in all I loved every minute of it."

As The Fireman, McCartney was hidden under a yellow rain hat, sunglasses and black balaclava, over which he wore headphones throughout the performance. In this disguise he stood in the corner of the set, very still, playing either guitar (his Epiphone Casino), a whistle or keyboards. In the background, away from the cameras, a stressed, but excited, Youth mixed in recordings and samples and processed the audio, all live.

■ I had him with a guitar and a bass and then I fed that into the mix. It was a mad day because I only had that afternoon to set up. We had until eight o'clock, when it had to go out, to set up all the computers and tapes and do this 40-minute gig. I was kind of producing it, but we did it live. We had Pro Tools set up there. I was live on the desk, in the control room. McCartney was in the studio with loads of different instruments that he could plug in and feed into me and I'd sort of spin it in and dub them up and move on to the next one or something. I'd be playing all these different CDs, had the live Pro Tools stuff going, multi-tracks ... So I'd go from Pro Tools to multi-track, mix in a bit

**of CD, wound to the next track and just did a fly mix with all that sort of going on with him playing.**

Youth and McCartney conjured up huge, instrumental, panoramic versions of tracks from the *Rushes* album, beginning with a 21-minute version of 'Watercolour Guitars'. The album's original guitar loops were overlaid with more guitar counter-melodies from McCartney, with Youth blending dialogue from unknown sources deep into the mix. Ambient in the extreme, it was three minutes into the broadcast before any drums were heard. Youth mixed in the organic, arpeggioed keyboard loops another three minutes later. The performance then moved seamlessly into brand-new Fireman material, including new piano/percussion breaks, guitar solos and drum loops.

In an abstract, ambient sense, the music performed at The Fireman event was an emotional tribute to Linda McCartney. In the epic opening take on 'Watercolour Guitars', McCartney singing "Let me love you, always" was looped and mixed in by Youth, as was – perhaps more poignantly still – the sound of horses running. From this, Youth and McCartney moved into something far more disorientating. In an eight-minute revision of 'Bison', the random, post-rock instrumentation from the album was mixed with live wailing, whistling and keyboards by McCartney. A 'mainstream' approach would have been hard pushed to convey McCartney's mental turmoil, but it is all too graphic in 'Bison'.

The footage was broadcast, and recorded for the archives, from a variety of cameras. Some poised, some handheld. All soft-focused. This first Fireman performance was also the public's first sight of the Fireman's penchant for naked women. Soft-porn pics of sixties-style babes – some with feathers, another sitting in the lotus position, another with a big stuffed animal toy – were intercut with the live footage as it was broadcast across the web. Other video had been prepared, too – a toy penguin, film of McCartney playing his Hofner bass, a figurine of a fireman, a graphic crying "Oh Yeah!" With spotlights, strobes and other vivid lighting effects moving across the set, McCartney had come close to recreating the 'Carnival of Light' Rave for 1998. Well, as close as you could get when viewing through a one inch-sized box on a computer screen.

Back in 1973, both Paul and Linda McCartney had been 'interviewed' for the final track on Pink Floyd's *Dark Side of the Moon* in a session that inspired the next section of the Fireman webcast. Floyd's piece had made a great impression on Youth, too. "The thing where they've got the spoken word at the end, you know, 'I've always been mad' ... They had set up a load of questions," he recalls fondly. "I don't know which member of the band's idea this was, but they got all their roadies and people who were working in the studio and people who were around to sort of answer these questions and they recorded that and they used snippets of it." Although Paul and Linda's vocal tapes ended up on Floyd's cutting room floor, Wings guitarist Henry McCullough's voice can be heard on the final album.

"McCartney had been recording an album in Abbey Road while Pink Floyd were doing *Dark Side of the Moon*," Youth told me, "and he really liked that idea. He sort of hung out with them while they were doing it and thought it was a really brilliant idea. And he said, 'Why don't we do that for this Fireman thing?' I said, 'Yeah, that's a really good idea.'"

The Fireman's question-and-answer session took place about halfway through the webcast. McCartney acted as spokesperson, although he didn't actually 'speak'. An engineer off-camera spoke the question, McCartney would then hand the answer on a piece of paper to a woman sitting beside him who read it out. According to Youth, the questions came from various sources – "different people who worked on the farm and people in the studio ... Then we'd just start ringing people up after a while and just recording the conversations. We compiled some mad questions like 'Have you ever seen God?' or 'Have you ever seen a UFO?' or 'Have you ever had an out of body experience?' and things like that. It was good but it was a bit weird as well, because they were people who worked for him and they obviously were revealing intimate details of their lives in a way and it felt a bit like an interview sort of thing." Video footage and stills had also been prepared to cut in to the The Fireman's 'interview'. So when the question of The Fireman's love for naked women came up, a black-and-white photo of a naked man (with strategically placed fireman's helmet) appeared on screen.

Although McCartney would remain in full disguise throughout, he blew his cover at the end by giving a classic thumbs-up to the camera: Paul 'Fab Macca Wacky Thumbs Aloft' McCartney, as future Pet Shop Boy Neil Tennant would often refer to him while writing for *Smash Hits* in the early 1980s. Taking Pink Floyd's lead, The Fireman managed to deliver an interview as avant-garde as the music. Here it is in full. For the first time ever in print.

■ **Question:** How do you like other contemporary rock or techno-artists like Prodigy, Marilyn Manson, Smashing Pumpkins, or Nine Inch Nails?
**Fireman:** We like the Prodigy for breakfast, Marilyn in the bath, Pumpkins for tea and Nine Inch Nails for bedtime.
**Question:** I want to know why 'Palo Verde' has that name. Is it in Spanish, sorry, I don't speak good English?
**Fireman:** Nay nay, you speak good. 'Palo Verde' is green tree found where no trees grow.
**Question:** Why no naked man? Over half of us want one of them too.
**Fireman:** Show us the money. We go all the way.

**Question:** Is the CD being released in the US and when will The Fireman play live?

**Fireman:** Yes to the US. Live depends on seasonal cycles.

**Question:** What does *Rushes* music desire to symbolise to the people?

**Fireman:** *Rushes* desires only the fertility of the imagination.

**Question:** What initially inspired these recordings?

**Fireman:** Inspiration is derived from the cosmic creative force of the universal fire.

**Question:** How do you classify your music?

**Fireman:** Ambient dreams in rainbow arches describe the circles of The Fireman.

**Question:** What is the significance of the naked woman on the inner sleeve of *Rushes*?

**Fireman:** The symbolism of the unknown naked woman is an ancient mystery. We do not have her number.

**Question:** What inspired you to do this album?

**Fireman:** Night skies, flowing streams and whipped cream fire extinguishers.

**Question:** What is the Fireman's musical bent and where did he learn to play so fluidly?

**Fireman:** Hidden in the *Rushes*, the Fireman smoothes his bent hose daily.

**Question:** Maybe I'm just not deep enough but I just don't get the web page. Could you explain?

**Fireman:** The purpose is to meet you at your fireplace.

**Question:** How many instruments were used in making *Rushes*?

**Fireman:** Countless numbers.

**Question:** Are the sounds of the horses on 'Palo Verde' taped from your horses?

**Fireman:** Live wild horses rushed past our mike. They are owned by no one.

**Question:** How did The Fireman get his nickname?

**Fireman:** The Fireman is no nickname – simply a warm place in the head.

**Question:** What would you consider the best listening conditions for the new music?

**Fireman:** Best conditions vary from planet to planet.

**Question:** So what is it, Fireman? You said we wouldn't believe... briefs, boxers, union shorts, non-women edibles?

**Fireman:** The answer is... what is your question, oh naked one?

**Question:** A clue to the new direction? Can we expect more of the same?

**Fireman:** More of the same would involve less of the rest.

**Question:** Is it your intention for the music to be played when people relax and what is influenced by Youth?

**Fireman:** News of cosmic relaxation influence all decisions made by the burning man.

**Question:** Does the sentence 'The Fireman is no mason' use an anagram to say 'The Fireman is soon man'?

**Fireman:** No, no, Sam, it ain't no anagram.

**Question:** How is your belly for spots?

**Fireman:** The Fireman's belly is clear and facing towards a bright future.

With the pseudo-interview over, McCartney, still in disguise, got back on guitar for a 30-minute rendition of 'Fluid' (taking the webcast 10 minutes over time). Drum-free guitar lines were piped through from the mixing room by Youth, onto which McCartney added his own and improvised whistle melodies. It was an atmospheric mix, with Youth holding off bringing in the track's spaced-out rhythm section until well after seven minutes of McCartney's improvisations, then moving in elements from 'Palo Verde' much later. Listeners had 20 minutes of blissed-out, stripped 'Fluid' mixing before they heard the track's familiar piano loop. Midway, there was guitar feedback that would normally give backroom knob-twiddlers heart attacks, but this was all left in, only adding to the performance's otherworldly quality – and pointing the way to McCartney's even more extreme musical experiments in the future.

If the Fireman webcast was McCartney's final full-blown version of the 'Carnival of Light' or Technicolour Dream raves, then for Youth it was the natural follow-on from Land Of Oz and the long-form DJing (explored in Chapter Ten) which shaped the early career of The Orb.

With random, heavily reverbed guitar chords crashing in and out, a voice then became audible. "Thank you for coming in… Signing off…" spoke a distant-sounding McCartney through the primitive webcast link before the two of them broke into a few hardcore bars of an unreleased Fireman track and then shut the whole thing down completely. At the end, just four words filled the screen: "The Fireman Loves You."

The Fireman webcast (which was so oversubscribed it was replayed twice later that year, nearer the album's release date) was McCartney's longest and most extreme live avant-garde performance to date. But one or two surprising fragments had come before it. 'Stella May Day', for example, a buzz-saw guitar instrumental from 1995…

When Stella McCartney entered Central St Martins college in the early nineties, it had already produced two designers who had changed the face of British fashion – John Galliano and Alexander McQueen. Stella was 23 when she graduated in 1995, having already worked in Savile Row and, at just 15, with Christian Lacroix. By 1997 she was chief designer for Chloe, dispelling myths that her appointment was a mere publicity stunt with a debut collection deemed "sensual and romantic" by *Vogue* magazine. Remaining as staunchly anti-leather as her mother was anti-meat, Stella McCartney once used Queen's 'Killer Queen' as the music to a catwalk show which had the pro-hunting Camilla Parker Bowles sitting right on the front row.

For her final, graduate catwalk show back in 1995, Stella met with criticism for being the only student whose runway models included Naomi Campbell and Kate Moss. Stella also called in her father to write and record the music for the catwalk show. But the press didn't pick up on this 'nepotism' headline at all. Why? Most likely because they wouldn't have realised in a million years that what they heard was by Paul McCartney.

Instead of providing something traditionally McCartneyesque, or in the vein of the middle-of-the-road love songs he presented to other family members as gifts, he provided something extreme and experimental, even by the standards of the fashion world. 'Stella May Day' simply comprises a huge distorted guitar strum, repeated over and over (and over), punctuated only by an ascending seven-note riff. On one hand it's avant-garde, on the other it's pure Jimi Hendrix.

Perhaps the closest musical relation to McCartney's guitar-fire for 'Stella May Day' is Robert Fripp. Since leaving King Crimson in 1974 for a solo career, Fripp has produced the most experimental, organic ambient guitar rock ever recorded. Having collaborated with modern experimental outfits such as The Orb and Future Sound of London, Fripp's post-millennium output has centred around a guitar/electronics hybrid, often played live, to create long, low-key instrumental soundscapes. A territory which McCartney himself would explore in 1999.

When McCartney's music meets other media, whether it be fashion (resulting in 'Stella May Day') or art (*Liverpool Sound Collage*), it often veers off into the avant-garde. There couldn't be a better example of this than *Feedback*, a sound/art installation McCartney created for the first ever exhibition of his paintings, which took place in Siegen, the birthplace of Rubens, in Germany in May 1999.

This debut exhibition was a true coming-out of another side of McCartney's work. He assembled friends and family for the opening, and refused to sign autographs, perhaps feeling that any visitors should be there to see a relatively unknown painter, not a world-famous rock musician. He had been painting for almost 18 years before showing his work publicly and, when he did, he took great care in the presentation of his canvases and how they related to his life. He book-ended the exhibition of oils with two separate installations. At the entrance was a mini-exhibition of Linda McCartney's photographs of her husband at work at the easel. At the far end was an avant-garde sound and video installation, entitled *Feedback*, which he had designed to act as a bridge between the music he was associated with and this new side of his creative character.

Linda McCartney had steered her husband into the art world in the early eighties when she arranged for him to visit one of his inspirations, abstract expressionist master Willem de Kooning. De Kooning had a studio not far from the McCartneys' residence in Long Island. "Watching him in his studio gave me such a buzz – he was the guy who released my painter's block," McCartney remembered years later. Another inspiration came from Linda, when she bought him, as a birthday present, one of Magritte's original easels. McCartney's 18 years of private painting had produced almost 500 canvases by the time Wolfgang Suttner, owner of the Kunstforum Lyz gallery in Siegen, finally had him agree to exhibit his work.

Seventy oil paintings were shown in total. Huge, highly abstract works combining expressionism, pop art and surrealism. Some peaceful, but many intimidating – and all much more akin to McCartney's avant-garde musical experiments than the music he is more well known for. His oil work is highly layered, using carving, scratching and other techniques to tell his stories visually as opposed to musically. The 70 exhibits included various portraits (John Lennon, Andy Warhol, Charlie Watts, David Bowie and of course Linda McCartney). His off-the-wall portrait of Queen Elizabeth II was the visual equivalent of his cheeky performance of The Beatles' 'Her Majesty' at the Queen's Golden Jubilee concert in June 2002.

The gallery planned for 20,000 visitors but 37,500 arrived in total, including over 10,000 from outside Germany. The exhibition was a success and established McCartney as a painter in his own right, unlike the legions of rock musician-cum-painter wannabes. "I didn't want an exhibition to be based on my celebrity," he told *USA Today*. "I met people who said, 'Oh, I'll give you an exhibition.' When I said, 'But you haven't seen my paintings,' they said, 'It doesn't matter.' But you know what? It does."

The media may have concentrated on the oil paintings but the piece that really showed McCartney the musician in a new light was *Feedback*. The gallery's catalogue described the installation coldly, but intriguingly, as:

■ Video installation: six monitor screens mounted in dark grey steel columns, each 173 x 54c x 39 cm; video tape; blue light focused on loud speaker openings. Overall dimensions approx. 17 x 3 metres.

The same tape is started at different times in each of the six columns, resulting in random overlapping of the soundtracks, so that the music heard is never the same twice.

McCartney had been recording guitar feedback experiments for some years. He decided that, for visitors to Siegen, this pure noise, rather than music and songs, would make the natural bridge between his established output and the oils on display. The video and audio material was improvised and recorded on a number of separate occasions. McCartney used harsh white noise to express his feelings, treating this continuous instrumental soundtrack as some kind of emotional diary. As a result some sections are aggressive, others passive, depending on the mood he was in when he recorded them.

The video shows Paul standing against a plain white background grinding feedback out of his guitar (the Epihone Casino, as used for the Fireman webcast). To his side are a stack of amplifiers, with two microphones on long booms hanging above him. At one stage the guitar is abandoned altogether for the ultimate instrument of industrial music – the chainsaw. McCartney's assistant John Hamill managed some of the filming, including one section where McCartney is seen sitting on a bed generating more guitar feedback. In the foreground is a projection of his shadow, also playing guitar. As the shadow is right-handed, and McCartney is left-handed, the finished section looks like an abstract memory of the young Lennon and McCartney composing together, eye to eye.

McCartney had been recording these feedback sounds from day to day at his home studio. Elsewhere on his farm he had been chopping away at undergrowth to clear a path with his chainsaw and it occurred to him that the machine itself had similar musical qualities to the sound of random, resonating guitars. So he took the saw into the studio, recorded it and mixed it into *Feedback*. During the video he recreated 'playing' the chainsaw – wearing a protective face shield, but still surrounded by amplifiers and boom mics. The finished video then cuts quickly back to the guitar – with McCartney still obscured by headgear – to disorienting effect as the boundaries between machine and music begin to blur.

He had first been impressed by the musical qualities of instrument/machine accidents when recording 'I Feel Fine' with The Beatles. As they walked from the recording studio to the control room to listen back to their work, John Lennon had leaned his guitar against an amplifier, which was turned down but still switched on. The guitar and amplifier started feeding back, with the A string resonating across the whole studio. "It was like magic for us," McCartney said, remembering how he and Lennon rushed straight into the control room to ask the technicians how such a sound could have been produced.

The finished *Feedback* film was presented in a tactile, interactive way at the Siegen gallery. McCartney designed six free-standing steel monoliths, each housing a television set and pair of speakers, a visual throwback to the debut performance of Stockhausen's 'Song of the Youths' at Cologne's WDR Studios in 1956.

Aside from the gun-grey steel of the monitor columns, and the black-and-white video images, *Feedback* only used one colour. Each tower was lit with an alluring blue light, just as Stockhausen had lit his 1971 'Trans' symphony in violet. When pairs of speaker grilles were drilled into each column, the monoliths took on human form, the speakers reminding McCartney of a woman's breasts.

Each played the *Feedback* video but started at different times, with random delays between them. This element of chance created a theoretically unending performance, the first since the avant-garde loop at the end of *Sgt. Pepper's Lonely Heart's Club Band* and McCartney's most Cage-inspired work to date. With six monoliths layering the *Feedback* audio over each other, a whole new sound was produced which was unique to each day of the exhibition. No two viewings were ever the same, scuppering McCartney's plan to hover a microphone over the Stonehenge-like creation and record one of the performances.

As the monoliths piped the music around the gallery, visitors were puzzled. Some even passed through the installation unwittingly. It called to mind other avant-garde installations from 40 years before. Like the giant radio station speakers which poured out Stockhausen's pure noise symphonies in Cologne. Or even Bell Labs' intercom system, which Max Mathews linked up to his pioneering electronic musical instruments for late-night broadcasting.

McCartney was messing about with the boundaries between film and performance as far back as 1973. For the *James Paul McCartney* TV special, Wings performed 'Big Barn Bed' from *Red Rose Speedway* to an audience of TV sets. "I go to the films to hear the soundtrack," he said later in the same programme, "the picture becomes a background." Introducing 'Live and Let Die' he said with typical modesty, "They've just filmed a background to some music I wrote … and I must admit the film helps the music work."

The random, evolving improvisation of *Feedback* can be traced to McCartney's exposure in the 1960s to John Cage, with what he described (to Stockhausen's annoyance) as 'indeterminacy', or, as McCartney himself described *Feedback*, "the opposite of synchronisation." "Playing the music on several machines simultaneously, but with a short interval of delay between each one, then produces yet more random effects, new patterns of sound," McCartney noted of *Feedback*. "These random events are like nature," he concluded, "where, for instance, there is never the same rainstorm twice."

McCartney's "rainstorm" analogy addressed the very essence of Andrew Poppy's speech quoted in Chapter One, where Poppy discussed performance in the age of electronics and recordings. Has recorded sound killed live performance? Has the multinational corporate machine for CDs and DVDs pushed live spontaneous music to the side? Why, come to think of it, are people happy to buy a CD when it only allows them to listen to the same set of performances over and over and over again? In post-millennium consumer clutter, the machines used to bring music to our ears have enslaved us. Poppy could have been talking about *Feedback* when he mused:

■ The focused and controlled moment of spontaneity that can live for ever in the object of recorded music casts a shadow over the live event. The live event

> becomes the acoustically compromised, one chance to get it right. The audience's expectation is palpable yet indistinct and various. The live event begins to appear untenable … At some point, the shadow cast by recording over performance is so dark that recording starts to believe that performance is dead. Or insignificant or forgotten.

McCartney, of course, wasn't the only musician attempting to address what Poppy had noticed. Three years earlier, SSEYO had strived to achieve the same effect using computer programmes and produced KOAN. As McCartney would with *Feedback*, it placed time and tempo in the hands of the user, as well as numerous other variables, and then drew on processing power and chance operations to produce unique organic soundscapes that were never the same twice. Brian Eno was impressed by KOAN and began using a term for the whole area McCartney had veered into – generative music.

Eno claimed to have invented the term himself but it actually had a much longer heritage. The year after Cornelius Cardew's death, Edwin Prevost and AMM recorded an album entitled *Generative Themes* (1982). This was the first musical application of the 'generative' creative style described by the great Brazilian thinker Paulo Friere.

In 1963, Edgar Win warned that "Listening to a gramophone or a tape recorder, or to any of the more advanced machines of electro-acoustical engineering, is like listening to a superior kind of musical clock." Years later (33 1/3 years later, coincidentally), Eno, inspired by SSEYO's output and subconsciously steered by AMM, noted that "Until 100 years ago, every musical event was unique: music was ephemeral and unrepeatable, and even classical scoring couldn't guarantee precise duplication. Then came the gramophone record, which captured particular performances and made it possible to hear them identically over and over again." Eno agreed with Win, deciding that future generations would find this hi-fi-induced, performance-destroying slavery absurd. At a conceptual level (generative music) and at a practical level (*Feedback*) are the seeds of a new revolution that might avert this and change the very essence of how we appreciate music itself.

In practice, many visitors to the Kunstforum Lyz would sit for hours at a time among the columns to fully absorb its atmosphere. Its generative nature meant the music varied wildly. Sometimes minimal tones, at others a full guitar rockout, totally overdriven and abrasive. The listener could imagine anything among such atonal strummings. The theme from *The Dam Busters*, a horror movie soundtrack, a chill-out room are all elements that visitors 'thought' they heard coming through the severe, discordant and random guitar abuse.

The concept of noise as music may have been new to McCartney and the audience he took it to, but it had existed for years as the essence of the ambient industrial movement. As the label would suggest, ambient industrial is a subtle, subliminal take on noise. *Feedback* certainly satisfied all the criteria of industrial music which, as Jon Savage noted in the seminal Industrial Culture Handbook, *RE/Search*, include the use of "anti-music", "extra-musical elements" such as video and TV, and "shock tactics." Although few artists concentrate solely on ambient industrial music, the likes of Coil, Nocturnal Emissions and Zoviet France have all produced landmark releases in this area.

Writing for *Epsilon*, the definitive ambient music resource, Peter Werner once attempted to describe, if there could be such a thing, a "typical" ambient industrial work. "[It] might consist of evolving dissonant harmonies of metallic drones and resonances," wrote Werner, " extreme low frequency rumbles and machine noises, perhaps supplemented by gongs, percussive rhythms, bullroarers, distorted voices and/or anything else the artist might care to sample (often processed to the point where the original sample is no longer recognisable)." There is a heat and intensity to ambient industrial/noise music, as evidenced in the soundscapes and recordings by Ovum, Bedouin Ascent, Aube, 8 Frozen Modules and others, whose albums sound like the musical equivalent of jet engine symphonies or metro tunnel echoes.

IFTAF, the organisation behind Chapter Four's Vegetable Orchestra, have played in the pure noise arena too, with their *Rough* CD compilation. The original ambient industrial piece, of course, was Stockhausen's 'Song of the Youths'. Following its debut at Cologne's WDR Radio studios in the early sixties, it formed the basis of the avant-garde movement which influenced McCartney and Lennon later in the decade.

"You could describe noise music as almost the total lack of music in sound," explains Adam Sykes, founder of the avant-garde record label Iris Light. He first ventured into the field by releasing *Stared Gleam*, the debut album by Japanese artist Aube in 1997. It mixed a very hypnotic ambience with huge amounts of noise, all of which were derived from a single source: a small lightbulb!

■ However, within that context you have to ask what is music? Is music confined to the obvious definition of having a beat, rhythm, verse and chorus? A jack hammer or drill can make just as interesting sounds and prove equally as engaging when used within the context of being percussive or to drive the beat, a huge wall of sound can be equally as cathartic or as emotive as the most romantic love song.

Noise is sound, music is sound. The difference can be minimal but the effects can also be the same ... Noise is a diverse genre that although [it] doesn't have mass appeal it does have a very real place in the world of music, and is always going to be something either loved or hated, just as with art.

On one hand, the music McCartney made for *Feedback* could be described as generative or ambient industrial. To most listeners, however, it will sound like pure hell. When the ultimate rock history is written, it would be a worthy inclusion in a chapter on the world's most unlistenable records. This would place it alongside the likes of *Pagan Muzak* by Non (a record which was designed to be played at any speed), Painkiller's *Guts of a Virgin* (a Japanese thrash metal/jazz fusion), or the legendary Borbetomagus, a trio whose performances (and records) would consist of as much random, unstructured noise as they could generate from two saxophones and a guitar.

Just as he had tried new musical styles under pseudonyms – lounge as Thrillington, and ambient as The Fireman – McCartney took on a new persona for his painting: Mr Blendini. On deciding to begin painting he found he suffered from an almost complete artistic block. "I had this big block in my head that only people who went to art school were allowed to paint," he told the BBC. "But when I got to 40, I realised this block was madness. I wanted to paint and the only person not allowing me a canvas was me." Mr Blendini became a mind game he devised to get over this. He would imagine himself as this fictional painter, who focused on blending colour so the joins and textures of his work would become almost invisible. In doing this he learned to stop thinking of himself as McCartney the musician and released his artistic vision as Mr Blendini the painter.

The Siegen exhibition was a daring attempt to break out of his mainstream pigeonhole by using experimental music as well as art. Given the quality of his work and the critical reaction it received, McCartney quickly left behind the tag of 'rock painter' often attributed to his musical peers. Writing for the *Times*, critic John Russell Taylor was impressed. "These are the works of someone who, in front of a blank canvas, thinks and feels in paint," he decided, calling McCartney's pictures "challenging: They force the spectator to react."

Traditional rock and pop music failed as a channel for McCartney's grief and emotions after the passing of Linda. It offered therapy – most obviously from the first major project he threw himself into, a covers album of rock and roll standards from his youth called *Run Devil Run*. But he is yet to record (or at any rate release) any original music that is as disturbing as that time must have been. When Linda is addressed in song these days, whimsy is more apparent than the confusion and longing heared in *Rushes*, the Fireman webcast or *Feedback*. To say nothing of the "anguish" John Russell Taylor found in McCartney's paintings on display in Siegen. "Many of them might be taken to mirror a personal anguish in McCartney," he concluded. "If there is autobiography here, it emerges directly from McCartney's unconscious. Which is just what painters do – real painters, that is."

In 2002, a second exhibition of McCartney's visual work, *The Art of Paul McCartney*, was staged in Liverpool, but the *Feedback* installation was not shown and Siegen remains its only appearance to date. Perhaps by then he had rediscovered the ability to take risks, which had been one of the most entertaining aspects of the middle and late period Beatles. "I know a lot of people will just automatically not like it because it's me, but that's okay," McCartney said of the then-unknown critical reaction to the Siegen exhibition. "It's always risky to do something outside your own field. But I think I've always been taking risks. Back when I was a part of The Beatles, a lot of what we did was risky."

By the time he reached Siegen, McCartney had spent well over a decade focused on the middle of the road. But *Feedback*, the Fireman webcast, the Kunstform exhibition and its critical reception provided confirmation that his work with Youth and other private experiments were as important as his traditional albums. It also confirmed that this surrealist music – and art – had a deeper emotional depth than much of his mainstream work.

# FIFTEEN

## REAL GONE DUB MADE IN MANIFEST IN THE VORTEX OF THE ETERNAL NOW

The BBC was getting curious. CNN was excited. And *Rolling Stone* were beside themselves. In 2001 the spotlight turned on the hitherto secretive Fireman in a big way. And all because of one seven-letter word: Beatles. That year McCartney won a joint Grammy nomination with Youth and Super Furry Animals for their mindbending collaboration with artist-extraordinaire Peter Blake, *Liverpool Sound Collage*.

The story of what, for a moment, became absurdly known as a 'new' Beatles record began with Peter Blake in Liverpool in 1999. The city's newly opened Tate Gallery asked the *Sgt. Pepper* sleeve designer to oversee their 'About Collage' exhibition. As the gallery would announce, Blake "has contributed significantly to the development of the technique since his student days and has also amassed a fascinating collection of collages in his studio." So, from April 2000 Blake presented classic examples of collage by artists including Kurt Schwitters, Joseph Cornell and Jean Dubuffet alongside his own work and special commissions from celebrities and unknowns. But this exhibition was not just about painting. Collages of clothing, furniture and ornaments were also featured. As was collaged music, courtesy of Paul McCartney.

Born in 1932 in Kent, Peter Blake is widely regarded as the leader of the British pop art movement. At the end of the 1960s, just as McCartney decamped from central London to the Scottish highlands on the break-up of The Beatles, Blake left London (where he had been teaching at the Royal College of Art) for rural Avon. From their new bases, McCartney and his wife formed Wings while Blake, his wife and five other artists formed a new art movement, the Brotherhood of Ruralists. By the end of the millennium most major European cities had hosted exhibitions of Blake's work.

"Obsessive and personal" was how Simon Napier-Bell described the art and the imagery of modern sample-based music. And this was exactly what Blake was looking for as a musical accompaniment to his newest exhibition. Why sit with a guitar and strum an ode to Liverpool when the sounds, smells and characters found on the city's streets could be recorded and cut-and-pasted into a new style of music?

■ *About: relating to; on the subject of; near or close to; on every side of.*
   *Collage: an art form in which compositions are made out of pieces of paper, cloth, photographs, etc pasted on a dry ground; any collection of unrelated things.*

These were the two dictionary definitions on which Blake and Tate Liverpool curator Natalie Rudd based their exhibition. Rudd had been at the gallery for four years by that stage and was the perfect curator for the exhibition. She had tracked Blake's work for years and combined a passion for his work with a down-to-earth approach to the visual arts. "What is really interesting about him [Blake] is this late flurry of creativity that he's having," she told me. "I'm quite interested in how artists work when they get old and how they do often have this kind of late surge."

■ Peter contacted the Tate in Liverpool with regard to an exhibition that he wanted to do. It had been in his head since the late '80s I think. This idea called 'About Collage' and the notion that collage could extend conventional boundaries. For him, collage was something that could be stuck to something else, be it in the physical sense or in the aural sense. He was really keen that it could be quite a creative exhibition and that it need not just be objects stuck to walls. Obviously the Tate was thrilled to be working with Peter on an exhibition of this kind and immediately said yes, we'd love to work with him on the exhibition. I was the curator there at the time, so I got to work with Peter on the show.

Natalie Rudd found Blake's devotion to collage as an art form "infectious... He even said that his life was a collage really, that he dips into all these different things and it all escalates into this kind of collage lifestyle." The finished exhibition explored Blake's fascination and pulled from many unexpected sources, as Rudd explained:

■ It was made up of various categories. One category was Peter's selection of collage from the Tate collection. The second category was Peter's collection of collage. He's been collecting for years, which was where the idea came from.

The third category was Peter's collages. So most of it was actually fairly conventional collages as artworks really, that were kind of hung on walls. Then Peter introduced this fourth category and he really wanted to make connections with Liverpool. So he started to borrow collages by, for example, Paul McCartney, John Lennon, Holly Johnson and Robbie Williams. So he kind of built up this entourage of north-western musicians-cum-collagists...

Holly Johnson had been making art for quite a long time and Peter happened to stumble across one of his shows, in London I think it was, and he was really struck by Holly's work and invited him to contribute. They've been quite good friends since... Robbie Williams went round to see Peter's studio, which is quite an amazing kind of collage environment really, it's full of stuff and arranged with Peter's vision. He just went to look round one day and was so inspired by Peter's approach that he decided to go away and make a collage, he made two actually, and Peter was thrilled that he'd kickstarted this kind of collage craze, and he decided to include Robbie's works in the show and he was happy to do that...

I think often Peter worked in this way, he started off with an initial idea and it led off in different directions. It goes from being quite a conventional show about collage to being something that's much more like an environment reflecting his different interests.

At the final event Dada sat next to Victorian engravings, which sat alongside anything from pop art to ice-cream parlour placards. All mediums were explored – ranging from collaged dresses to screens, bottles, scrapbooks and trinkets. The more visitors absorbed what was on display, the more the boundaries blurred between the creative impulse and the hunter-gatherer instinct. A classic example was Tracey Emin and Sarah Lucas' 'The Last Night of the Shop 3.7.93', a blanket covered with their collection of pin badges. A rarely seen collage by John Lennon was also included. Only David Vaughan's 'lamp post with ticket' was missing...

When Blake commissioned new works from friends and other artists, McCartney (who had adorned the gatefold sleeve of *Red Rose Speedway* with pop art collage back in 1972) contributed a piece called 'The World'. This was a crucifix-shaped collage of faces. Some plain, others disturbing, they ranged from a painted self-portrait and a family photo to a screaming man and a bull. "He didn't say at all who they were," remembers Natalie Rudd. "It was quite soon after Linda died and we were all thinking that the woman in the centre looked quite like her ... He was never keen to expand on what it represented."

'The World' stood close to an equally dark collage by John Lennon from the late fifties (itself clearly inspired by the paintings of Stuart Sutcliffe). On Peter Blake's suggestion, McCartney augmented 'The World' with an avant-garde audio collage, using Liverpool as its theme. A direct successor to 'Carnival of Light', this was to become McCartney's most high-profile avant-garde work to date.

Blake had fused music with art at previous exhibitions. "When he was doing his Tate retrospective in 1983 down in London, Ian Dury made a piece of music to go with the exhibition called 'Peter the Painter'," explains Natalie Rudd. "'Peter the Painter' was the overall soundtrack to the show and then his entire work was arranged thematically. So in his pop room he had rock and roll and Elvis Presley and then when he went to live in the country in the 1970s he had Vaugan Williams and Elgar playing, so every room had this kind of soundtrack … I think subconsciously it [Liverpool Sound Collage] grew out of that, but I think also that every exhibition he does he tries to turn into a kind of environment."

For 'About Collage', Blake wanted to install music and individual tracks as displays in their own right. The remix revolution explored in Chapter Nine had not only blurred the boundary between avant-garde music and pop, but also between mainstream music and collage. "Why do you think musicians respond so readily to collage?" Natalie Rudd asked Blake in a conversation taped to launch the exhibition. "It is very much in the air," he replied. "In most bands there is someone who went to art school. The other link is the idea of sampling, or the collaging of sounds from various sources. I have followed Paul McCartney's career as an artist, so when 'About Collage' emerged, I suggested that he made a collage, perhaps from sound, which he has pursued…"

McCartney was inspired by the parallels Blake had drawn between art and avant-garde music. "Paul was immediately really enthused by the idea," according to Rudd. "He had this kind of flurry of creativity before the show in response to Peter's brief and just kind of went collage-crazy."

Like a musical chain letter, and in the style of the remix experiments of Sprawl and Dot Recordings, Liverpool Sound Collage was mixed in a circle. First, McCartney himself reworked the sounds and atmospheres he'd taped to create 'Plastic Beatle', an eight-minute collage and his first truly solo avant-garde release. These sounds were then passed on to Super Furry Animals, and then to Youth, to create their own versions. While this was going on McCartney made a second, even more daring, collage, 'Made Up', before taking the Super Furry Animals piece and editing it down into a bizarre three-minute single.

Before the first collage could be made the source material had to be gathered. McCartney took this from three major sources, all closely connected to the city in question. Tapes of old Beatles studio rehearsals were used for 'Plastic Beatle' (credited on the sleeve to Paul McCartney, The Beatles). Elsewhere on the album are excerpts from his Liverpool Oratorio and, for 'Made Up', McCartney drew on specially recorded tapes of Liverpool street chat and noise.

If Rushes is a confusing album for traditional McCartney fans, they were soon soothed by its mellow ambience. 'Plastic Beatle', however, is full-throttle experi-mentation. The first half of this eight-and-a-half minute track comprises a recycled Ringo Starr drum loop, industrial noise from the Mersey and snippets of McCartney and John Lennon in the studio. Following a breakdown of backwards piano, the beat is back with an odd, catchy vocal loop which eventually collides with a sam-ple of rock and roll guitar from The Beatles' sessions filtering back into the track.

The final breakdown comes with a rapid-fire section of The Beatles playing, shouting, singing, arguing and laughing. The vocals are overlaid on each other, making a radiant sound array which eventually tails off into at least two minutes of ambient street noise and movements on the Mersey. "Full of inspired word-play," wrote one journalist on hearing 'Plastic Beatle', savvily describing it as "a trance version of the [Beatles'] Christmas messages…"

The source of The Beatles voices and samples was a tape dating back to 8 November 1965, which had been plundered at least once before for other proj-ects. "I think it had to be negotiated," said Super Furry Animals' Gruff Rhys of the fact that McCartney was re-using sounds of the other three Beatles. It had to be approved by George Harrison, Ringo Starr – "and Yoko. Because it featured her man, you know."

In November 1965 The Beatles were in the process of recording vocal overdubs for George's song 'Think for Yourself' (although at the time it was known as 'Won't Be There With You'). A tape recorder was set up in the studio to catch The Beatles talking between takes, the plan being to edit jokes and chat into the third of The Beatles' Christmas fan club records. This was the start of the band using the fan club flexidiscs as an experimental outlet, an idea which grew with each successive instalment, as explored in Chapter Two. This time, however, the finished fly-on-the-wall tape was rejected in favour of something more structured, so at least half an hour of Beatle studio talk remained in the can for future projects.

The first time it was used was for *Yellow Submarine*. The fly-on-the-wall tape hears how Lennon had been having trouble hitting the right notes for the third and final verse of 'Think for Yourself'. So he, McCartney and Harrison did an a cappella rehearsal. This was then looped and incorporated into the *Yellow Submarine* soundtrack.

Ringo Starr was not present for the 'Think for Yourself' vocal overdubs, but George Martin, as well as John, Paul and George, can be heard talking on the rehearsal tape. The references the band make as they work give a truer insight than any interview into their motivations and inspirations at that time. TV (*Juke Box Jury, Supercar, Stingray,* adverts and jingles), their own songs ('Yesterday', 'Do You Want To Know a Secret?'), comedy (from Frankie Howerd to Woody Woodpecker), as well as boxer Rocky Marciano, Cynthia Lennon and Humphrey Bogart all figure in the conversation.

The unused 'Think for Yourself' tape gave Paul McCartney ample material to include in his 'Plastic Beatle' sound collage. Other sources were used, too. *The Beatles Anthology* videos provided an instant source of archive chat, namely McCartney's "must be all right" (at 00:46 in 'Plastic Beatle', from take 13 of 'I'll Be Back'), Starr's "a lovely time" (at 03:38 and 07:00, from the guitar version of 'Goodnight'), and Lennon's "cause it's our song any road, innit?" (at 00:39, which was found on a tape from 1 March 1964, preceding take 1 of a recording of 'I Call Your Name').

The samples may sound random on a first listen. But repeated listens show that, in the few seconds of dialogue attributed to each Beatle, McCartney manages to paint a picture of their personalities. Hearing banter between the four of them from such a creative peak as *Rubber Soul* is intriguing, and hearing how four musicians played – verbally – together is captivating. It would be wrong to think that this – or most other Beatles archive recordings – 'sheds new light' (a phrase too often used in cases like this) on the band. That's not the point. 'Plastic Beatle' and *Liverpool Sound Collage* are about firing the listeners' imagination so they can complete the story themselves.

Certainly in the case of John Lennon, McCartney selected simple phrases that showed his humour and sense of fun. Two of Lennon's attempts to stir the band into action in the *Rubber Soul* session pop up – "Okay, Paul, you ready boy? This is it." (at 06:55) and an "All right, cut this tomfoolery out!" (at 06:57). The 'Think for Yourself' tapes provided most of the George Harrison samples. His "chinga chinga ching, boom boom boom" description of his guitar track is recycled into a new percussive fill at 03:33 and again at 06:04. McCartney sampled himself of course, too. He can be heard joking around with John imitating a preacher (at 06:18).

'Peter Blake 2000', Super Furry Animals' 17-minute collage of the same source material, was McCartney's first collaboration with the Welsh art/rock band. They had already sampled The Beatles on their single 'Happiness is a Worn Pun', but this was the project which led them to hire McCartney for vegetable-chewing duties, as explored in Chapter Four. As noted, it was a chance meeting at the *NME* awards between keyboard player Cian Ciaran and McCartney that led to their involvement in this new project. According to Gruff Rhys (vocals, guitar):

■ Paul took his phone number. We didn't expect anything to come of it, but he phoned and I think he sang 'Born Free' into his answering machine two weeks later. Cian came into a practice with a tape of Paul McCartney singing 'Born Free'! A few days later we were sat in our office in Cardiff, the Ankst office, with four big boxes of original Beatles master tapes with a heavy letter from the record company telling us not to take it down the market and sell it! And

> also he sent us a collage of interviews he'd done in Liverpool, when he did that
> Cavern comeback a few years ago. It's just one of those things you never
> expect to be doing…

The thought of The Beatles and Super Furry Animals on one record certainly got
the press excited as soon as word was out. "Super Furry Animals Remix The
Beatles" headlined *Dotmusic* on Wednesday 3 May 2000. Cian gave the first
description of this new creative process. "McCartney went around Liverpool with
a DAT recorder, talking to ordinary Liverpool people," he explained. "Everything
on the track is the sounds he gave us, but we've rearranged them as we see fit.
Of course the arrangement is going to be different to his, but some of the sounds
are so good you wouldn't want to touch them anyway."

In June 2000, the band were in Toronto performing tracks from their Welsh-
language album *Mwng* to a bemused but adoring crowd. "Perhaps it is ironic that
McCartney, leader of one of the world's most recognised melodic acts, has invited the SFAs under his fold," wrote Canada's *Chart Attack* magazine after Gruff
told them about the collaboration on the night of their Toronto gigs. "The band's
new album … concentrates on what it seems music has evolved away from,
which is essentially the point of music, the melody." But *Chart Attack*'s interviewer, Derek Nawrot, was by no means surprised, citing some of the band's
other notable achievements. "They've sold an armoured military tank to Don
Henley, sampled a Steely Dan song which uses the word "fuck" 52 times and
released it at Christmas, kept company with one-time dope kingpin and master
of disguise Howard Marks, and declared war on Celine Dion…"

'Peter Blake 2000', the Super Furries' finished work, is challenging, to say the
least. But not alienating in the slightest. Listening to this track is like watching
an artist create a collage, if that artist had 100 arms and a canvas the size of a
skyscaper. The musical equivalent is this – the word "rapidly" looped and repeated over and over again for three minutes, repeated faster and faster, so fast eventually that it becomes a single tone, increasing in pitch. The tone then slows and
becomes a word again, still looping, over 400 times per minute to begin with,
slowing eventually to become recognisable as "Liverpool".

Scattering some speech of "Peter Blake Sound Collage" around ends the first
five-and-a-half mesmerising minutes of the Super Furry Animals' piece, the first
'third party' remix of The Beatles to be heard since Phil Spector was let loose on
*Let It Be*. "20 minutes of hip-hop, almost opera" was how the band described the
finished track to VH-1, delighted that it was "featuring Ringo Starr on drums and
George Harrison on guitar and John and Paul on vocals, as well as strings … and
a choir recorded in Liverpool last year."

The track's entire bassline is a heavily processed George Harrison vocal loop.

Harrison's "It's okay. We know. I think we know. We just go chinga chinga ching. Boom boom boom," as used in McCartney's collage, comes up again in 'Peter Blake 2000' at 05:43. But the Super Furries take this one stage further, taking the rest of the speech – "The bit that John finally got just after that. And we'll do both of the do what you want to do" – and using the final words as a loop. "Do what you want to do. Do what you want to do. Do what you want to do. Do what you want to do." Sampling and resampling, Ciaran tore the treble off and rounded the corners until the "Do what you want to do" phrase became a single bass note bouncing to the rhythm of the original words. Gruff Rhys:

> ■ Our sounds had to come from either the Beatles material or the collage, so you weren't allowed to play a guitar over it or anything. So Cian sampled up loops of Ringo's drums and there's a sample going "do what you wanna do, do what you wanna do, do what you wanna do". I think Cian sampled that out of a conversation Paul was having in the studio with some of The Beatles. He changed that into a bassline and just basically cut up George's guitars and we had made loads of loops out of The Beatles. We did it in our friend Chris' studio in Cardiff, which is basically just one room in a living room and a computer set-up. It was like doing it at home. It was very relaxed. It must have taken a few weeks. Whatever we do, one of the six of us takes charge of a particular project, but the rest of the band is always there with an opinion. So we're an engineer's worst nightmare.

More than any track on *Liverpool Sound Collage*, Super Furry Animals succeeded in literally breathing new life into the Beatles. As the Harrison vocal bassline rumbles on, a Ringo Starr drum loop crashes in and the two set each other off on a six-minute groove. Ciaran's work was declared "utterly ingenious" by a reviewer for *Extended Playhouse*, who was blown away by his "transmogrification of a phrase casually spoken by George Harrison into the guitar riff forming the foundation for the music."

In the boxes of tapes delivered by Apple to Cardiff, Super Furry Animals found some more gems. "There were some jams in the studio sounding like they were warming up," remembers Rhys, "and I think there was stuff like the string section from 'Eleanor Rigby' and conversations between John and Paul. There wasn't any complete unheard songs or anything, just a lot of messing about in the studio, of George and Ringo jamming." Some of this can be heard buried away in their collage, like the end music from 'Magical Mystery Tour' (at 09:24 and again at 10:09, behind McCartney singing). Ciaran and the band also created a whole scat section by sampling individual "boom boom booms" from Harrison's off-the-cuff studio chat and time-scratching them across another of

Starr's drumbeats which they found on the tapes.

From this collage an entirely new song was created. The Harrison vocal 'bassline', across Starr's archive drumbeat, was topped off by a sample of Paul singing "Free now, gotta be free now" – all of which had been found on unrelated archive tapes. It was catchy, startlingly different, and its potential fired McCartney's imagination. Unbeknown to the Supper Furries, he took their track, added elements from the other collages, some new source material and chopped it down to just three-and-a-half minutes. Clearly he had the desire to put *Liverpool Sound Collage* on a more public platform, producing 'Free Now', a single-length edit of the Super Furries' track.

"We were a bit pissed off, because he went and edited it himself," said Gruff Rhys, "and we thought we could have made a mix that was three minutes long without editing it. If we knew he wanted to make a short version, we had very strong ideas ... So as punishment, we made him chew some celery and an apple."

'Free Now' is a workable edit of some of the main ideas from the album, a musical equivalent of a souvenir postcard from the Tate Liverpool shop. Quite different to seeing one of the full-sized 'About Collage' artworks in the main gallery. But one thing 'Free Now' does show is that, despite McCartney's classical leanings, he hasn't lost his spirit of musical adventure. He veered to one side of the road with the Liverpool Oratorio and veers to the opposite extreme with 'Free Now', as he tears pop music to shreds and layers it across three minutes of sound.

Unlike Super Furry Animals and McCartney himself, Youth was fairly frugal with the amount of Beatles dialogue used on his track. Only four lines of dialogue from the 'Think for Yourself' vocal overdubs tape feature in his 17-minute collage, which he titled, in true Orb style, as if it were a cross between a sci-fi movie and a Buddhist mantra: 'Real Gone Dub Made in Manifest in the Vortex of the Eternal Now'. It appears on the final LP after linking sections of choral music, fittingly enough lifted from McCartney's classical venture of 1991, *Liverpool Oratorio*.

Youth's collage stands out from anything else on the album as it is spiked throughout with electronic pulses, stabs and ripples – not original but created by processing the original source material into unrecognisable oblivion. Sparring with this is a loop of Ringo Starr's drumming, sounding funky and loose when combined with the dub bassline Youth cooked up from other parts of McCartney's source material.

Dialogue from all four Beatles can be heard in Youth's collage, which is the most persistent, rhythmic and upbeat on the whole album. McCartney ("Hang on. John's just broken a string"), Starr ("Mal, will you come down and fix the seat"), Harrison ("The bit that John finally got") and Lennon ("Oh well, I can get back of it") were all pasted across the track.

More than a collage, '...Vortex' is the musical equivalent of driving through a raging electrical storm. There are some new voices trapped in there – as a modern-day McCartney can be heard asking "What's your name? Where're you from?" These are the first instances to be heard on *Liverpool Sound Collage* of McCartney's other major source of material – his audio tour of Liverpool, gathering voices and sounds to be used as paints in the palette for his, Youth's and the Super Furry Animals' sound collages.

It was the night of Tuesday 14 December 1999. McCartney was returning to where it all began – the Cavern Club in Liverpool – for his first gig there in 36 years. When Linda McCartney died the year before, his music splintered in different directions. He resisted the temptation to dwell on dark ballads. Or if he didn't, he resisted the temptation to release them. Instead McCartney pressed on with the ethereal *Rushes* project with Youth and then went back to his roots with the *Run Devil Run* album of rock and roll covers.

It was in promoting *Run Devil Run* that McCartney came up with the idea of returning to the Cavern, where he played to a capacity crowd of 300. Like *Rushes*, a live internet broadcast was also set up. But with the music being slightly more mainstream, and with McCartney not using a pseudonym, millions more connected up. In fact, in cyberspace the gig brought the house down, literally.

Few realised it at the time but 14 December 1999 was actually used to record two McCartney projects. Before the Cavern gig took place McCartney took a stroll around his home town and, tape recorder in hand, proceeded to chat to the locals. Ordinary Liverpool people – surprised shoppers, students, passers-by, a woman serving in a fish and chip shop – all became absorbed into the audio collage.

The chat with students was recorded on a visit to the Liverpool Institute for Performing Arts, which McCartney had launched some years before. From there to some words from "the lady who gets me my chips when I'm back in the 'Pool," as he described a woman who pops up and congratulates The Beatles on winning various millennium music awards. Talk from the soundcheck for the Cavern concert can also be heard. And all of this is glued together with the daily noises of the River Mersey and the Mersey Tunnel which runs beneath it.

"My name's Anne," says a fan who McCartney interviewed with his DAT recorder, ready to immortalise her words on 'Made Up', a track which dwells less on Beatles out-takes (using the same four Youth chose) and more on an audio tour of the city McCartney grew up in. This, the first voice heard on the tape, is Anne Williams who, in a typical exchange, is asked by McCartney: "What do you think of Liverpool?" "I love it," she says, "and I'm made up that you keep coming back here all the time." Working to this premise, the track could have become a self-indulgent tourist board soundtrack, were it not for the fact that McCartney spontaneously interviewed real people. As a result the next two voices that pop up – Mark and Pauline – choose San Francisco when asked what their favourite city in the world is.

Car horns, a passer-by's rendition of 'Mary Had a Little Lamb', "Who are you looking at?!", McCartney's rendition of 'Maggie May', and other audio snippets are pasted across a background canvas of organ chords and more choral work from the *Liverpool Oratorio*, underpinned by heartbeat-style bass drum pulse and a rhythm track like a ticking clock.

From the streets outside McCartney moves to LIPA, where various students pop up and there's talk of the Sound Technology Programme and the In The City music conference. "We're doing a sound collage thing for Peter Blake," says McCartney as he approaches some students with his DAT recorder, "and it's all about Liverpool, so I'm going to get these girls now talking Liverpoolian." The next scene is the Cavern Club – cue the sound of screaming and shouting fans one second, followed by the confusion in Paul's car on arrival the next. As they park, time warps backwards to snippets of the Beatles getting ready to perform 30 years before. Unlike its visual equivalent, it's easier to trick the brain and skip backwards and forward in time with sound collage.

'Made Up' is a captivating 13-minute McCartney's-eye (or rather ear) view of the world. Some of the pieces of collage are there on purpose and others – like all the best pieces of avant-garde music – are there by accident. Like the interference from a passing mobile phone that his tape recorder inadvertently picked up (at 09:26).

The finished audio collages were piped as ambient sound around the Tate Liverpool gallery, much to the surprise of some visitors. "It kind of goes quiet and then loud in places," remembers Natalie Rudd, "and some of us would sit up and go, 'Oh, what was that?' There was a spot where you could listen to it ambiently and a spot where you could listen to it more actively," she says of the small sound installations that were set up to give the music collages as much focus as their visual counterparts.

When Tate visitors sat down at these sound booths they could see and hear for themselves the graphic parallels between the world of collage and sample-based avant-garde music. "This definitely occurred to Peter," Rudd reveals. "It was very much part of his notion of being 'about' collage. It is collage really, but 'categorically' speaking it's not, and he was interested in blurring that. The whole notion of sampling was something that he was definitely interested in, and that's why he wanted Paul to make this thing, to make this musical connection." Blake and Rudd at one point planned to blur this even further by incorporating a special concert into the exhibition. "We were going to very much direct the content of the concert towards this notion of sampling as the key thought behind the show," she says. "It was definitely thought of in that way."

Before *Liverpool Sound Collage* was released, anonymous-looking white label DJ promos of 'Free Now' began to emerge, not credited to either The Beatles,

Paul McCartney or Super Furry Animals, but just to Sound Collage. It instantly created a buzz with DJs, which was furthered when McCartney talked about the promos to a UK newspaper, telling them the track was set for release and was "a new little piece of Beatles … 'Free Now' is an outbreak from my normal stuff," he added. "It's a little side dish that is not to be confused with my other work. It's more underground than what you usually hear from me but I like to be free enough to do this sort of thing."

*Liverpool Sound Collage* was never quite destined to go out as The Fireman album # 3. Instead it was released with no artist name on the front cover at all. But the inclusion of archive studio chat from John, Paul, George and Ringo led to individual artist credits for The Beatles for the first time since 'Free as a Bird' and the *Anthology* releases. 'Plastic Beatle' and 'Made Up' were credited to 'Paul McCartney, The Beatles', while 'Peter Blake 2000' was attributed to 'Super Furry Animals, The Beatles'. The final single edit, 'Free Now', was then credited to 'Paul McCartney, The Beatles, Super Furry Animals'.

The record shop owner's nightmare of the artist-less album was, with this credit list, a media dream come true. Just as McCartney had issued a press statement in 1970 kicking off the whole 'Beatles split' fury, his comments on *Liverpool Sound Collage* and its "manic Beatles single" 30 years later had the totally opposite effect. "Beatles Back In Business" screamed *People* magazine. "Beatles Get Back With A Dance Track," cried CNN. "In 1995, it was thought that 'Free as a Bird' and 'Real Love,' from the first two volumes of *Anthology* respectively, would be the last Beatles records ever released," mused an eager VH-1. "After all, what 'Beatles' tune could follow recordings that grafted demos of John Lennon singing onto new tracks recorded by Paul McCartney, George Harrison, and Ringo Starr? And yet, McCartney has completed what he calls a new Beatles track, which he will release as part of the *Liverpool Sound Collage*…"

'Free Now' was eventually shelved as a single. "At a certain point we were contemplating releasing it on our label Placid Casual," remembers a bemused Gruff Rhys. "It got a bit weird for a moment. We thought we were going to be releasing The Beatles on our label. That could have been very weird but that didn't happen." While McCartney explained to the media how and why the album was created, his "new little piece of Beatles" comment was enough to place this avant-garde work on the world stage. Even if most of the media were likely to completely misinterpret the entire project.

"The Beatles are making another attempt for the charts with a dance track put together by Sir Paul McCartney," rambled CNN's reporter. "It is the first original work by The Beatles since McCartney, George Harrison and Ringo Starr regrouped in 1995 to record the John Lennon song 'Free as a Bird' in memory of their slain colleague."

The *All Music Guide*, a noted archive of independent rock history, stepped in to set the record straight, recognising that the frenzy over The Beatles' involvement was due in no small part to a certain Paul McCartney. "The hype mill, stoked in part by McCartney himself, promoted this CD as nothing less than a posthumous chapter in The Beatles' saga," wrote Richard Ginell. "Nonsense, for this is really just the latest of McCartney's excursions into electronica, an interest of his that dates back to The Beatles' boundary-shredding experiments with musique concrète and the Moog synthesiser in the 1960s." Their review was simple. "As a listening experience ... it grows on you, provided that you drop any expectations of this being a long-lost Beatles album."

Perhaps an album like this would always have been just too much for CNN to comprehend. The *College Music Journal*, on the other hand, managed to get their heads round it completely. *Liverpool Sound Collage* "finds Macca cutting and dubbing bedroom grooves ... into five pieces of shambling sonic schizophrenia," they reported. They found a "funky musical landscape" in the assembled beats and samples and had the foresight to warn listeners of, say, Fiona Apple and the like that "these are not your standard verse-chorus-verse compositions". McCartney's 'Plastic Beatle' and Youth's 'Real Gone Dub Made in Manifest in the Vortex of the Eternal Now' were their favourites from this "engaging listen."

Another magazine that understood where *Liverpool Sound Collage* was coming from (while avoiding getting sucked into the hype around 'Free Now') was Belgium's *Progressive World*. A "contemporary audio canvas which at times holds the balance between The Orb and Faust" was how John 'Bo Bo' Bollenberg described the album. "Collage is an art form in which compositions are made of pieces of paper, cloth, photographs, etc ... pasted on a dry ground; any collection of unrelated things," the magazine noted. "It's especially the latter which is very appropriate to the work on this disc. The separate elements don't mean a thing yet it's the way in which the various parts fit together like a jigsaw which makes this experiment worthwhile." Bollenberg was particularly fond of Youth's 'Real Gone Dub Made in Manifest in the Vortex of the Eternal Now' collage. "It's where early Can, Neu!, Cluster and Kraftwerk get under the varnish of the rock tradition to enter the chill-out world," he declared, the track's array of technical bleeps and beats clearing evoking a roll-call of German electronic pioneers.

On the web, the *All Music Guide* agreed that Youth's piece shone out. "The most effective segment is the one credited solely to Youth," they wrote, "where the pitchless electronic sounds are at their wildest and the disembodied Beatles voices and ghostly choruses are hauntingly adrift in a high-tech netherworld."

Not every journalist was quite so ecstatic. And for those who were annoyed by the hype and didn't like the album either, the results weren't pretty. In Canada, Mike Bell, writing for the *Calgary Sun*, managed to see past the 'Beatles-talking on record again' euphoria in a piece headlined "If you're Paul McCartney, apparently you can release any old damn thing you please." Maybe abstract sample-collage was just not his thing. "Lifted from the context of the exhibit," wrote Bell, "this ambient soundscape made from a mish-mash of noises ... is an annoying exercise in indulgence that wouldn't have seen the light of day without Sir Paul's name attached to it."

In the US, Barnes & Noble immediately saw Paul McCartney and The Beatles' name on the disc and decided to warn shoppers. "While it's certainly interesting to hear Macca deconstruct snippets of Beatle music, layering semi-recognisable riffs with spoken word, bits of found sound, and the like, the five-part Collage doesn't hold together – either conceptually or sonically – well enough to merit repeated listenings," the chain declared. "Committed McCartney followers – at least more open-minded ones – will be more likely to take the time to decipher what's going on in 'Peter Blake 2000' and 'Real Gone Dub Made in Manifest in the Vortex of the Eternal Now.' But if your fandom doesn't stretch too far past the songs that appear on *Beatles 1*, head for another disc." Presumably Barnes & Noble's reviewer, David Sprague, forgot he was addressing the millions who had welcomed the avant-garde into the mainstream in the first place when they bought 'Revolution 9', the Christmas flexis, 'Tomorrow Never Knows' and *Sgt. Pepper*.

The hype around the 'return' of The Beatles and the controversy as to whether *Liverpool Sound Collage* was actually music combined to create one positive effect. It put McCartney's experimental side in front of a new, much broader audience. This third 1990s attempt at something completely 'out of the box' was recognised at the Grammy Awards of 2000. *Liverpool Sound Collage* sat alongside albums by Fiona Apple, the Cure, Radiohead and Beck in the Best Alternative Music Album category. It "almost looked like a misprint," commented Yahoo!. Gruff Rhys from Super Furry Animals was less surprised.

▪ I think they sent us a Grammy certificate a few months ago. After being involved in that project hardly anything surprises me any more. It was something we could never have imagined doing two and a half years ago or at any point before doing it. I don't know how much value there is in a Grammy anyway. McCartney's very well known so he's going to be up for a Grammy for anything he does I suppose ...We were really pleased with what we'd done and also as a tall story it's amazing. I think he was working on a whim ... He's probably not used to people being so up-front really. He reacted well to that and he had a telephone relationship with Cian. It must be good for him to do things on a whim sometimes.

Misprints aside, *Liverpool Sound Collage* had finally drawn McCartney's avant-garde dabblings out of the closet. And won him and his collaborators acclaim in the process. The dub, cut-up, sample-driven experimentation was certainly not new, not even for McCartney. But given that a mainstream audience, lured in by the inclusion of Beatles mementos, was exposed to its vocal basslines and electrical storm effects, it stood as a challenging question mark over the very nature of music itself. "The best collages are inspiration-intensive, and audio collage has the added intensity of making a lucid message while subverting linear continuity," concluded *Extended Playhouse*. "As such, *Liverpool Sound Collage* is mesmerising..."

## SIXTEEN

# MUSIC MADE FOR FAMILIES AND NEUROSES

*If I listed all the things I like, it would be embarrassing. I'm a*
*Gemini, so it's natural that there are a lot of things I like to do.*
*I used to shrink away from them and think, "That's not my thing."*
*Now I've learned that if there's something I really love to do, why*
*should I repress that passion?*

**Paul McCartney, 2002**

**C**ollaborators as diverse as Super Furry Animals, Allen Ginsberg, Youth and Yoko Ono had combined to make the 1990s McCartney's most prolific avant-garde period to date. But also his most secretive. From *Flowers in the Dirt* onwards he had successfully won back his audience, and his image as rock and roll songwriter, which had been eroded with the middle-of-the-road hits and misses of the 1980s. As such, 'The Ballad of the Skeletons' had been the only experimental 1990s recording that bore his name on the cover. With the final musical notes of the 20th century already a distant memory, it will be intriguing to see how McCartney handles his hidden, almost schizophrenic musical personality in the 21st century. Maybe, having reached the final chapter of this book, his cover's been blown.

There's no doubt that – despite the sceptical views of the people who have heard it – 'Carnival of Light' was a turning point for both The Beatles and pop culture. It's one of the earliest instances of a contemporary pop band playing with the sounds and compositional techniques of the avant-garde composers of the forties and fifties. To say nothing of the way it was presented – a rave environment which was embryonic and experimental at the time but now, over 30 years later, is a vital cultural commodity. As this book was being finished, McCartney was completing his first major tour for ten years. The Driving USA concerts heralded what some call the return of Maccamania – a heady combination of a strong solo album (2001' s *Driving Rain*), the live airing of 21 Beatles songs per concert, and not just an audience but an entire country going through a musically assisted healing process after a major tragedy.

From the 'Carnival of Light' rave to Soft Machine to Gong, Daevid Allen is still on the road, too. Touring the world in 2001, I spoke to him after gig 43 out of a total of 62. He had no doubts that events he, McCartney and David Vaughan witnessed at the Roundhouse and elsewhere in London were a true turning point. "And then further down the track the party scene began from a fresh generational level … an energetic octave above where we left off … and here we all are today," he mused. "I am happy to think of ourselves as icebreakers for rave culture … and even happier to say that we of Gong are still on this path tonight."

Like Allen, McCartney was too busy creating to think deeply about his inspirations or cross-fertilisations of styles and genres. He's just ploughing forward on something which David Vaughan describes as his "continual inward journey." McCartney has professed on numerous occasions to be uninterested in the kind of dates and details that many fans and some authors spend great chunks of their lives cataloguing in minute detail. "A particularly obsessed musician of my acquaintance," wrote Brian Wilson biographer George Byrne, "possesses no less than three CDs' worth of outtakes of 'Vegetables' alone – yet he still walks the streets and is allowed to vote."

Conveniently, all sides of McCartney's musical personality can be traced back to his first post-Beatles album, McCartney. Rock and roll, pop ballads, instrumentals (some chirpy, others experimental), orchestral and a healthy dose of the avant-garde. "Listening to it is like hearing a man's personal contentment committed to the sound of music," wrote the *NME* when the album appeared in April 1970.

When critical reaction to solo McCartney product wasn't so good, it was his cosy, home-spun balladeering that came in for the most criticism. But Mike Keneally has a different take on this. "Critics who found it [*Ram*'s lyrics] smug or overweening say more about their own unhappiness than about Paul's ability to make a good album on his own terms," he told me. "I've never gone to Paul McCartney for profundity and anyone who expects it from him really ought to face reality. It's clear from the earliest Beatles music that Paul's agenda was to make memorable pop songs which a lot of people would want to buy. When that goal was no longer tempered by the headier concerns of John and George, a lot of people turned away – but Paul never promised more than he gave."

Although in no way avant-garde, Keneally's favourite McCartney album, Thrillington, couldn't have been more experimental. And that experimental spirit still resounds today from the other collaborators who hid behind Percy 'Thrills' Thrillington's ram-shaped mask. "As for today, I'm still making dance/jazzy type tracks in my home studio carrying on my RAH Band stylie," says Richard Hewson, who has made the transition from sixties pop to modern electronic music more easily than most. During his interview for this book he was finishing a new Fireman-style album of pure trance called *Orkestronic*.

McCartney could have been referring to this musical schizophrenia when he sung "I'd appreciate it if you'd help me find the other me" in 1983's 'Pipes of Peace'. An odd reference in an era generally judged as his most middle-of-the-road. But there are parallels with and traces of his avant-garde spirit throughout that decade. The *Give My Regards to Broad Street* film is perhaps so loathed because people know that McCartney can do so much better. That's why fans rarely tolerate experiments (or experimental works) – by their very nature they can fail as often as they succeed. Certainly the album that pre-empted that decade, *Back to the Egg*, was schizophrenic, as Laurence Juber remembers:

■ *Back to the Egg* was an album that had some interesting cross-currents going. On one level it was an English folk pop record, kind of on the back of *London Town*, but on another level it was a rock and roll record ...The band was really put together to kick some ass. The band had its own momentum, but Paul was kind of leaning, as he ended up in the '80s, much more towards the more mainstream pop thing ... The whole album has been reassessed. It got dismissed at the time but now, when you look back at it, and you look at it in the context of the Wings output, it's probably one of the more interesting records.

While the results may have been mixed, 1980's *McCartney II* was a brave attempt on two counts. Firstly, its willing – and playful – assays with synthesisers and electronic music. Secondly, the fact that so many of the tracks from these highly experimental recording sessions were released on the final album for the public to offer their judgment. Despite the fun McCartney was clearly having in the studio, computer music was at that point considered to be completely devoid of human emotion. But by 1997 Bjork, an artist who has succeeded more than most in gaining both pop and avant-garde credibility, was describing how this had changed on *The South Bank Show* (which for its inaugural programme in 1978 had covered the recording of the *McCartney* album). "I find it so amazing when people tell me that, that electronic music has not got soul, and they blame the computers ... like there's no soul here. It's like you can't blame the computer, if there's not soul in the music it's because nobody put it there."

Despite these continuing prejudices, many areas of avant-garde music have been around for decades longer than is generally acknowledged, with even 'turntablism' and DJing being traced back to the 1940s. Steve Anderson, who created one of McCartney's first major remix reincarnations with 1993's 'Deliverance', can trace remixing back to the roots of rock and roll. "I've always said that my favourite arrangers such as Vince Mendoza, Nelson Riddle and Jeremy Lubbock were the remixers of their time," he told me. "The melody and lyrics were done and it was their job to represent it in the definitive way depending upon who was to sing it."

If this direction can be traced back, it should be possible to trace it forwards. The Black Dog tries, but fails. "When the youth of the '60s found themselves in the pages of Ginsberg's 'Howl' and in the music from The Beatles, it was a catalyst for new thought," Keir Jens-Smith told me.

> ■ But will today's youth only hear the message in an Eminem rap, a gangster lyric, a rock song or a pre-toned pop song? Where are the free thinkers? Where are the voices? Where are the artists not driven by 'the corporation' or a simplistic desire for money or fame? If we made celebrities out of writers and great fame was on offer from writing books or poetry, we'd have a sudden surge of new writers. These days people just want fame, and talent goes discouraged and un-nurtured; more often than not it's an inconvenience to the defined process of 'manufacturing' a star. Is there any passion left in the world today to even start a new movement, be it a literary or musical one? Will anyone care enough about anything other than themselves for long enough to create something for 'the bigger picture' and the good of the world? Doesn't anyone want to preach free thought and free thinking any more? And is this where it got us, for the minorities to have separated down into small subcultures and microcosms of society, with no voice?

Adam Sykes, who spoke up for noise as a pure musical form in Chapter 14, agrees. Jens-Smith and the Black Dog may tackle the Beat poets and Sykes may distribute random white noise, but both are trying to push against a tide of mediocrity which is threatening to drown pop music at the start of the new century. There could be no blunter way of doing this than the chainsaw/feedback duets which McCartney unveiled at Siegen in 1999, as Sykes notes:

> ■ I think it's important because it has an effect on the listener, it isn't puerile easy listening music for the non-thinker. Not everyone wants to listen to 'pop' music all the time or music with obvious song structures. I think it is very expressive music that, once tapped into by the listener, can be a lot more fulfilling than the latest single by the newest manufactured pop explosion. Music can be challenging, it can be more than a three-minute pop song to give the

> listener a break from reality and it should be something that leaves a mark on
> the listener - and with noise that mark can be both physical and mental.

Keir Jens-Smith's point about music and its effects on listeners is fundamental, and reminiscent of a comment from David Sprague about Liverpool Sound Collage in Chapter 15. Although McCartney is seen as the middle-of-the-road, when in reality he dances all over it, perhaps his dedicated fans actually are. There's a strong possibility that the millions who bought *Wingspan* and the *Beatles Anthology* would be rather upset if they heard something like 'Real Gone Dub Made in Manifest in the Vortex of the Eternal Now', the 17 minutes of electro dub on *Liverpool Sound Collage*. Upset enough to be wary of buying a 'normal' McCartney album like *Driving Rain* in the future. Being pigeonholed is one thing. Being open-minded is another.

To continue the thread from Chapter One, pigeonholing makes life easy for shops as well as critics, to say nothing of music buyers themselves. "More than three decades after the break-up of the Beatles, Paul McCartney is still – with some degree of prudence – pigeonholed as that band's most pop-driven member," wrote Barnes & Noble when stocking the shelves with *Liverpool Sound Collage*. "Well, if that perception wasn't altered by his forays into classical music, it will certainly get a jolt from this compelling but decidedly odd disc," which they described as "combining '60s-rooted cut-and-paste techniques with state-of-the-art technology" while warning buyers that it was "anything but 'pop'."

Following all the 'unknown' works covered in this book, *Liverpool Sound Collage* was McCartney's final coming-out as an experimental musician. He didn't put his name on the cover, but he didn't deny he'd made it either. "From now on it's not only Yoko Ono who will be remembered for her fair share of avant-garde," wrote *Progressive World*. "Only time will tell whether *Liverpool Sound Collage* will find its place next to *Two Virgins* and *The Wedding Album*." The *College Music Journal* agreed. "Most think of John Lennon as the most experimental and unpredictable Beatle, but judging from Paul McCartney's millennium release, Sir Paul has a daring artistic side as well ... Not as daring as say, Lou Reed's *Metal Machine Music*, but not exactly what you'd expect from Mr McCartney."

The 1990s was McCartney's most productive decade for avant-garde releases. It was by no means limited to The Fireman's *Rushes* and *Strawberries Oceans Ships Forest*, the *Feedback* installation and *Liverpool Sound Collage*. As the 1980s ended he spent the Christmas break of 1989 working at home on wild, atmospheric soundtrack material. In May 1999 he returned to the spirit of the solo synthesiser *McCartney II* album and recorded his most blatant attempt at modern dance music to date, with an internet-only techno track. He followed this up at the beginning of the next decade with a lengthy instrumental chill-out remix session. In the new century, McCartney continued his policy of airing new avant-garde works as part of his live-show warm-up music and, taking the idea of avant-garde pop to its ultimate extreme, joined a select few daring musicians to have played live and jammed with another species.

Taking these 1990s developments in order…

McCartney's Big World tour of 1989 put him firmly back into the rock mainstream, but with a credibility that had been lacking earlier in the 1980s. When he stepped off the stage at Madison Square Garden on 15 December 1989, he only gave himself two weeks off before embarking on 17 live dates in the UK on 2 January 1990. But his experimental urges were not dampened by either the return to rock or his hectic schedule. During this short Christmas break he spent time at home alone working on six bizarre instrumental tracks with a film soundtrack – no particular film – in mind.

The finished material totalled just 14 minutes but explored a variety of styles across six different tracks. In 'Right', McCartney presents two minutes of pure glacial ambience mixing chimes, choral voices and what John Cage might have described as 'prepared piano'. The accompanying piece, 'Wrong', was far from serene, with shifting orchestra parts, manic vocal percussion (human beatbox style) and random timings. It sounded like a follow-up to 1970's tribal 'Kreen-Akrore', another soundtrack looking for a film. 'Payment' was a simple piece of meditational piano, Satie style, playing off a Spanish guitar. The other tracks – 'Justice', 'Punishment' and 'Release' – were more conventional soundtrack material, high on drama but made with sparing use of conventional instrumentation.

McCartney's experimental soundtrack eventually found its film thanks to his long-term associate in all things animation, Geoff Dunbar. Dunbar had directed the short film and video for McCartney's 'We All Stand Together', testament to his longstanding fascination for the Rupert the Bear cartoons, which he had bought the rights to as far back as 1970.

In the early nineties McCartney commissioned Dunbar to bring to life the drawings of the French artist Honoré Daumier. An artist of various media, Daumier was born in 1808 and pioneered the art of caricature. Dunbar was no stranger to bringing to life images from a bygone age. In 1975 he had won acclaim in Cannes for Lautrec, which did the same for Toulouse Lautrec's Can-Can drawings as he would do for McCartney's Daumier. Character design and layouts on the film were handled by another polished animator, Nicolette van Gendt, who had previously worked on *Who Framed Roger Rabbit*.

Dunbar tackled Daumier's heritage with great skill and, setting the finished animation to McCartney's six short musical experiments, *Daumier's Law* received its premiere at the 1992 Cannes Film Festival. It went on to win a BAFTA for Best Animated Short that same year. Dunbar has continued working with McCartney and, more recently, they collaborated on the animated feature Tropical Island Hum and another short film, Tuesday. The former is aimed at children but with an ongoing animal rights theme; it appears to have been put on ice following the death of Linda McCartney, who was very involved in the film's development.

*Tuesday* was voiced by Dustin Hoffman and received another BAFTA nomination after opening at the Venice Film Festival. In fact, *Tuesday* is a classic example of what the public and media expect from Paul McCartney versus what he produces. McCartney's appearance at the rain-drenched Venice Film Festival for Tuesday's premiere made news around the world not due to the story (a tale of strange unfolding events in an American town) or its soundtrack, but because of photos of McCartney playing air guitar with his umbrella when he arrived.

While in recent years Geoff Dunbar's animation has revolved strictly around Beatrix Potter and children's tales, in the mid-seventies he shared another passion with McCartney – playwright Alfred Jarry. Dunbar's homage to Jarry, the 1979 animation Ubu was acclaimed on release as a shocking, daring and compelling visual feast. At the same time, McCartney began working on a musical project inspired by the same Jarry material, but it would not appear until 1995.

*Oobu Joobu* was McCartney's attempt at zoo radio, inspired by *Life With the Moons*, an anarchic BBC Radio series by Keith Moon and Viv Stanshall of the Bonzo Dog Doo-Dah Band. (*Life With the Moons* was loved by Lennon too, inspiring his second album with Yoko Ono, *Life With the Lions*. The title was also a reference to the post-war radio comedy *Life With the Lyons*). By the time *Oobu Joobu* finally aired on the radio (in the US via the Westwood One network), it was a 17-part series featuring many regular slots like 'Cook of the House' (a recipe by Linda) and 'Rude Corner' (tracks from McCartney's Spirit of Ranachan home studio, which he had renamed Rude Studios). Everything was linked with mad whiz-bang special effects and general radio chitchat, reminiscent of Kenny Everett in his heyday. McCartney aired many rare tracks from his archives across the series, including soundcheck recordings, unreleased demos and – for those with a keen ear – a small smattering of avant-garde efforts.

When US listeners tuned into show number eight of *Oobu Joobu* they would have been surprised to know that it was McCartney behind the first two songs played that night. The first was simple enough, an instrumental synth soundscape of analogue chords and programmed percussion dating from the mid-nineties. It showed that McCartney hadn't lost the spirit of the electronic instrumentals of *McCartney II*. The second was wonderfully avant-garde. A claustrophobic piano track, drowning in reverb, with a falsetto voice drifting in and out singing "so lucky". Unsurprisingly, no more than one minute of this track was aired. This was primetime US radio, after all. Another instrumental '90s synth experiment also cropped up in show 13, the unreleased 'Mambo Baby'.

'Hot Soup – Jammin Fools' was an archive experimental track which McCartney aired on *Oobu Joobu*. A complex, wild electronic rhythm pattern, scat singing and sampled glass-smashing combined to produce a track like no other he has ever made. Although most of the music played by DJ McCartney on *Oobu Joobu* was his own, he did use the series to air some of his non-mainstream musical tastes. Reggae played an important part, with tracks by Toots & The Maytals,Winston Scott, Bob Marley, while various old 7" singles (many missing their artist details) got an airing too. *Oobu Joobu* also put some major doses of world music onto the American airwaves. This is another non-mainstream musical passion of McCartney's which dates back to the experimental 'Kreen-Akrore' on his eponymous 1970 solo album.

From the archives of Peter Gabriel's Real World label, McCartney played an extract from *Arcane*, an album of freestyle collaborations recorded by eight countries' worth of musicians who had spent a week at Real World studios in 1995 communicating only through music. One track, a collaboration between the UK's Simon Jeffes (Penguin Café Orchestra) and a Terkmenistn wedding band, was a tribute to John Cage. 'Cage Dead' was composed using only the notes C, A, G and E. McCartney aired 'Chinese Canon' from Arcane, another track overseen by Simon Jeffes.

The world music thread in *Oobu Joobu* also gave McCartney the chance to play music from Bulgaria (the Sofia Women's Choir singing 'Rodina, Song of the Father Land'), the Burundi tribe and Camaroon across mainstream American FM. Of the latter, he explained: "Listen to this, this is music form the Bula Dance by the Baka Tribe, who are the pygmies of the equatorial African forest. You didn't know that, did you? Their instruments are iron blades, struck against each other, rattles and a rafia pole, laid on the ground and struck with sticks. Wow."

Conversationally, environmental causes were high on the agenda with celebrities dropping in to talk about water wastage, vegetarianism and so on. Coming full circle with one of the sound innovators who had inspired him decades before, McCartney spent the last section of the final *Oobu Joobu* show in conversation and at the piano with Brian Wilson. Wilson talked about The Beatles and *Sgt. Pepper* and McCartney talked about the Beach Boys and *Pet Sounds*.

Oobu Joobu was just one of scores of mid-1990s projects McCartney embarked on while taking a break from public life. While continuing to record the demos that would eventually form his 1997 *Flaming Pie* album, he divided 1994 between preparations for *The Beatles Anthology* and co-promoting vegetarian issues and products with Linda. 1995 was spent working almost completely on experimental projects. The year began with the recording of 'Hiroshima Sky is Always Blue' with Yoko Ono and their respective families. In May he recorded 'Stella May Day', having, the previous month, prepared a special version of

'Maybe I'm Amazed' for *The Simpsons* TV show. Known as the 'Recipe Remix', this version of the classic 1970 solo track featured a Linda McCartney Lentil Soup recipe recorded for *Oobu Joobo* played like a subliminal message – backwards and deep in the mix!

In 1999 McCartney recorded a new song as the theme for Linda McCartney's latest vegetarian foods publicity drive. But anyone expecting to hear a guitar-based poem on the joys of going veggie was in for a shock. Instead, McCartney delivered a manic, modern techno track and, if that wasn't enough of a wake-up call to baby boomers, its only vocals were cut-and-paste samples of 'Penny Lane'.

The idea had first come about in 1998 when Julian Clark, the general manager of a cycling team, approached Linda McCartney Foods as a possible sponsor. The Linda McCartney Pro Cycling Team was thus born, on Linda's condition that all members of the UK team be strict vegetarians. Both Linda and Paul became quite involved with the team. Paul would call team members direct when they had success, contacting Australian David McKenzie when he won a stage of the Giro d'Italia. Just months before she died, Linda McCartney attended a photo shoot with the team, who had dubbed themselves the Clean Machine. "Cycling was going through a drug crisis at the time," remembered Stuart Howell, who designed the Linda McCartney Pro Cycling Team website, "so the team and its riders were keen to be seen as clean and healthy, and the only vegetarian cycling team on the planet."

Racing around Europe, Linda's team went from strength to strength after her death and Paul, who was fighting to keep his late wife's vegetarian campaigning alive, invited them to his Sussex home to find out more. An impromptu tour of his home recording studio ensued at which point the idea of a tie-in song – to attract people to the team's website – came up.

McCartney went to Abbey Road and came back with 'Clean Machine', his first full-on electronic dance track, using a standard four to the floor house drumbeat and pre-set, clichéd bassline. It sounds nothing like anything he had attempted before, or since, The Fireman included. While not exactly a classic of its type, it made it quite clear that, when it comes to the ever-evolving world of music, technology and rhythm, Paul McCartney is determined to try anything at least once. He recorded two versions of 'Clean Machine', the Main Version and – exactly as a young house producer would do for the clubs – a second mix with an extended DJ intro.

If 'Clean Machine' had received a full release it would have dumbfounded anyone who heard it. Partly because of the type of music and partly because of who made it. Even as far as McCartney's non-mainstream works go, it's a full-frontal experiment in the modern club scene. A website was the perfect place to let such an experiment leak out. "Once the tracks were put on the web site, the hits almost doubled," remember Stuart Howell. "We had hundreds of site visitors emailing us to say they loved the tracks and asking were they could obtain a copy!" Although the Linda McCartney Pro Cycling Team disbanded in 2001, it remains the most bizarre platform for one of McCartney's musical ventures to date.

During our interview sessions for this book, Youth was working at McCartney's studio on a special mix of material from The Fireman's *Rushes* album. The finished result of organic ambient jamming, based around the track 'Auraveda', was to give The Fireman its biggest audience yet. Youth turned out to be working on the pre-show music for McCartney's 2002 Driving USA tour, though at the time this return to touring after eight years was strictly under wraps. "It goes through four different kinds of terrain, it starts really quietly and slowly builds up to this big crescendo," Youth explained. "But that was intensely hard work because I only had two days. It was like doing it in half an hour."

Other music used in this stadium entry compilation included the minimalist classic 'Gymnopedie No 1' by Erik Satie (which had also received an airing on *Oobu Joobu*), 'The Very Thought of You' by Nat King Cole, extracts from McCartney's *Working Classical* and two tracks that had been used on previous tours, 'Singalong Junk' and 'The Family Way'.

For the first time, the music accompanied live action. In surreal scenes inspired by Cirque-Du-Soleil, a host of colourful characters – a woman in Victorian costume, a carnival strong man, a flamenco dancer, a stiltwalker, living statues – entered the auditoria as the audience found their seats. "It came from originally we were thinking of having a support act, but it gets difficult because you have to move their stuff off stage and yours on," McCartney explained in a live web-chat just before one of the Driving USA concerts. "So I thought of having the audience come in rather than have them feeling like an auditorium. Then it turned into having them seem like they didn't know how they got there. Then I worked with Youth, and that was it basically. It just gets the audience in and gets them into the atmosphere."

When McCartney's then-fiancée Heather Mills recorded a charity single in 2001 it looked and sounded like any other fund-raising song. The fact that Paul McCartney had produced it gave it a boost of publicity but hardly encouraged his fans or followers to whisk it off the shelves. But those who did buy the single would have heard McCartney's first solo chill-out work, away from his collaborations with Youth. 'Voice' was accompanied by a seven-minute ambient remix, which McCartney called Paul's Mellow Extension. It was trancey, pulse-oriented music – a natural follow-on from the Teutonic beats of the first Fireman album, *Strawberries Oceans Ships Forest*, and the Reich-inspired minimalism before it. And on top of the beat was overlaid some delicate ambient piano.

Paul's Mellow Extension of 'Voice' is remarkable on three counts. First, because it is such a break from any style he has worked in before, or rather such a progression of his various avant-garde experiments to date. (Quite unlike his first solo experiment in modern dance music, 'Clean Machine'.) Secondly, because he put his name to it. It wasn't on the web, it wasn't under a pseudonym. It was an instrumental electronica soundscape that he had 'admitted' to. And finally, the Mellow Extension is notable because it is such an accomplished example of modern chill-out.

Peter Gabriel is an artist who has presented his avant-garde work to the public in completely the opposite way to Paul McCartney. Gabriel has never used pseudonyms and, rather than playing it safe with his mainstream work, has run advertising campaigns encouraging fans to "Expect the Unexpected." Although both artists have a strong admiration for each other (they recorded a track together in 1986, 'Politics of Love', which remains at unreleased demo stage), they present themselves in quite opposite ways. But "Peter Gabriel's got a different type of public expectation," Youth maintains, "because people expect him to be a bit off-centre anyway, whereas McCartney is the centre."

■ McCartney's always going to be compared to what he did in The Beatles. I think he accepts that and doesn't really care. But he is still, I think, incredibly ambitious in what he wants to achieve as an artist. Obviously his songwriting is a big thing, but I don't think he always feels in that space to do that material, and in between that, he can do his choral music, his painting and explore other landscapes of his emotional terrain.

But commercial considerations clash against avant-garde experiments today more than in any other era of rock music, as the Black Dog noted. "I think all those [60s] guys now are finding it a bit harder," says Youth, "because ten years ago anything, some of his worst work I think, would still sell a couple of million. Boom. Now it's not. And it's not just McCartney, it's all those guys of that generation. Mick Jagger and all those guys are finding it harder to command that instant fan-base that they used to have."

In 2002, Peter Gabriel told McCartney about his visit to the Language Research Facility in Atlanta, where their apes are so highly developed they can play music. McCartney paid a visit too and although playing his most mainstream music – 'Eleanor Rigby' and a new song written especially for the occasion – jammed along with perhaps his most avant-garde collaborators to date, brother and sister bonobo apes. "The fact they could recognise and understand 800 words was pretty astounding," McCartney said afterwards, "and we found ourselves actually communicating with them easily. We played some music – the male ape and I jammed a little and his sister joined in with us. He played keyboards and she played drums. It was wild."

Jamming with apes, however much of a stunt or a laugh (film cameras just happened to accompany McCartney on his visit to the Language Research Facility), is a classic example of one of McCartney's motivations in his avant-garde work. Musically he has never ceased to take risks. Even though he's cautious about what he lets the public hear. He may carefully protect his mainstream image but that belies a genuine spirit of adventure, finding new sounds and tackling emotions and ideas in new ways through music. Something that has been apparent for over 40 years. During those 40 years, McCartney has also been an incredibly prolific artist. And when he is out of the public eye he is always creating, most likely something in avant-garde vein.

Another motivation behind McCartney's avant-garde work is his addiction to keeping up with the times, in terms of musical instruments, song structure and record production. By the same token his interest in music, as a listener, continually develops and tries to keep up. Among the inspiring factors in that, of course, are his children; just as in his mainstream work, they have been a major inspiration in his avant-garde work. But not all of the motivations behind McCartney as avant-garde composer are positive forces. Paranoia and Paradise syndrome are just two further factors, and equally important ones, that drive him to produce the work examined in this book.

McCartney is undoubtedly an extremely prolific musician, and this allows him to spread his work into new styles and experiments. As a songwriter, his prolific nature is legendary. For 2001's *Driving Rain* album he had 22 songs recorded and finished, from which he chose 15. And there's a legacy of finished but unreleased albums (*Cold Cuts* being one Holy Grail for collectors). When the rest of his *Flowers in the Dirt* band were resting during the massive world tours of 1989 and 1990, McCartney, right up until Christmas Eve, was finishing his avant-garde soundtrack for *Daumier's Law*.

'Check My Machine' is one McCartney recording that's proof of his avant-garde style and prolific nature. As related in Chapter Eight, it was recorded, as its title implies, to try out new recording gear but turned into a mad electronic workout – which, coincidentally, was exactly how New Order's dance classic 'Blue Monday' came into being too.

It was hard to believe that the same person who recorded 'Check My Machine', 'Secret Friend' and their accompanying tracks could record 'Ebony & Ivory' and 'The Girl is Mine' in the same period. That's the surprising and infuriating thing about McCartney as an artist. Genres are meaningless to him. He has a sense of adventure when it comes to almost every style of music. Steve Anderson, who recorded McCartney doing Jamaican toasting and laying his Hofner bass sound onto a progressive trance 12", agrees. "He wants to have a go at everything and why not," he told me. "He is continually creating and challenging himself, which a lot of people who have achieved what he has would probably not be doing and slowing down.

"I loved the *Run Devil Run* album as it sounds like everyone is enjoying themselves and has such an energy to it," he adds, "but then again, I was that six-year-old being played rough Cavern tapes." As it turns out, rock and roll has had just as much of an impact on the new generation of dance producers as the psychedelic era. It all goes back to getting off your face in a club and letting go, basically. So one of McCartney's most 'techno' collaborators actually has an affinity with his rawest, earliest recordings.

■ My dad is responsible for my education in music and has been since I was born. So when the other kids were on 'Nelly the Elephant' I was listening to rock and roll, blues, jazz and classic Sinatra, Fitzgerald. My favourite period for The Beatles still remains the real rock and roll stuff, where it was rough round the edges and they were learning how to be a band. Obviously, as a record producer I admire the techniques pioneered on *Sgt. Pepper* and the whole end section of *Abbey Road* never fails to take my breath away.

Anderson remembers his progressive house remix of 'Hope of Deliverance' as one of his "proudest achievements ... I only wish I could have taken my dad along..."

McCartney's single most important skill – melody – allowed him to enter Anderson's works of progressive dancefloor trance, and then leave it, with his credibility more or less intact. His classical works – *The Family Way* (1967), *The Liverpool Oratorio* (1991), *Standing Stone* (1997), *Working Classical* (1999) and *Nova* (2000) – all succeeded, too, thanks to this melodic gift. If McCartney continues in the future to separate his surrealist tendencies from his mainstream albums, they'll most likely show up in the other media he is exploring. With McCartney's 'unknown' avant-garde work now becoming known, it should come as no surprise that his paintings aren't the wholesome, still-life equivalent of his *All the Best!* period in music. In fact, they are dark, disturbing onslaughts which, as Liverpool's Walker Gallery stated in 2002, "take risks, break conventions and flout expectations."

Of course, unlike most other musicians, McCartney doesn't actually need to be prolific at all. He works in other media, painting and film, but these are side projects. He has never left music for a new direction – like politics, movie acting, a quiet life or the kind of careers that enticed some of his contemporaries.

Chris Isaak, for one, still can't get over the fact that McCartney continues to produce new music at such a prolific rate. In 2001, they bumped into each other when they were recording albums in adjacent studios. They hung out together briefly, McCartney popping round to sing 'Happy Birthday' to Isaak. "It's mind-blowing that he's still in the studio working," Isaak said later.

> ■ What does he have to prove? If you gave me a billion dollars and I had his body or work behind me, I don't know, maybe I would build an exact replica of Disneyland in my backyard or something. I would probably lose the use of my legs because I would have people carry me around. But he seems really normal. I saw him driving a Chevy, and I was driving a Chevy. Of course, his was a brand new Corvette and mine was a '64 Nova. But it was still a Chevy.

As a musician in his own right, McCartney's key avant-garde collaborator, Youth, had been inspired both by The Beatles and by Wings. When he actually met McCartney and they started working together... "Then he had an even bigger influence on me," he told me, "because I was really inspired by how much he was doing. I felt that, here was a guy who'd achieved incredible success and could have just retreated into a reclusive decadence. And instead, what he's done is he's realised every dream he's ever wanted to do, he's taken that opportunity that he has to do it, and done it." That said, Youth recognises the critics' perception of McCartney and firmly believes this creative outpouring to be "at his peril." The pair forged a creative bond, outside just music. "I found we gelled on a lot of levels," he told me. "We had a good correspondence in what we liked, and poetry. I paint as well, and write, and he's really encouraged me to do that anyway, maybe not publish it, but just do it."

With McCartney turning 60 in 2002, this makes Youth and Isaak's observations even more pertinent. "As far as retirement is concerned, I'd never consider it, although I'm getting up toward retirement age," McCartney said on tour. "I think someone falsified my birth certificate because I can't feel it. I don't want to retire. I love what I do. I always said if people don't come to the shows, I'll do this as a hobby. I have a vision of me at age 90, being wheeled on stage very slowly, doing 'Yesterday'. At the moment, it's not like that. It's the opposite of that. We're loving it, the audiences are loving it, so while that's happening, I'm keeping on rocking."

Standing up to touring America with the verve of a 20-year-old, McCartney remains flippant when asked for the secret of his seemingly boundless energy. "I don't really know," he typed on a Driving USA webchat. "I've been a vegetarian for a long time, that might have something to do with it. I am just enjoying the whole thing. Enjoying playing with the band. I have a very nice woman in my life. I think all of that helps in my life to energise." In the same interview he alluded to his prolific nature. Although he said he didn't play much guitar outside the nightly concerts, clearly music was and is continually on his mind.

■ When I'm touring I don't really find myself sitting around playing acoustic, because you're doing so much in the day that time off is time off. I really just play whatever comes into my mind, it could be an old song that I learned when I first learned guitar, or something new, or someone else's song. Or I'm writing a song when I have time off. I just play nothing in particular and just see if an interesting idea comes out of that. It just depends on the mood you're in. I like doing it and always have one with me, but on tour I don't always use it that much.

It seems, too, that McCartney's eclecticism may spring from his optimistic outlook. "I tend to sort of listen to music, spot the good stuff, sort of ignore the mistakes," he told the press on the LA stop of his Driving USA tour, "and I just sort of think, 'Wow, that's great.' I'm a pretty positive person, you know, and I do try to see the good in everything. It just seems to me to be a good idea, because life is tough." In the same interview he tried to put his finger on where megastar musicians can lose the plot. "Believing their own myths, I think ... There are some people who just get too big for their own boots ... I think it's a very destructive thing. I don't think it's good for you or your self. It's certainly not good for the people around you."

2001's *Driving Rain* album followed the back-to-basics approach that McCartney alludes to. While not being part of his avant-garde lexicon, it became the first album to openly acknowledge some of his more unorthodox musical interests. "It's *White Album*-ish. It's very broad, and he hops from one style to another," promised *Driving Rain* producer David Kahne before the album's release. McCartney himself had chosen Kahne as a producer because he was "a little bit adventurous but not too pop."

Devised purely as a song album, McCartney's return to the pop fray after a long absence included tracks, like the ten-minute 'Rinse the Raindrops', which were clearly put together post-, rather than pre-, Fireman or *Liverpool Sound Collage*. "That's just one verse repeated over and over, but he never sings it the same way twice," said Kahne of the track, which clearly references McCartney's interest in trance music in its middle section. "The song goes through different cuts back and forth between different takes. It's a very aggressive, pushy song where he sings real low then real high – all over the place..."

*Driving Rain*'s 'She's Given Up Talking' sees producer Kahne in full Zooropa-style postmodern rock production mode, and there's at least one secret message mixed subliminally into the music which fans are yet to decipher. Are 'hidden satanic message' uproars appropriate for sexagenarian artists, or are they exempt?

In 2002 the strange, pivotal album *Back to the Egg* came up again. Continuing McCartney's enthusiasm for new styles, he allowed LA rapper Knoc-Turn'al to sample a section of one of the album's rockier highlights, 'Old Siam, Sir'. The sample is the foundation of 'Muzik', a track from the Dr Dre/Missy Elliot-produced album *LA Confidential Presents Knoc-Turn'al.*

Two of McCartney's most popular and, in places, most experimental albums have come out in periods of self-imposed isolation. But the music he will likely be remembered for most are his collaborations. Lennon and McCartney achieved their goal of becoming a modern day Rodgers and Hammerstein, eclipsing their original inspiration. And since the Lennon-McCartney songwriting team disbanded, McCartney has searched for a new partner to fill that void. Linda McCartney's musical worth will be continually debated but she was the first to fill the gap left by Lennon, acting as – in McCartney's view – a co-writer for much of the *Ram* album. How much of Linda's input remained on the finished LP is questionable, but she managed the main part of her role successfully – to give McCartney the sounding board he needed. Wings too, was based around the McCartney-Denny Laine partnership, followed by McCartney's unsuccessful 1980s period with 10cc's Eric Stewart. He followed this in the 1990s by teaming with Elvis Costello, "taking over a half share in the sweet and sour chemistry between McCartney and John Lennon", as Costello biographer Brian Hinton put it.

This songwriting process is mirrored in McCartney's avant-garde work too. Although often working and experimenting in isolation, his best work has been achieved as a duo. Laine, Stewart and Costello's total failure to even slightly inspire McCartney's avant-garde side – even Linda collaborated on 'Glasses' – makes Youth McCartney's most important collaborator in this area since John Lennon.

Those who are new to McCartney's avant-garde work would be forgiven for thinking that it is intense, premeditated highbrow stuff, especially given some of the influences charted in this book. Instead, he brings to his experimental music a sense of spontaneity that has characterised all his other songwriting. In 1971 McCartney told *Life* magazine that a lot of his music came from simply improvising in the studio. But he also explained that he didn't feel desperate to have all of these efforts mixed, pressed and duly distributed on vinyl. Experiencing the process, and the 'accidents' that often lead to new sounds and ideas, was enough. "Sometimes you don't want to share those moments," McCartney told *Life*. "Okay, the record-buying public didn't hear it, but you and I did. That's beautiful. That's real. The moment was temporary like everything is. Nothing in life really stays. And it's beautiful that they go. They have to go in order for the next thing to come. You can almost add beauty to a thing by accepting that it's temporary."

Spontaneity was the basis not only for the early Beatles recordings and much of McCartney's avant-garde work, but also for his most recent album. "It was all very spontaneous," David Kahne said of *Driving Rain*. "There were no rehearsals. He just brought the songs in and we started playing them. Basically, he'd show us a song on the acoustic guitar and we'd learn it. He wanted to do it very much in the way The Beatles used to record. Ringo and George never really heard the songs before The Beatles recorded them. So we just did it on the fly starting the first day."

Various people have also testified to how some of McCartney's best work has been written in an instant, on the spot. 'Picasso's Last Words (Drink To Me)' from Wings' *Band on the Run* was written when Dustin Hoffman set McCartney the challenge of writing a song on the spot. *Driving Rain*'s 'Loving Flame' was written in this way, too. "I actually wrote this one for Heather," McCartney explained. "I was in America and in the Carlisle Hotel, a very posh suite. I was on the 73rd floor and it was a fantastic big suite with a plate-glass window overlooking Central Park. To the side there was a black Steinway piano so it was like walking in Cole Porter's life, so I thought I've got to write a song if I get a chance. The next morning I wrote this one. It came very easily."

Of course, spontaneity and a spirit of experimentation mean that you only ever know if what you've created is valid until after the fact. It was the Asher family, as George Martin remembered in Chaper Two, who encouraged McCartney to explore new areas of music. And it was for Asher's band, Peter & Gordon, that McCartney first tried writing under a pseudonym to see if his work would stand up in its own right.

As McCartney was rehearsing his band for his 2002 tour, Peter Asher, now working in the business side of music, was taking the stage to deliver a keynote address at the SXSW music industry conference in Austin, Texas. "When people ask me for my recollections of 'historic moments', most did not seem so at the time," he told the assembled audience, before embarking on a series of anecdotes "in support of my thesis that sheer excitement and love of music is what should fuel our work and that we could be in the midst of just such historic moments now."

■ The first such occasion was in about 1963. Paul McCartney was living in the guestroom at our family home in London. My mother had a small music room in the basement, where she gave oboe lessons, which contained an upright piano. One evening Paul's friend John came over and they borrowed the room. A few hours later Paul came up to my bedroom and asked me if I wanted to hear a new song that he and John had just written which they clearly thought was quite good. I came down to the basement where they sat side by side at the piano and sang 'I Wanna Hold Your Hand' for the first time to an audience. I was overwhelmed.

Asher's speech was an attempt to mobilise the music industry workforce into finding 'historical moments' of their own in the work of new and emerging artists. For an artist of McCartney's age, stature and experience, Cole Porter would be an obvious inspiration, but his thirst for new music is a major motivation. Philippe Manoeuvre once asked McCartney what current music he listened to, for an interview on France's Canal Jimmy TV station. He listed some obvious influences (Elvis Presley, Nat King Cole, Fred Astaire and Frank Sinatra) but talked about new music too (Snoop Dogg, Cypress Hill and Wyclef Jean) and spoke at length about being in the audience at Nitin Sawhney's Royal Albert Hall concert, which Sawhney explained from his side of the stage in Chapter Nine.

Bass player to the stars and Thrillington insider Herbie Flowers has found his own niche, playing bass for music workshops, universities, arts centres and prisons. He plays jazz mostly, not pop or rock ("Possibly because it's so freeform – the complete opposite to being told what to play in sessions!"), and has strong views on the effects the ageing process has on artists, and how the pop world has changed. "Maybe it's just because I'm an old man now and don't run around playing on Shawaddywaddy records," he explains.

■ A lot of people don't like looking at me – because I am an obstreperous old bastard. Maybe it's because I like professionalism. Kids these days don't know who John Lennon is, and that's perhaps how it should be. People are quite stuck with the commercial side of music. Everyone's listening to stuff on the radio and TV but that's only a tiny percentage of the music that's being created. But broadcasters and labels decide between them what's going to fill the market. At the same time a lot of orchestras are drying up from lack of funds and people are walking around listening to machines, and players like me might as well be working in a factory!

When people get past 50 their ambitions can be an embarrassing disease. Look at Mick Jagger – is anyone really interested in that sort of stuff nowadays? The pop stars today are almost beginning to look like hamburgers as well as being sold like them. You see 25-year-old men with beer guts chasing the playlists. Maybe Cat Stevens had a point when he decided to stop making music for money and sing his kids to sleep instead...

"Singing the kids to sleep" is the classic view of McCartney, the middle-of-the-road family man balladeer. So it's surprising to find that his children and family have often provided the motivation for some of his oddest music. There could be no more extreme McCartney music than Liverpool Sound Collage, which is almost entirely based around childhood memories and homage to his family. It would be easy to assume that Strawberries Oceans Ships Forest was mixed and remixed by Youth in isolation. But he disagrees – even McCartney's techno-oriented album was a family affair. "We did that together," he told me. "Even on the mixing, he and Linda and were very involved. They were up till six o'clock in the morning while I was mixing it one night. I'd get a few hours on my own and then they'd come by."

As McCartney's children have grown up, he's written music for them accordingly. Wings' 'Marty Had a Little Lamb' single and 'Baby's Request' from *Back to the Egg* are obvious early examples. But as they grew up, so McCartney's music for them went more and more off the wall. 'Stella May Day', the post-rock/Hendrix freak-out detailed in Chapter 14, is one example. McCartney's private punk recordings are another. Back in 1977, punk was at its height and his daughter Heather was a Sex Pistols fan. So McCartney had a go at punk rock himself – at first he wrote and recorded the (thankfully) unreleased track 'Boil Crisis'. Then, during the making of *Back to the Egg*, he got Heather to scream the ingredients on the side of a carton of baby milk for his second punk attempt, the appropriately titled 'SMA'.

McCartney also had his children in mind when working with Nitin Sawhney on the drum & bass remixes of 'Fluid'. According to Sawhney, he was keen to create something at the time of Linda's death which his children could relate to. "He told me, 'This means a lot to me, this is kind of my little project,'" Sawhney says of their bedsit meeting. "He said, 'This is the kind of thing I think my son would be into' as well. He said, 'I'm not very relevant to that kind of club scene, so it would be quite nice if people on that scene could be into this kind of thing.'"

Family, spontaneity, a thirst for new music, partnerships – these are some of the key positive motivations behind both Paul McCartney's mainstream and avant-garde music. But they're balanced by darker psychological motivations. Paranoia is one. McCartney claims not to read his own reviews. "They have an effect on me: I either think I'm too great or I get paranoid," he warns. He does read John Lennon's posthumous reviews though. In the same era in which he was being slated for 'The Frog Chorus', his former partner in experimentation (who himself had written many a nursery rhyme) was being elevated, God-like, to the plateau marked 'genius'.

This started McCartney's various attempts to 'get the facts straight' – the 'who wrote what' biography *Many Years From Now*, the attempt to change the credits on 'Yesterday', and so on. George Harrison accused him of wanting to rewrite history, but McCartney had another story. "I became worried that the John legend would totally wipe out any of our contributions," he said later. "I'm sure I got paranoid about it, but, hey, that's normal for me."

In music paranoia becomes perfectionism, which sometimes can be taken too far. McCartney recorded overdubs to his Live Aid vocals the day after the charity concert, having suffered microphone problems on stage. He gathered Wings fans in Wembley after their final world tour to record further crowd noise for the accompanying live album.

Linda McCartney, too, once pointed to this insecurity as a driving force behind his music. "I don't dwell on what people say about me," she said. "I dwell on what people say about Paul, for some reason. Maybe it's because he can't handle it." This paranoia is supplemented by Paradise syndrome, as the *Daily Telegraph* suggested when McCartney reportedly reacted in fury to having one of the poems from his *Blackbird Singing* poetry anthology included in *Private Eye* magazine's 'Pseuds Corner'. "In his professional life at least, he suffers from Paradise syndrome," the paper suggested. "Having a perfect life he needs to find something to feel anxious about."

Psychologically or astrologically, Paul McCartney will continue to be the subject of examination and deconstruction. As a Gemini, his music and avant-garde tendencies are explicable to some extent. One moment he's working in private, the next he can only work in partnership. Sometimes he stretches sound to its limits with avant-garde recordings, the next he is a heads-down rock and roller. One moment he completes an entire song spontaneously, at others he labours for years over minor details. McCartney will often cite his star sign when attempting to rationalise his diverse musical interests. "I'm a Gemini and we're supposed to like this and that; it's slightly schizophrenic," he claimed on US TV while promoting both *Working Classical* and *Run Devil Run*.

McCartney's audience for his experimental music varies wildly – tracks for his kids, for himself, for catwalks or commissions – but not necessarily for the post-Beatles McCartney-loving public. This latter audience has been largely cordoned off from his more oddball output; for them he provides something entirely different. Which is the true McCartney? Both, of course. Neither side is more important than the other.

The fact that such opposite forms of music come from the same man can be infuriating to critics who need to have every artist safely tucked away in pigeon-holes. Some feel the need to repress artists of a certain genre or era and feel uncomfortable when they progress into new fields. When McCartney's debut art exhibition opened in Siegen, *Rolling Stone*'s coverage fell back on a theme that would have been contentious in 1969 but in 1999 came across as merely outmoded. "The creative rivalry that characterised John Lennon and Paul McCartney's musical relationship now extends to the visual arts," they reported. "Just a month after news broke of the first permanent display of Lennon prints at Liverpool's Mathew Street Gallery, seventy-three of Paul McCartney's 600 paintings have gone on display at the Kunstforum Lyz gallery in the German town of Siegen, and they're drawing rave reviews from art critics."

Pigeonholing aside, it's possible to gain a deeper appreciation of McCartney's well-known albums – like *Driving Rain, London Town* or *Off the Ground* – when they're placed in the context of avant-garde works such as *Feedback, Rushes, Liverpool Sound Collage* or even knockabout experiments like

*Thrillington*. And there is a whole new world of music and ideas that pushes the concept of music to its very limits (or at least the limits we can imagine thus far), a new world that McCartney is expressing himself through. At the personal level, these works, composing and recording styles open up a whole new window on the creative psyche. At the global level they open up the most extreme musical forms to a mass audience.

Six TV towers pouring ambient noise, chainsaw effects and random video. McCartney's *Feedback* installation – and the other music covered in this book – hopefully shed new light on one of the 20th century's most important composers. As McCartney said himself of *Feedback*, "It was through music that I broke free. I learned the rules of paradox, of random experiments in music." Youth has seen first-hand this free spirit and its thirst for new musical forms.

> ■ I think he does what he wants. I think he does exactly what he wants when he wants to do it, that's what he does, and he just thinks, "Well, if that's what I'm doing, I'll put it out." I don't think he has management in place that says, "Oh, that's not right, you'll do this or do that." He's definitely at the helm of that ship and for better or worse he sails wherever he likes and things just move into gear around that.

As a Beatle, a solo artist, a Fireman, as Percy Thrillington, Paul McCartney has pushed forward both the art of songwriting and his own "random experiments". But the work of this 'unknown' McCartney wouldn't have surprised Brian Epstein. The "gentleman of pop", as the original Cavern Club DJ Bob Wooler described him, saw boundaries blur and new musical directions splinter in 1967. In his last interview before his death, Epstein described all four of The Beatles as "four creative people whose minds burst with ideas ... they will always be exploring new horizons."

"You won't find them sitting back and saying they've come to the end and can go no further," Epstein added prophetically. "For them, the road has no end. They follow it, enthused with incentive and ambition and the insatiable urge to discover fresh things."

# EPILOGUE
# A BLIND TASTING

Having traced McCartney's musical travels from the sixties to the present day, from playing with the Gizmotron in Lympne Castle to trying drum & bass in Nitin Sawhney's bedsit, I thought I'd go on some travels of my own. I had one final question about McCartney's avant-garde music in mind. Is it any good?

I gathered tapes of the music – The Fireman, Percy Thrillington and McCartney's other experiments – and played them to established musicians in the alternative, dance and avant-garde fields. After all, the media reviews surveyed in this book were almost all written knowing that the avant-garde artist they were listening to was Paul McCartney. But what if people heard this material unawares, and free from any 'Frog Chorus' or even Beatles-induced baggage?

I started off by putting some Fireman music in front of Guy Fixsen from the band Laika. Laika have a unique sound that blurs the boundaries of rock, electronic and avant-garde music with subtle beauty. Their 1994 album *Silver Apples of the Moon* was described by *Mojo* magazine as "the missing link between the avant funk of Can and the ambient jungle heard on London's pirates." They took their name from the first living thing to leave planet Earth, the Russian dog Laika, which was blasted into space on Sputnik 2 in November 1957. "For us it made a good band name, firstly because we liked the sound of the word and we liked the association with being 'out there' in terms of experimentation, while at the same time being a warm furry organic thing," Fixsen once said.

Having worked with The Breeders, Throwing Muses and My Bloody Valentine, Guy Fixsen took Laika on the road in 2000, supporting Radiohead on their European tour. As *i-D* magazine noted, "Laika go where no other band dares to go," so Fixsen seemed the ideal person to check out 'Palo Verde' from McCartney and Youth's second venture as The Fireman, *Rushes*. 'Palo Verde' was the highlight of *Rushes*, with so many emotive sounds almost subliminally blended into its meditational, guitar-based mix. Funnily enough, Fixsen didn't guess that McCartney was involved but, curiously, the bass playing stood out to him.

> ■ I'm not much up on the art of the hair-splitting genre. I would file it in a rather large box labelled late '90s ambient electronica. It has that progressive rock tinge injected by a kind of Weather Report-ish bass solo which, although a little smug and over-muso for my tastes, has a nice polyrhythm effect on what is basically a 4/4 bassline amble. The found sound/horse ear candy is nice if a little plasticised with delay. The guitar chimes take me back to cokey late '80s recording sessions.

"Single white French males in Montmartre bedroom studios" was Fixsen's assessment of the people behind 'Palo Verde'. "It's part of the glue that holds many a fashionable 30-something's apartment together on a hungover Saturday afternoon," he decided, referencing the UK's almost saturation-point exposure to post-millennium chill-out albums. "Unlikely to change the world but part of a general complexity drift in music of late. Hard to justify the tag avant-garde, unless it was produced quite a few years ago." But did he like it? "I don't love it," Fixsen told me, "but it does a certain chill-out thing with a little grace to spare."

I wondered in what way Fixsen's views, or anyone's, would have been different if they had known this music was made by Paul McCartney. "If I had known I'm really not quite sure what I would have changed in my reply," said the man from Laika, "apart from the French bit, I guess! Well, there you go – Paul still smokes the odd spliff now and then, I guess," he concluded. "His more well-known stuff certainly has a much larger personality stamp on it."

I took a tape of the pure chainsaw and guitar feedback noise to play to LA's Ken Gibson, aka 8 Frozen Modules. No stranger to noise music, his 1997 album *The Confused Designer* contained tracks of pure noise (which at the time I described for readers of *DJ* magazine as simply "brilliant"). It was followed by the groundbreaking *Random Activities and Broken Sunsets* album, which *The Wire* magazine described as using "the precision of breakbeat programming to create a complex sonic terrain best explored with either headphones or a cinema grade surround system." Sticking to the 'blind tasting' idea, I made sure Ken had no clue that this music had been made by Paul McCartney when I asked him to describe what he heard.

> ■ It's running through some FFT fx ... possibly the spectral gate in Logic. I like the loud clicky 'wrong' sound that comes in occasionally like someone is pressing a microcassette recorder record button on Earth Day. When it cuts out, it's

my favourite part of the clip. A slight buzz, like they took a bathroom break due to diarrhoea or something. It really sounds like someone recorded a guitar jam on a microcassette recorder and did some minimal editing with it in Pro Tools or Logic. I would classify this as 'banana boat blues' or quite possibly 'experimental love music' or even just 'experimental'.

'Bison' was the rambling punk, or rather post-rock, jam recorded live by Youth and McCartney. It was like a wake-up call on the otherwise blissed-out *Rushes* album, pulling anyone who had drifted off to the album's chill-out atmospheres sharply back to reality.

■ I'm a big compression fan. I like loads of compression on everything, especially drums. I like the way the snare sounds in the mix. I also sort of like when the sampled vocal stuff comes in near the end of the clip. As a whole I don't like the track. It sort of bores me. I guess you would classify this as post-rock…

Although 'Bison' didn't sit well with Ken Gibson, *Feedback* (albeit just the audio part of the installation) had conjured some pretty graphic images in his head. But overall he was cautious about both tracks. "I wouldn't listen to either of these tracks on a normal day in the life. I don't hate them but neither stick out as being, well, something I'd listen to really. But there's a couple things about each track I can dig."

"Wow! Paul McCartney?" The 8 Frozen Modules man was certainly blown away when I told him who had made this music and asked him if knowing this beforehand would have changed his view. "Crazy. That would probably change it a bit even if I didn't want it to … Mmm … interesting … The drums almost sounded like Ringo, but not. Crazy."

Laika once contributed a track to *Whore*, a tribute album to the highly influential experimental band Wire. As soon as their debut album was released in 1977, Wire became one of the most influential bands of the punk generation. *Pink Flag*, as it was known, contained 21 of the most nerve-wracking, primally energised songs of the era. With typical punk ethos, the four piece of Colin Newman (guitar, vocal), Bruce Gilbert (guitar), Graham Lewis (bass, vocal), and Robert Gotobed (drums) decided to learn how to play their instruments after deciding to form a band. Having disbanded in 1979 at the height of their popularity, they reformed to produce more avant-garde albums in the mid and late 1980s, like 1988's *A Bell is a Cup (Until it is Struck)*. These and their punk records were true crossovers between art experiments and songs.

"Strange task… but interesting!" said Colin Newman when I asked him to talk to me about some experimental music tracks but refused to say who they were by. I had decided that Newman, with his Wire heritage, was ideally placed to listen to tracks by The Fireman. Unsurprisingly, 'Bison' stood out (especially when I asked him who he thought had made it):

■ Sounds like a group, sounds like it was played live, even samples played in real time. It has a feel not unlike a kind of breakbeat track only done live. Quite like the distorted bassline, the guitar is a bit out of the aesthetic. I think this style is something that could be quite moody and a lot more heavy and dark if it was done in a tougher way. I don't think the percussion adds anything although I like the rest of the elements. The music is possibly made by jazzers or stoners (or both!). I could define it with a bunch of entirely meaningless genre classifications but won't bother. If it was a bit tougher it could be very effective live, I like stuff which is moody and I do like this but I think I already said how it could be better!

I also managed to get a snippet of the soundtrack to McCartney's *Feedback* installation into Newman's eardrums. And his comments on this were even more pertinent.

■ It's got that "I am an individual and I just don't care" vibe. For me this is more self-consciously 'experimental' than the first one; either that or the author is an extreme naïf. Sometimes people who do stuff like this edge genius or can be just totally self-indulgent. I like it because the 'musical' content is quite moody and a bit eerie in a nicely unsettling kind of way but I can't say I'd spend hours listening to it.

"Interesting!" Newman was more than surprised when I told him that Paul McCartney had recorded *Rushes* and *Feedback*. "One thing which is quite weird is that when I heard the second piece [*Feedback*] the first thing I thought was 'Revolution 9', but then I dismissed it as not being relevant! I think in general the dismissal of McCartney in favour of Lennon is a bit unfair, although 'Mull of Kintyre' (not to mention 'Ebony & Ivory' and 'The Frog Chorus') did him no favours at all. However, I must say I also think 'Imagine' is the most overrated Beatle-connected piece of music, full stop!"

With McCartney now able to embrace areas such as remix, techno and chill-out, he is working with an extra audience in mind – DJs. "DJs are the curators of modern sound," DJ Spooky once told me. They are also the driving force behind how new music, in the dance field, is discovered, developed and promoted. So I decided to takes some tapes of early Fireman material and some McCartney solo dance material across town to Chris Coco.

DJ, journalist, artist and remixer, Coco started DJing acid house at Brighton's influential Zap club and now plays all over the world as well as compiling chill-out compilations such as the acclaimed *Acoustic Chill* (2001), *Solar Spectrums* (2000) and *Real Ibiza* (1999). He has DJd in Ibiza for some years. "Ibiza has got that other side to it that is nothing to do with cheesy clubs," he says. "Total hedonism means not just partying and taking loads of drugs but doing whatever gives you the most pleasure, whatever that might be. That's what Ibiza is really good for, so that's why I really love it."

In 2002 Coco took chill-out to a new level with *Next Wave*, an album featuring collaborations with legendary singer-songwriter Nick Cave, author Iain Banks and samples of veteran dissident activist Noam Chomsky. The year before he wrote the liner notes for Ministry of Sound's *Chill Out Session*, the UK's biggest selling chill-out album ever. I started by hiding the artist name and playing Coco the first two tracks from *Rushes* – the entire suite of 'Watercolour Guitars' and 'Palo Verde' – and asked him what he thought and if he would DJ something like this…

> ■ It's a bit of a slow builder, or in other words it's boring at the beginning. But it has a good electro sound, very now, and a euphoric feel that is enhanced by the vocals. Though it is long, over eight minutes, new elements keep coming in to keep the interest. Yes, I could play this in one of my downtempo sets. I wonder what it is…

I refused to say. Instead, I skipped back a few years and played 'Sunrise Mix', the closing track on The Fireman's debut, *Strawberries Oceans Ships Forest*. He spotted it was from 1993 straight away, but didn't cast it off by any means:

> ■ More traditional ambient/chill with little sequences, funny noises and pads. This is the kind of thing you hear a lot of in Ibiza. It's nice but sounds a little bit old-fashioned now. It's also incredibly long. I'm all for things stretching out and having space to develop but for me the optimum length for a chilled track is still only about five minutes. Maybe that's because if you're DJing it's pretty daft to play 20-minute tracks – it doesn't say much about your style or ability to build a set.

With all this unknowing positive feedback for McCartney's avant-garde work, I decided to go the whole hog and play Coco a recording of 'Clean Machine', McCartney's solo house track released only on the worldwide web. It had to be the Extended Mix as the other released version featured the 'Penny Lane' sample more overtly and might have given the game away.

■ This one I don't really like at all. Again it sounds a bit old-fashioned. It bounces along in a traditional housey fashion but doesn't really do anything or make me feel anything. It sounds like the spill-over from a dodgy rave down the road… !

In Battersea I found Mike Flowers living in what de described as "a permanent state of flexitime." He was the artist who flew in the face of rock's biggest revival of the 1990s (with all its Oasis vs Blur hype) by championing the cause of easy listening as a hip alternative. The Mike Flowers Pops' cover version of Oasis' 'Wonderwall' (recorded, appropriately, in mono) sat so perfectly on the edge of parody and quality that it was a European top ten chart hit.

Away from the charts Mike Flowers continues to experiment with exotica on collaborations with the likes of Aphex Twin and Luke Vibert and compilation appearances alongside Pizzicato 5, Devo and others. There could be no one better to listen to McCartney's venture into the world of easy listening and exotica, recorded as Percy 'Thrills' Thrillington. For Mike Flowers it bought back a flood of thoughts on how The Beatles managed the rare task of mixing experimentation with sales. I played Flowers the *Thrillington* album and he immediately spotted some of the trademark sounds of this alter ego. The musicianship, 'dry' drum sounds, Beach Boys-influenced vocals and even the overall sound of Abbey Road Studio Two all stood out. But his favourite bit was the end of the wild, 'watery box'-based exotica version of 'Too Many People' with what Flowers called "Walrusesque cellos".

■ I was at a friend's the other day and he played me one of the Beatles *Anthology* CDs. Some of Paul Mac's 'messing about' recorded therein put me in mind of the Thrillington you played me. I think he led a jokey, lounge (ie, the lounge of a northern social club) rendition of one of their songs. It seems all Paul Mac's output is essentially nostalgic, with 'Yesterday' being the apotheosis of this tendency. Not to mention being the most recorded tune, which must surely be the litmus of truly light music. I'd never heard the *Anthology* recordings before and I was very impressed by the fun, lighthearted, irreverent and, dare I say, unprofessional atmosphere of the sessions … the only conditions for producing extraordinary beat music?

Flowers points to an easy listening or exotica thread that runs through the more mainstream work of McCartney, as well as that of his sixties contemporaries. As well as 'Yesterday', he also mentioned 'Long and Winding Road', 'Michelle' and George Martin's *Yellow Submarine* soundtrack. Warming to this theme, he played me 'America Drinks…', 'Duke of Prunes', 'Peaches' and 'Twenty Small Cigars' by The Mothers of Invention. The Beach Boys straddled exotica perfectly on *Pet*

*Sounds* with 'God Only Knows' and followed it with elements of the doomed *Smile* and their work with Van Dyke Parks in general. 'Sunday Morning' was one of a few tracks by the Velvet Underground that Flowers also fits into this thread, to say nothing of 'Femme Fatale' and 'Candy Says' ("especially its 'doo, doo wah' outro").

> ■ *Thrillington* also reminds me of 'America Drinks and Goes Home' by The Mothers of Invention, who I'm sure I've read in interviews or music journalism of the time, Paul Mac was a fan of. I get the feeling from early interviews – before he got media-sussed – that Zappa had, in return, been in awe of the Beatles despite himself … I guess that at the time ('65-'70) there was a rivalry between The Beatles, The Mothers of Invention, The Beach Boys and the Velvets for the pop avant-garde higher ground, with each recording 'edgy', groundbreaking music. It's interesting to note that each act could also 'get easy' at the drop of a bippetty-boppetty hat...

The Beatles and the sixties still cast a shadow in the minds of all the musicians I talked to. It's the root of everything for them, it seems. "You know you've succeeded at something when others not only try to emulate you, but embrace your ideas and help them evolve," says the Black Dog. "Writers follow Ginsberg, and to this day bands still sound like The Beatles. The trouble is that when Ginsberg died, the world knew there would never be another voice to replace him."

When we sat in the studio meditating to the Ginsberg/Glass/McCartney (with more than a little help from Kaye/Mansfield/Ribot) recording 'Ballad of the Skeletons', Keir Jens-Smith began to worry about the future of poetry itself. Which in turn led to the question of just how few creative channels the youth of today, as opposed to the Beatles generation (or the Beat generation before them), have available to them, avant-garde or otherwise.

> ■ Here, in music with Paul McCartney, people may still discover Ginsberg's message and his words. And it isn't even ironic that a larger degree of new ears to his mouth will discover him through music, which is now the only culture outside of movies that exists to a younger generation who have yet to go through a 'movement' or live through a war. A generation that finds its cultural home in the music scene, and the words of mass-produced 'youth bands' speaking to them, as opposed to those of great writers or poets.
>
> Did the work of Ginsberg and the Beats influence popular culture even more than we give credit? It's clear that they had a huge influence on other artists, who are in turn expressing their own inspired words to a new audience. If the music in the 50s and 60s was all about love and heartbreak, and the literary movement that followed offered up new words, then the music and lyrics of

today's music scene are heavily laden with sex and rebellion and voices of anger and dissatisfaction. Lyrics offering an alternative and painful honesty – which was the shared vision of the Beats. If the new generation won't read, then music, film and TV offer the only messages they'll receive, there's little space for imagination or interpretation, it's all presented to you in a finished package.

An epilogue is perhaps not the right moment to open up a discussion on the musical worth of one genre (say avant-garde) versus another (for example mainstream pop). Possibly because there is no discussion at all. In conversation with Trevor Horn and Lol Creme in 1999, we cooked up an abstract view on this subject. Horn, of course, was one producer who managed to fly in the face of McCartney's return to back-to-basics when he worked on the wacky electronic track 'Ou est le soleil?'. Creme was the inventor of the Gizmotron device, which had changed the sound of Wings' *Back to the Egg* album.

> ■ **Horn:** I don't know if one piece of music is better than another piece of music. I think it's maybe better for you at the moment, whether or not it's intrinsically better. It's an interesting thing I've often thought: could you take a piece of music that was digitally recorded, which is in actual fact a stream of numbers. Then if you had two streams of numbers and one was a good record and one was a crap record, how could you tell from the numbers? Could you tell it from the numbers? Could you look at those numbers and be able to tell, "This is a crap record"?
> **Creme:** And if you could identify the number which when associated made the things that put people off, could you remove them and replace them with numbers that did the right thing? Is that what you're saying?
> **Peel:** Well, you know what this is, don't you? This is genetically modified music!
> **Creme:** Yes! I think we'll have to get before the United Nations.
> **Horn:** GM Music!

But whatever the genre, be it the pure ambient noise of *Feedback* or the comic singalong of 'The Frog Chorus', it has to connect with the listener in some way in order to succeed. Few musicians could be considered more avant-garde than Tim Cole, whose SSEYO system of generative music takes McCartney's *Feedback* installation to another level. Instrumental, esoteric and challenging in the extreme, Cole told me that SSEYO's work is still made with a simple emotional connection with the listener in mind.

> ■ As everyone is hardwired to seek meaning, you look to find meaning in generative/avant-garde material as in everything else. If not enough meaning can be found, then it can be hard to relate to as you are not engaging with it (again,

depends if engagement is a desired outcome). They say that the most music pleasure is experienced by the composer, then the performer and then the audience. If you are the creator of a generative environment then you can enjoy the context because you made it. Unless you are using the sound environment as a pure backdrop, to engage the emotions of the audience is the tricky part, as you must somehow find resonance with the listener.

No matter how the music covered in this book sounds today, it will sound completely different to the ears of listeners in ten or 20 years' time. In the late 1940s Schoenberg dumbfounded the Parisian elite with a symphony not for instruments but for radiogram turntables. Nearly 60 years later and turntable music is the norm, not only being listened to but being created in every teenager's bedroom. So how will the futuristic noise-scapes that McCartney produced for *Feedback*, or the dialogue-as-bassline contortions of *Liverpool Sound Collage*, be heard in another 60 years' time? By its very nature, anything described this century as avant-garde or postmodern certainly won't be in the next, as Mike Flowers mused:

■ It rather puts paid yet again to the idea that postmodernism is anything remotely new, or even that it was something that Prince had dragged in. The term may have been coined fairly recently, but the practice of what it describes sure wasn't! And it certainly didn't start in 1973 as some have suggested. Ask Stravinsky in the 1930s! As Constant Lambert pointed out in 'Music Ho', Stravinsky, under Diaghilev's influence, realised that the geographically exotic (like Debussy's orientalism, his own 'primitive' *Rite*) was already no longer exotic, and that 'time travelling' raids of musical pillage would have to be made to keep a 20th century audience's novelty-craving attention! … resulting in the wonderful 'Pulcinella'. Lambert also bleats that the adjective most often heard in the contemporary music scene (1930s) was 'amusing', suggesting that there was a lack of 'authentic emotion' to be had. Ah well, plus ça change...

Other experimental musicians' views of McCartney's work is one thing, but what about the next generation of musicians? What will they think of sound experiments from the past 40 years, or even McCartney's mainstream music from the seventies? Colin Newman and his son bring our story full circle:

■ I heard 'Band on the Run' a couple of weeks ago in the car bringing my 13-year-old home from school. He found it laughable that something so "random" and peculiar could have ever been considered to be pop music! People often say that over time the avant-garde becomes pop, but perhaps the same is also true the opposite way round...

# APPENDIX ONE

# LISTENING

### Chapter 1

The Beatles - Please Please Me (Parlophone PCS 3042, 1963)The Beatles - With the Beatles (Parlophone PCS 3045, 1963)

The Beatles - The Beatles' Christmas Record (Lyntone Recordings LYN 492, 1963)

The Beatles - A Hard Day's Night (Parlophone PCS 3058, 1964)

The Beatles - Another Beatles Christmas Record (Lyntone Recordings LYN 757, 1964)

The Beatles - Beatles For Sale (Parlophone PCS 3062, 1965)The Beatles - Help! (Parlophone PCS 3071, 1965)

The Beatles - Rubber Soul (Parlophone PCS 3075, 1965)

The Beatles - The Beatles' Third Christmas Record (Lyntone Recordings LYN 948, 1965)

The Beatles - 1962-1966 (a/k/a The Red Album, Apple PCSP 717, 1973)

The Beatles - Live! at the Star-Club in Hamburg, Germany; 1962 (Lingasong LNL 1, 1977)

The Beatles - Live At The Hollywood Bowl (Parlophone EMTV 4, 1977)

The Beatles - Live At The BBC (Apple PCSP 726, 1994)

The Beatles - Anthology 1 (Apple PCSP 727, 1995)

### Chapters 2 and 3

The Beatles - Revolver (Parlophone PCS 7009, 1966)

The Beatles - Pantomime: Everywhere It's Christmas (Lyntone Recordings LYN 1145, 1966)

The Beatles - Sgt. Pepper's Lonely Hearts Club Band (Parlophone PCS 7027, 1967)

The Beatles - Christmas Time Is Here Again (Lyntone Recordings LYN 1360, 1967)

The Beatles - The Beatles (ak/a The White Album, Apple PCS 7067/8, 1968)

Yoko Ono/John Lennon - Unfinished Music No. 1, Two Virgins (Apple SAP-COR2, 1968)

The Beatles - The Beatles 1968 Christmas Record (Lyntone Recordings LYN 1743, 1968)

The Beatles - Yellow Submarine (Apple PCS 7070, 1969)The Beatles - Abbey Road (Apple PCS 7088, 1969)

George Harrison - Electronic Sound (Zapple 02, 1969)

John Lennon/Yoko Ono - Unfinished Music No. 2, Life With The Lions (Zapple 1, 1969)

John & Ono - The Wedding Album (Apple SAPCOR 11, 1969)

The Beatles - The Beatles' Seventh Christmas Record (Lyntone Recordings LYN 1970, 1969)

The Beatles - Let It Be (Apple PCS 7096, 1970)

The Beatles - From Them To You (Apple LYN 2154, 1970)

The Beatles - 1967-1970 (a/k/a The Vlue Album, Apple PCSP 718, 1973)

The Beatles - Magical Mystery Tour

(Apple/Parlophone PCTC 255, 1976)

The Beatles – Anthology 2 (Apple PCSP 728, 1996)

The Beatles – Anthology 3 (Apple PCSP 729, 1996)

The Beatles – 1 (Apple 7243 5 29970, 2000)

## Chapters 4-5

The Beach Boys – Smiley Smile (Capitol, 1967)

Paul McCartney – McCartney (Apple PCS 7102, 1970)

Paul and Linda McCartney – Ram (Apple PAS 10003, 1971)

Brung To Ewe by Hal Smith (Apple SPRO 6210, 1971) 2

Wings – Wings Wild Life (Apple PCS 7142, 1971)

Paul McCartney & Wings – Red Rose Speedway (Apple PCTC 251, 1973)

Wings – Band on the Run (Apple PAS 10007, 1973)

Wings – Venus and Mars (Capitol PCTC 254, 1975)

Wings – Wings at the Speed of Sound (Parlophone PAS 10010, 1976)Wings – Wings Over America (Parlophone PCSP 720, 1976)

Wings – London Town (Parlophone PAS 10012, 1978)

## Chapters 6-8

Percy 'Thrills' Thrillington – Thrillington (Regal Zonophone EMC 3157, 1977)

Percy 'Thrills' Thrillington – Uncle Albert/Admiral Halsey (Regal Zonophone 7" EMI 2594, 1977)

Wings – Wings Greatest (Parlophone PCTC 256, 1978)Wings – Back to the Egg (Parlophone PCTC 257, 1979)Paul

McCartney – McCartney II (Parlophone PCTC 258, 1980)

Paul McCartney – Temporary Secretary/Secret Friend (Parlophone 12" R 6039, 1980)

Paul McCartney – Tug of War (Parlophone PCTC 259, 1982)

Paul McCartney – Pipes of Peace (Parlophone PCTC 1652301, 1983)

Paul McCartney – Give My Regards To Broad Street (Parlophone PCTC 2, 1984)

Paul McCartney – Press To Play (Parlophone PCSD 103, 1986)Paul McCartney – Pretty Little Head (Remix by John Tokes Pottoker)/Write Away/Angry (Parlophone 12" 12R 6145, 1986)

Paul McCartney – All the Best! (Parlophone PMTV 1, 1987)

Paul McCartney – Flowers in the Dirt (Parlophone PCSD 106, 1989)

Paul McCartney – Tripping The Live Fantastic (Parlophone PCST 7346, 1990)

Paul McCartney – Unplugged, The Official Bootleg (Parlophone CDPCSD 116, 1991)

## Chapter 9

Paul McCartney – No More Lonely Nights (Arthur Baker Remix)/Silly Love Songs/No More Lonely Nights (Ballad) (Parlophone 12" 12R 6080, 1984)

Paul McCartney – No More Lonely Nights (Mole Mix) (EMI 12", 1984) 2

Paul McCartney – Spies Like Us (Party Mix)/Spies Like Us (Alternative Mix (Known To His Friends As Tom))/Spies Like Us (DJ Version)/My Carnival (Party Mix) (Parlophone 12" 12R 6118, 1985)

Paul McCartney – Figure of Eight/Ou est le Soleil?/Ou est le Soleil? (Tub Dub Mix) (Parlophone 12" 12RX 6235, 1989)

Paul McCartney – Ou est le Soleil?
(Shep Pettibone Edit) (Capitol US CD
DPRO-79836, 1989) 2
Paul McCartney – The Steve Anderson
Remixes (Deliverance/Deliverance (Dub
Mix)/Hope Of Deliverance)
(Parlophone 12" 12R 6330, 1992) 2
The Fireman – Fluid/Appletree
Cinnabar Amber/Bison (Long One)
(Hydra 12" HYPRO 12007, 1998) 2
The Fireman – Fluid (Out of Body and
Mind Mix)/ Fluid (Out of Body Mix)/
Fluid (Out of Body with Sitar Mix)/Bison
(Hydra 12" HYPRO 12008, 1998) 2
The Fireman – Fluid (Out of Body and
Mind Mix)/ Fluid (Out of Body Mix)/
Fluid (Out of Body with Sitar Mix) (Hydra
CD single HYPRO CD008, 1998) 2
Paul McCartney – Silly Love Songs:The
Remixes (EMI CD CDP 000587, 2001) 2

## Chapters 10-15

The Fireman – Strawberries Oceans Ships
Forest (Parlophone PSCD 145, 1993)
Allen Ginsberg – The Balld of the
Skeletons (Mouth Almigty/Mercury sin-
gle 697 120 101-2, 1996)
The Fireman – Rushes (Hydra 4 97055-
1, 1998)
Linda McCartney – Wide Prairie
(Parlophone 4 97010-1, 1998)
Liverpool Sound Collage (Hydra LSC01,
2000)
Paul McCartney,The Beatles, Super Furry
Animals – Free Now (Hydra 7", 2000) 2

## Chapter 16

Bonzo Dog Doo-Dah Band – New Tricks
(Remastered) (includes I'm The Urban
Spaceman, Castle, 2001)

The Family Way (Original Motion Picture
Soundtrack) (Decca LK 4847, 1967)
Paul McCartney & Carl Davis – Paul
McCartney's Liverpool Oratorio (EMI
Classics PAUL 1, 1991)
The London Symphony Orchestra con-
ducted by Lawrence Foster – Paul
McCartney's Standing Stone (EMI
Classics CDC 5 56484-2, 1997)
Paul McCartney's Working Classical
(EMI Classical CDC 5 56897-2, 1999)
Paul McCartney – Choba B CCCP
(Parlophone CDPCSD 117, 1991) Paul
McCartney – Off the Ground
(Parlophone PCSD 125, 1993)
Paul McCartney – Paul Is Live
(Parlophone PCSD 147, 1993)
Paul McCartney – Flaming Pie
(Parlophone PCSD 171, 1997)
Paul McCartney – Oobu Joobu, Ecology
(Best Buy OOBU #5, 1997) 2
Paul McCartney – Run Devil Run
(Parlophone 523 3042, 1999)
Heather Mills – Voice (includes Paul
McCartney's Mellow Extension,
Coda, 1999)
Paul McCartney – Wingspan, Hits and
History (Parlophone 532 8762, 2001)
Paul McCartney – Driving Rain
(Parlophone 535 5102, 2001)
Peter and Gordon – Ultimate Collection
(includes every Lennon & McCartney
composition, EMI, 2002)

## Notes

All releases listed here are UK albums,
unless otherwise stated.
1 These releases are flexidisc EPs.
2 These releases are promotional
singles/EPs.

# APPENDIX TWO
# FURTHER LISTENING

### Chapters 1-3

Daevid Allen – The Death of Rock & Other Entrances (includes 'The Switch Doctor' – only release of poem/tape collage material, Shanghai, 1984)

AMM – The Crypt, 12 June 1968 (early live recording, Matchless, 1995)

AMM – Generative Themes (Matchless, 1982)

AMM – Laminal (3CD live compendium, Matchless, 1995)

BBC Radiophonic Workshop – BBC Radiophonic Music (includes various Delia Derbyshire tracks, BBC Records, 1971)

Luciano Berio – Many More Voices (includes Thema (Omaggio a Joyce), RCA Victor, 1998)

William Burroughs – The Best of William Burroughs, From Giorno Poetry Systems (a comprehensive 4 CD set with photographs by Gus Van Sant and Allen Ginsberg, Mouth Almighty, 1998)

William Burroughs – Dead City Radio (Mercury, 1990)

John Cage – 25-Year Retrospective Concert of The Music of... (includes Imaginary Landscapes series and Williams Mix, Wergo, 1994)

John Cage – HPSCHD (Nonesuch, 1969)

John Cage – Cage, Music for Trombone (includes Fontana Mix, Etcetera, 1993)

John Cage – Music Of Changes (Wergo, 1982)

Cornelius Cardew – Piano Music (Music Now, 1991)

Cornelius Cardew – We Sing for the Future! (New Albion, 2002)

Cornelius Cardew – Four Principles on Ireland (Ampere, 2002)

Ray Cathode – Time Beat/Waltz In Orbit (Parlophone 7", 1962)

Chemical Brothers – Dig Your Own Hole (includes Setting Sun, Astrelwerks, 1997)

Claude Debussy – Greatest Hits (Sony Classics)

Claude Debussy – Prelude A L'Apres Midi d'Un Faune (Deutsche Grammaphone)

Philip Glass – Glass Masters (3CD compilation of early work, Sony Classical, 1997)

Philip Glass & Ravi Shankar – Passages (Private Music, 1990)

Grateful Dead – The Golden Road 1965-1973 (a detailed 12 CD overview, WEA/Rhino, 2001)

Jimi Hendrix – Are You Experienced? (Universal/MCA, 1967)

Jimi Hendrix – Axis, Bold As Love (Universal/MCA, 1967)

Jefferson Airplane – The Worst of Jefferson Airplane (RCA, 1970)

The Mothers of Invention – Freak Out (Ryko, 1966)

Pink Floyd – The Piper at the Gates of Dawn (EMD/Capitol, 1967)

Pink Floyd – Saucerful of Secrets (EMD/Capitol, 1968)

Erik Satie – Quintessential Satie (Olympia, 2001)

The Scratch Orchestra – London, 1969 (recording of first perfornce, Die Stadt)

The Scratch Orchestra - Great Learning Disc (Deutsche Grammaphone, 1971)
Peter Sellers - A Celebration of Sellers (68 track box set including Shadows On The Grass and various George Martin productions, Angel, 1993)
Ravi Shankar - Live At Monterey (EMD/Angel, 1967)
Ravi Shankar - Full Circle, Carnegie Hall 2000 (EMD/Angel, 2001)
The Soft Machine - Turn Ons, Volume 1 ('67-era Speakeasy live tracks, Voiceprint, 2000)
Karheinz Stockhausen - Gesang der Jünglinge (Stockhausen Complete Edition 3, 1955)
Karheinz Stockhausen - Mikrophonie I (Stockhausen Complete Edition 9/ Sony, 1964)
Karheinz Stockhausen - Telemusik (Stockhausen Complete Edition 9, 1966)
Karheinz Stockhausen - Hymnen (Stockhausen Complete Edition 10, 1967)
Karheinz Stockhausen - Prozession (Stockhausen Complete Edition 11, 1967)
Karheinz Stockhausen - Kurzwellen (Stockhausen Complete Edition 13, 1968)
Karheinz Stockhausen - Aus den siebenTagen (Stockhausen Complete Edition 14, 1968)
Karheinz Stockhausen - Trans (Stockhausen Complete Edition 19, 1971)
Karheinz Stockhausen - Sirius (Stockhausen Complete Edition 26, 1977)
Morton Subotnick - Silver Apples of the Moon (Nonesuch, 1968)
James Tenney - Selected Works (includes Collage 1, Artifact Recordings, 1996)
The White Noise - An Electric Storm (mid-60s Delia Derbyshire, Island, 1992)

Various Artists - Computer Music Currents 13 (inclues various Max Mathews pieces, Wergo)
Various Artists - Music From Mathematics (Decca, 1964)

## Chapter 4

The Beach Boys - Pet Sounds (Capitol, 1966)
The Beach Boys - Pet Sounds Sessions (Capitol, 1997)

The Beach Boys - Classics, Selected By Brian Wilson (Capitol, 2002)
John Cage - John Cage/Christian Wolff (includes Cartridge Music, Mainstream, 1962)
Das Erste Wiener Gemüseorchester - Gemise (IFTAF, 1998)
Daswirdas - Branches (live interpretation of Cage's Branches and Child of Tree (Edition Wandelweider, 1992)
Super Furry Animals - Lianfairpwllgywgyllgoger Chwymdrobwlltysiliogoygoyocynygofod (In Space) (Ankst EP, 1005)
Super Furry Animals - Fuzzy Logic (Creation, 1996)
Super Furry Animals - Mwng (Placid Casual, 2000)
Super Furry Animals - Rings Around The World (Epic, 2001)
Various Artists - Hearings 1-6 (IFTAF, 1999)

## Chapter 5

Aphrodite's Child/Vangelis - 666, Apocalypse of St John (includes the track Altamont, Vertigo, 1970)
Apollo Four Forty - Electro Glide In Blue (includes the track Altamont Super-

Highway Revistited, Sony, 1997)
John Cage/Steve Reich - Three Dances/
Four Organs (Angel, 1973)
Donovan – Barabajagal (Columbia,
1969)
Donovan – Open Road (Columbia,
1970)
Donovan – HMS Donovan (BGO1971)
Brian Eno – Another Green World
(EG, 1975)
Brian Eno – Discreet Music (EG, 1975)
Christopher Eschenbach & the Houston
Symphony Orchestra – Schoenberg's
Pelleas Und Melisande (Koch, 1995)
Mozart – A Different Mozart (includes
Adagio for Glass Harmonica, Imaginary
Road, 1984)
The Alan Parsons Project – Tales Of
Mystery & Imagination (Mercury, 1975)
The Alan Parsons Project – I Robot
(Arista, 1977)
Lee 'Scratch' Perry – Super Ape
(Island/Mango, 1976)
Lee 'Scratch' Perry – Return of the
Super Ape (Lion of Judah/Mango, 1977)
Lee 'Scratch' Perry – Roast Fish,
Collie Weed & Corn Break (Lion
of Judah, 1978)
Lee 'Scratch' Perry – Scratch on the
Wire (Island, 1979)
Pink Floyd – Dark Side of the Moon
(EMI, 1973)
Steve Reich – Live/Electric Music
(Columbia, 1969) Steve Reich – Four
Organs/ Phase Patterns (Shander,
1971)Steve Reich – Drumming
(Multiples, 1972)
Steve Reich/Philip Glass/John Adams –
The Ultimate Minimal (Warner Music
Japan, 1995)

Various Artists – New Sounds In Electric
Music (CBS Odyssey, 1967) Various
Artists – Wired, Music Futurists
(Rhino, 1999)
Various Artists – Reich Remixed
(Nonesuch, 1999)
La Monte Young – The Well Tunes Piano
(Gramavision, 1994)

## Chapter 6

David Bowie – Space Oddity
(Virgin, 1969)
David Bowie – Diamond Dogs
(Virgin, 1974)
Martin Denny – Exotica 1 & Exotica 2
(Scamp, 1996)
Juan Garcia Esquivel – Loungecore
(Camden, 1999)
Mike Keneally – Nonkertompf (Exowax
Recordings, 1999)
Mike Keneally – Wooden Smoke
(Exowax Recordings, 2002)
Arthur Lyman – The Very Best of Arthur
Lyman (Varese, 2002)
Harry Nilsson – Nilsson Schmilsson
(RCA, 1971)
Lou Reed – Transformer (BMG, 1972)
Various Artists – Late Night Sounds In
Stereo (Marble Arch, 1968)
Various Artists – Easy Tune (Drive
Inn, 1995)
Various Artists – The Cocktail Shaker-
New Groove Kitsch and Space-Age Pop
(Irma, 1997)
Frank Zappa – The Best Band You Never
Heard In Your Life (features Mike
Keneally, Barking Pumpkin, 1991)
Frank Zappa – Make a Jazz Noise Here
(features Mike Keneally, Barking
Pumpkin, 1991)

## Chapters 7-8

10CC – The Very Best of (includes I'm Not In Love, Polydor, 2001)

Frankie Goes To Hollywood – Liverpool (includes Lunar Bay, ZTT, 1986)

Peter Gabriel – Peter Gabriel (features Jerry Marotta, Virgin 1980)

Peter Gabriel – Security (features Jerry Marotta, Virgin 1982)

Introducing the Bass and Guitar Gizmotron (Gizmo, Inc./Evatone promotional flexi-disc, 1980)Laurence Juber – LJ (Solid Air, 1998)

Laurence Juber – Altered Reality (Narada, 1999)

Laurence Juber – Mosaic (Solid Air, 1998)

Laurence Juber – Different Times (Solid Air, 2001)

Terry Riley – In C (Columbia, 1968)

Terry Riley – A Rainbow In Curved Air (Columbia, 1969)

The Smith Quartet – Good Medicine (includes compositions by Terry Riley and Andrew Poppy, Glissando, 2000)

Sparks – Terminal Jive (Oglio, 1979)

## Chapter 9

Artful Dodger – It's All About the Stragglers (FFRR, 2000)

Art of Noise – (Who's Afraid of) the Art of Noise?' (ZTT, 1984)

Art of Noise – The Best of Art of Noise (China, 1989)

Art of Silence – artofsilence.co.uk (JJ Jeczalik solo, Permenant, 1995)

Arthur Baker – Breakin, Perfecto Presents Arthur Baker (Perfecto, 2001)

The KLF – The White Room (KLF Communications, 1991)

Thurston Moore – Root (Lo

Recordings, 1998)

John Oswald – Plunderphonic Plexure (Avant, 1993)

Nitin Sawhney – Beyond Skin (Outcaste, 1999)

Nitin Sawhney – Displacing The Priest (Outcaste, 1996)

Nitin Sawhney – Prophesy (V2, 2001)

Tape-Beatles – A Subtle Buoyancy of Pulse (Staalplaat, 1998)

Various Artists – Endlessnessism (Dot Records, 1997)

Various Artists – Chinese Whispers (Sprawl, 1996)

## Chapter 10

808 State – Quadrastate (includes Pacific State, Eastern Bloc, 1990)

David Bowie – Earthling (Virgin, 1997)

Brilliant – Kiss the Lips of Life (Food, 1986)

Dido – No Angel (includes production by Youth, BMG, 2001)

Thomas Fehlman – Flow 1990-1998 (Apollo, 1998)

Gabrieli/Montiverdi – Antiphonal (includes Vespers Of The Blessed Virgin, Sony Classics)

James – Seven (produced by Youth, Mercury, 1992)

Killing Joke – Pandemonium (Volcano, 1994)

Killing Joke – Democracy (Volcano, 1996)

The KLF – Chill Out (KLF Communications, 1990)

Laibach – Let It Be (Mute, 1998)

Marathon – Movin (inclues Youth remix, Ten 12", 1992)

The Orb – Adventures Beyond The Ultrsworld (Island, 1993)

The Orb – Cydonia (Island, 2001)
The Orb – Orblivion (Island, 1997)
The Orb – UFOrb (Island, 1993)
The Orb – UFOff, The Best of
(Island, 1998)
Sun Electric – Via Nostra (Apollo, 1998)
ST Melody – QTopia (inclues Youth
remix, Solid Pleasure 12", 1991)
System 7 – System 7 (Ten, 1991)
System 7 – 777 (Wau/Big Life, 1993)
System 7 – Point 3 (Butterfly/Big
Life, 1994)
T.D.F. – Retail Therapy (WEA, 1997)
U2 – Pop (Island, 1997)
The Verve – Urban Hymns (includes
production by Youth, Virgin, 1997)
Various Artists – Red Hot & Blue (includes
U2 remix by Youth, Chrysalis, 1991)
Various Artists mixed by Youth & Eddie
Richards – Heavy Duty Breaks
(Illuminated, 1984)
Youth & Ben Watkins – The Empty
Quarter (Illuminated, 1984)

## Chapter 11

Lenny Kravitz – Mama Said (Virgin,
1991)
Sean Lennon – Into the Sun (Grand
Royale, 1998)
Sean Lennon – Half Horse, Half
Musician (Grand Royale, 1999)
Yoko Ono – Onobox (6CD retroscpec-
tive covering 1970-1985, Rykodisc, 1992)
Yoko Ono/IMA – Rising (Capitol, 1995)
Yoko Ono – Bueprint for a Sunrise
(Capitol, 2001)
Peace Choir – Give Peace a Chance
(Virgin, 1991)
Motoharu Sano – Time Out (features
Sean Lennon, Sony Japan, 1987)

Stuntman – The Right Channel (features
Sean Lennon, Twitcher Records, 1994)

## Chapter 12

Black Dog – Unsavoury Products
(Hydrogen Jukebox, 2002)
Bob Dylan – Live at Budokan (features
David Mansfield, Columbia, 1978)
Allen Ginsberg – First Blues, Songs
1975-81 (also features David Mansfield,
John Hammond Records, 1981)
Allen Ginsberg – The Lion For Real
(Mouth Almighty/Mercury, 1989)
Allen Ginsberg – Cosmopolitan Greetings
(Migros-Genossenschafts-Bund, 1993)
Allen Ginsberg – Holy Soul Jelly Roll,
Poems & Songs 1949-1993 (4 CD
overview, Rhino, 1994)
Allen Ginsberg & Kronos Quartet –
Howl, U.S.A. (Nonesuch, 1996)
Allen Ginsberg – Jack Kerouac Mexico
City Blues, 242 Poems read by...
(Shambhala Pubs Audio, 1996)
Allen Ginsberg – Howl & Other Poems
(Fantasy Records, 1998)
Philip Glass – North Star (Virgin, 1977)
Philip Glass – Einstein On The Beach
(Tomato, 1979)
Philip Glass – Glassworks (CBS, 1982)
Philip Glass – Powaqqatsi
(Elektra/Nonesuch, 1988)
Philip Glass & Allen Ginsberg –
Hydrogen Dukebox (Elektra/
Nonesuch, 1993)
Philip Glass – The Essential Philip Glass
(Sony Classical, 1993)
Philip Glass – Music In The Shape of a
Square (Stradivarius, 2002)
David Mansfield – Heaven's Gate sound-
track (EMI/Liberty, 1980)

Marc Ribot – Rootless Cosmopolitans (Island, 1990)

Marc Ribot – Yo! I Killed Your God (Live Shrek) (Tzadik, 1999)

Patti Smith – Horses (features Lenny Kaye, Arista, 1975)

Patti Smith – Easter (features Lenny Kaye, Arista, 1978)

Suzanne Vega – Suzanne Vega (produced by Lenny Kaye, A&M, 1985)

Suzanne Vega – Solitude Standing (produced by Lenny Kaye, A&M, 1987)

Various Artists – Howls, Raps & Roars, Recordings From SF Poetry Renaissance (features Allen Ginsberg, Fantasy Records 1993)

## Chapter 13

Aube – Substructural Penetration (Iris Light, 1995)

Aube – Stared Gleam (Iris Light, 1994)

Tim Didymus – Float (SSEYO, 1997)

Brian Eno – Generative Music 1 (SSEYO, 1996)

Jamuud – Niskala (SSEYO, 1997)

Andrew Poppy – The Beating Of Wings (ZTT, 1985)

Andrew Poppy – Alphabed (A Mystery Dance), (ZTT, 1987)

Andrew Poppy – Poems and Toccatas (Bitter & Twisted, 1992)

Andrew Poppy – Ophelia/Ophelia (Impetus, 1995)

Andrew Poppy – Rude Bloom (ArtGallery, 1995)

## Chapter 14

Laurie Anderson – Big Science (Warner Bros., 1982)

Ash Ra Tempel – Discover Cosmic (introductory compilation, Ohr, 1977)

Michael Brook – Hybrid (Editions EG, 1985)

Michael Brook – Cobalt Blue (4AD, 1992)

Harold Budd – The Plateaux Of Mirrors (EG, 1980)

Brian Eno – Music For Films (Polydor, 1978)

Brian Eno – Music For Airports (Ambient, 1978)

Brian Eno – Apollo (EG, 1983)

Brian Eno – Music For Films vol.2 (EG, 1983)

Brian Eno – Thursday Afternoon (EG, 1985)

Brian Eno – Instrumental (compilation, Virgin, 1994)

Brian Eno & David Byrne – My Life In The Bush Of Ghosts (Sire, 1980)

Brian Eno & Robert Fripp – No Pussyfooting (EG, 1973)

Brian Eno & Robert Fripp – The Essential Fripp & Eno (Gyroscope, 1994)

Fridge – Ceefax (Output, 1997)

Robert Fripp – November Suite, Live At Green Park Station (DMG, 1997)

Robert Fripp – *The Gates of Paradise Vol. 1, The Outer Darkness (DMG, 1997)*

Labradford – Mi Media Naraja (Blast First, 1997)

Laraaji – Day Of Radiance (EG, 1980)

Moby – Early Underground (Instinct, 1993)

Moby – Ambient (Instinct, 1993)

Mike Oldfield – Tubular Bells (Virgin, 1973)

Mike Oldfield – Hergest Ridge (Virgin, 1974)

Mike Oldfield – Tubular Bells 2 (Reprise, 1992)

The Shamen – Boss Drum (includes Youth remix, Sony 12", 1992)

Tortoise – Millions Now Living Will
Never Die (City Slang, 1996)
Ui – Lifelike (Southern, 1998)
Various Artists mixed by Paul Oakenfold
& Danny Rampling – A Voyage Into
Trance (Dragonfly, 1995)
Various Dragonfly Artists – The
Technical Use of Sound In Magick
(Dragonfly, 1996)
Various Dragonfly Artists – Parallel
Youniversity Presents The Warp
Experience (Dragonfly, 1997)
Various LSD Artists – Dr. Alex Paterson's
Journey Into Paradise (Liquid Sound
Design, 2001)
Various LSD Artists – East Of The River
Ganges (Liquid Sound Design, 2001)
Various Muzak Artists – Muzak 60th
Anniversary (Muzak, 2000)

### Chapter 15
Can – Anthology, 1968-93 (Mute, 1995)
Cluster – Stimmungen (introductory
compilation, Sky, 1984)
Ian Dury – 4000 Weeks Holiday (includes
Peter the Painter, Polydor, 1984)
Faust – Faust (Polygram, 1972)
Kraftwerk – Autobahn (Warner, 1974)
Neu! – Volume 1 (Astralwerks, 1972)

### Chapter 16
Bjork – Vespertine (WEA, 2001)
Black Dog – Spanners (Warp, 1995)
Black Dog – Music For Adverts (And
Short Films) (Warp, 1996)
Cypress Hill – Stash (Sony, 2002)
Fatboy Slim – The Fatboy Slim/Norman
Cooke Collection (remix/pseudenym
compilation, Hip-O, 2000)
Wyclef Jean – Masquarade (Sony, 2002)

Knoc-Turn'al – LA Confidential Presents
Knoc-Turn'al (TBC, 2002)
Bob Marley – Anthologies 1-3
(Dealmakers, 2000, 2001)
Snoop Dogg -Death Row's Greatest Hits
(Death Row, 2001)
Toots & The Maytells – 54-46 Was My
Number, Anthology 1964-2000
(Sanctuary, 2002)
Various Artists – Arcane (Real World, 1995)
Various Artists – Burundi, Traditional
Music (Ocora, 1988)
Various Artists – Cameroun, La Musique
des Pygmees Baka (Auvidis, 1990)
Various Artists – Heart of the Forest, the
Music of the Baka Forest People of
Southeast Cameroon (Hannibal, 1993)

### Epilogue
8 Frozen Modules – The Confused
Designer (Trance, 1997)
The Mike Flowers Pops – A Groovy
Place (London, 1999)
The Mike Flowers Pops Meets Aphex
Twin – The Freebase Connection (Lo
Recordings, 1996)
Laika – Silver Apples Of The Moon (Too
Pure, 1994)
Laika – Sound Of The Satellites (Too
Pure, 1997)
Colin Newman – A-Z (Beggars Banquet,
1980)
Colin Newman – Bastard (Swim, 1997)
Various Artists mixed by Chris Coco –
Solar Spectrums (Obsessive, 2000)
Various Artists mixed by Chris Coco –
Acoustic Chill (Organic, 2001)
Wire – Pink Flag, 154, Chairs Missing
(3CD compendium, EMI, 2000)
Wire – High Time (Orchard, 2002)

# APPENDIX THREE

# SELECTED ARTICLES AND WEBSITES

## Chapters 1-3

'Revolutions from Scratch' (Julian Cowley, The Wire, December 2001); 'Lost Beatles Track "Will not be released"' (Annanova, 4 June 2001); 'Lost Beatles Track Set For Macca Movie; (The Daily Thing, 4 June 2001); 'The History of The Beatles' Most Mysterious Unreleased Track' (Abbey Road Beatles zine); 'AMM' (Rob Young, The Wire, February 1995); Record Collector magazine (June 1993), 'Paul McCartney, From Liverpool to Let It Be' by Howard A. DeWitt; Julian Palacios 'Lost In The Woods' (Boxtree/Macmillan).

Abbey Road: www.best.com/~abbeyrd/
Annanova: www.ananova.com/
The Beatles official site: www.thebeatles.com
Paul McCartney official site: www.paulmccartney.com

## Chapter 4

'The Beet Goes On as Musicians Dig Rhythm and Greens' (Peter Finn, Washington Post, 17 April 2001); 'Super Furry Animals' (Designer, 2001); 'Sir Paul Eats With The Animals' (BBC News, 18 April 2001); 'Interview – Super Furry Animals' (BBC Southampton, 25 September 2001); 'A Super Furry, Bizarre Time With Super Furry Animals In London' (Kelly Gateson, Stage, 2 October 2001).

The Daily Thing: the_captain00.tripod.com
Designer: designermagazine.tripod.com
Institute for Transacoustic Research: www.iftaf.org
Super Furry Animals: www.superfurry.com
Brian Wilson: www.brinwilson.com

## Chapters 5-9

'On Our Wavelength' (Boazine issue 7); 'Violent 1969 Altamont Concert Crushed Flower Power' (Associated Press, 06 December 1999); 'Life and Death at Altamont' (Nick Aretakis, Pop Politics); 'Paul McCartney Interview' (Richard Meryman, Life Magazine, April 1971); 'Thrillington' (Matt Hurwitz, Good Day Sunshine, 1995); 'The Rebirth of Easy Listening!' (Ian Peel, DJ Magazine, 1995); Incognito (Mark Lewisohn, Club Sandwich); 'Nitin Sawhney – The New Sound Of UK Asian Music' (John Oswald, Music Week, 21 Oct 1996); 'Hiding In The Limelight' (John Shearlaw, The Mighty Organ,); 'Nitin Sawhney Interview' (Amazon, March 1998); 'The Beatles, India, and the Counterculture' (Neal Sawhney, 2 June 1997); 'Pirates on the High (C)s – The Unacceptable Face of Plagiarism' (EST magazine); 'Plunderphonics' (John Oswald, Recommended Records Quarterly, Vol.2 #1, 1987); 'Beatles Orientalis – Influences from Asia in a Popular Song Tradition' (David Reck, Asian Music Vol.

XVI/1, 1985); 'Outcaste Presents…'
(Rosie Wild, The Big Blue Spot, 1999).

Amazon: www.amazon.co.uk
The Big Blue Spot:
www.thebigbluespot.com
Laurence Juber: www.laurencejuber.com
The Mighty Organ:
www.themightyorgan.com
Mike Flowers: www.mikeflowers.co.uk
Mike Keneally: www.keneally.com
Muzak: www.muzak.com
Nitin Sawhney: www.nitinsawhney.com

## Chapters 10-11

'The Plastic Ono McCartney Band'
(David Fricke, Rolling Stone, 6 April
1995); 'Paul McCartney Interview' (Tony
Bacon, Bass Player, August 1995);
'Hiroshima Sky' (Hiro Satou, 4
September 1995); 'Approximately
Infinite Universe' (Sari Gurney, 1996);
Beatles Book (May 1995 and August
1995); 'Yoko Ono, Vie Et Ouvre (Yellow
Submarine, 2000); 'Ono-McCartney
Reconciliation Tape' (The Los Angeles
Times, 5 August 1995); 'This Week' (The
New York Times, 29 September 1997);
'On the Razzle with Randy' (Randy
Gener, The Village Voice, 3 June 1998);
'Pop Features – Yoko Ono' (Michael
Small, Hotwired, 14 June 1996); 'A Love
Song for Yoko? Don't Be Silly' (New
York Daily News, 1998).

Approximately Infinite Universe:
www.kaapeli.fi/aiu/
Hiro Satou: www.yk.rim.or.jp/~y_satou/
Hotwired: hotwired.lycos.com/
Yellow Submarine: www.yellow-sub.net

## Chapter 12

'The Bard His Own Self' (Bob Holman,
About.com, April 1997); The collected
works of Steve Silberman; People maga-
zine (25 November, 1996); 'Allen
Ginsberg Dying of Liver Cancer' (Steve
Silberman, Wired, 3 April 1997); 'How
Allen Ginsberg Thinks His Thoughts'
(Dinitia Smith, New York Times 8
October 8 1996)

Bob Holman: poetry.about.com
David Mansfield:
members.aol.com/smashprod/
Steve Silberman: www.levity.com/diga-
land/ginsberg96.html

## Chapters 13-16

'Rushes' (Michael Henningsen, The
Weekly Wire, 14 June 1999); Aural
Innovations (issue 7, July 1999); 'Beatles
Get Back With A Dance Track' (CNN, 15
August 2000); 'Liverpool Sound Collage
analysis' (Tom Brennan, 2001); College
Music Journal (23 October 2000); the
archives of the Tate Liverpool; 'What A
Wonderful World' (Lyndsey Parker,
Launch, 5 February 2000); Beatlology
Magazine (Vol. 4 No. 1, 2001);
Progressive World magazine; 'Magical
Mystery Tour Enters 21st Century;
(Dotmusic, 15 August 2002); 'Peter Blake
Biography' (Gallery Online, 2000);
'Mersey Stream' (Extended Playhouse,
2001); 'About Collage' (Beatle City,
2000); 'No Shell Out!' (Q magazine, May
2001); 'McCartney Takes Winding Road
to Painting' (Edna Gundersen, USA
Today, 11 August 2000); 'Love Me Do'
(Nigel Farndale, The Telegraph, 17 May

2002); 'A Day in the Life' (Las Vegas Review-Journal, 5 April 2002); 'Paul McCartney Jams With Apes' (Ananova, 20 June 2002).

Beatle City: beatle-city.merseyworld.com/
Tom Brennan: home.earthlink.net/~tomjbr/Tom/Beatles/
Extended Playhouse: www.inspiracy.com/ep/
Gallery Online: www.galleryonline.com
Iris Light: www.irislight.demon.co.uk
Launch: launch.yahoo.com
Liverpool Sound Collage official site: www.liverpoolsoundcollage.com
Progressive World: www.progressiveworld.net
Rushes official site: www.fire-man.com
SSEYO: www.sseyo.com
Tate Liverpool: www.tate.org.uk/

## Note on Website Addresses

URLs and web articles are famous for being there one minute and off-line the next. If any URLs listed here are found to be inactive in future years, readers will most likely find copies stored at The Internet Archive, "a digital library of Internet sites and other cultural artefacts in digital form" at www.archive.org.

# APPENDIX FOUR
# BIBLIOGRAPHY

Badman, K.: The Beatles, Off the Record (Omnibus Press, 2000)

Badman, K.: The Beatles, After the Break-Up (Omnibus Press, 1990)

Beadle, J.: Will Pop Eat Itself? (Faber & Faber, 1993)

Born, G.: Rationalising Culture, ICRAM, Boulez and the Institutionalisation of the Musical Avant-Garde (University of California Press, 1995)

Broughton, F. (ed.): Time Out Interviews 1968-1998 (Penguin, 1998)

Cage, J.: Silence (Wesleyan University Press, 1973)

Cardew, C.: Stockhausen Serves Imperialism (Latimer Press, 1974)

Carter, D. (ed.): Spontaneous Mind (HarperCollins, 2001)

Cauty, J. and Drummond, B.: The Manual, How To Have A Number On the Easy Way (KLF Publications, 1988)

Daumier, H.: Lawyers and Justice (1971)

Eno, B.: A Year with Swollen Appendices (Faber & Faber, 1996)

Fields, D.: Linda McCartney, A Portrait (Renaissance, 2000)

Francastel, P.: Art and Technology in the Nineteenth and Twentieth Centuries (Zone Books, 2000)

J. Giroux: The Haiku Form (Tuttle, 1974)

Glinsky, A.: Theremin, Ether Music and Espionage (University of Illinois Press, 2000)

Home, S.: Plagiarism – Art as Commodity and Strategies for its Negation (Aporia Press, 1988)

Ives, C.: Daumier Drawings (Yale University Press, 1993)

Kahn, D.: Noise Water Meat, A History of Sound in the Arts (MIT, 1999)

Kakehasi, I.: I Believe in Music, Life Experiences and Thoughts on the Future of Electronic Music by the Founder of the Roland Corporation (Hal Leonard, 2002)

Kurzweil, R.: The Age of Spiritual Machines, When Computers Exceed Human Intelligence (Viking, 1999)

LaBelle, Brandon and Christof M.: Writing Aloud, The Sonics of Language (Errant Bodies Press, 2001)

Lanza, J.: Elevator Music, A Surreal History of Muzak, Easy-Listening, and Other Moodsong (St. Martins, 1994)

MacDonald, I.: Revolution in The Head, The Beatles Records and the Sixties (Pimlico, 1995)

Madinger, C. and Easter, M.: Eight Arms To Hold You, The Solo Beatles Compendium (44.1 productions, LP, 2000)

Martin. G and Pearson W.: With a Little Help From My Friends, The Making of Sgt. Pepper, Vol. 1 (Little, Brown & Company, 1995)

Miles, B.: Paul McCartney, Many Years From Now (Vintage, 1997)

Miles, B.: The Beatles Diary, Volume 1 – The Beatles Years (Omnibus Press, 2001)

Napier-Bell, S.: Black Vinyl White Powder (Ebury, 2001)

Peel, I: Future Visions, Music & The Internet (Future Books, 1996)

Prendergast, M.: The Ambient Century, From Mahler to Trance – The Evolution Os Found in the Electronic Age (Bloomsbury, 2000)

Pritchard, D. and Lysaght, Y.: The Beatles, An Oral History (Hyperion Press, 1999)Provost, L.: Honore Daumier, A Thematic Guide to His Oeuvre (1989)

Nyman, M.: Experimental Music, Cage and Beyond (Studio Vista, 1974)

Reich, S.: Writings on Music, 1965-2000 (Oxford, 2002)

Reighley, K.: Looking for the Perfect Beat, The Art and Culture of the DJ (MTV, 2000)

Rule, G.: Elektro Shock!, Groundbreakers of Synth Music (Miller Freeman, 1999)

Ruscol, H.: The Liberation of Sound: An Introduction to Electronic Music (Prentice Hall, 1972)

Shapiro, P.: Modulations, A History of Electronic Music, Throbbing Words on Sound (DAP, 2000)

Shuker, R.: Understanding Popular Music (Routledge, 1994)

Tamm, E.: Brian Eno, His Music and the Vertical Colour of Sound (Faber & Faber, 1989)

The Beatles: The Beatles Anthology (Apple Corps Ltd., Cassell & Co., 2000)

Thompson, A.: Stompbox, A History of Guitar Fuzzes, Flangers, Phasers, Echoes, & Wahs (Miller Freeman, 1997)

Toop, D.: Exotica (Consortium, 1999)

Toop, D.: Ocean of Sound, Aether Talk, Ambient Sound and Imaginary Worlds (Serpents Tail, 1995)

Turner, S.: A Hard Day's Write

(Carlton, 1994)

Van den Heuval: The Haiku Anthology (Simon & Schuster, 1986)

Various: 1000 Days That Shook the World (Mojo Special Limited Edition, 2002)

Various: The Beatles 1962-1970 (NME Originals, 2002)

Various: The New Grove Dictionary of Music and Musicians (Macmillan, 2000)

Various: The Rough Guide to Rock (Rough Guides, 1997)

Various: The Virgin Guinness of Popular Music (Guinness 1992)

Wilson, B. and Gold, T.: Wouldn't It Be Nice, My Own Story (HarperCollins, 1991)

Yuasa: Basho, The Narrow Road to the Deep North and other Travel Sketches (Penguin Books, 1974)

# INDEX